George Berkeley, Alexander Campbell Fraser

Selections from Berkeley

With an Introduction to the Problems of Modern Philosophy fopr the Use of

Students in Colledges and Universities

George Berkeley, Alexander Campbell Fraser

Selections from Berkeley
With an Introduction to the Problems of Modern Philosophy fopr the Use of Students in Colledges and Universities

ISBN/EAN: 9783744671095

Printed in Europe, USA, Canada, Australia, Japan

Cover: Foto ©Thomas Meinert / pixelio.de

More available books at **www.hansebooks.com**

SELECTIONS FROM BERKELEY

ANNOTATED

AN INTRODUCTION TO THE PROBLEMS OF
MODERN PHILOSOPHY FOR THE USE
OF STUDENTS IN COLLEGES
AND UNIVERSITIES

BY

ALEXANDER CAMPBELL FRASER, D.C.L. Oxon.

EMERITUS PROFESSOR OF LOGIC AND METAPHYSICS
IN THE UNIVERSITY OF EDINBURGH

SIXTH EDITION

OXFORD
AT THE CLARENDON PRESS
1910

PREFACE TO SIXTH EDITION

IN this edition the verbal expression of the contents of my Introduction to the *Selections*, as well as of the prefatory notes and annotations, has here and there been made I trust more luminous. But abstract words and ambiguous words are persistent enemies, especially in philosophy and theology.

It is hoped however that the book is thus somewhat better fitted for its intended use, as a text-book and aid to reflection on the spiritual constitution of the universe. It touches questions raised by contemporary Materialism and Agnosticism in the three centres of philosophical interest, namely, the material world, the human spirit, and God ; as well as on the final relations of our scientific interpretation of nature to moral and religious faith. The annotations point to a Realism that is fundamentally Spiritual, although after a native rather than a German type ;—this instead of either dogmatic Materialism, or abstract philosophic Omniscience, or total Nescience—all subject to patient and candid comparative examination by the student.

This selection from the classical works of a philosopher who appeared at a critical time in the evolution of modern thought, and who was long inadequately understood and appreciated, has I learn been found apt to stimulate meditation about the ultimate rationale (as far as man can pursue it) of this embodied mortal life of ours, in its scientifically interpretable physical environment, among those engaged with philosophy in academical institutions in this country and abroad and otherwise.

A. CAMPBELL FRASER.

October, 1910.

CONTENTS

	PAGE
HISTORICAL INTRODUCTION	ix

FIRST PART

PHILOSOPHICAL PRINCIPLES CONCERNING MATTER AND SPIRIT

PREFATORY NOTE	3
I. INTRODUCTION TO THE PRINCIPLES . . .	7
II. RATIONALE OF THE PRINCIPLES . . .	32
III. OBJECTIONS TO THE PRINCIPLES . . .	57
IV. CONSEQUENCES OF THE PRINCIPLES . . .	90
A DIALOGUE CONCERNING THE PRINCIPLES . .	117

SECOND PART

THE VISIBLE WORLD A DIVINE LANGUAGE

PREFATORY NOTE	169
I. A NEW THEORY OF VISION	175
II. DIVINE VISUAL LANGUAGE: A DIALOGUE .	220
III. THE VISUAL LANGUAGE VINDICATED . .	268

THIRD PART

SIRIS, OR THE UNIVERSE UNITED IN GOD

	PAGE
PREFATORY NOTE	283
A CHAIN OF PHILOSOPHICAL REFLECTIONS . .	287
INDEX	331

HISTORICAL INTRODUCTION

The design of the *Selections* is to afford appropriate mental exercise to students of Psychology, Inductive Logic, and Metaphysics, who desire to discuss and determine questions at the foundation of human life and knowledge, raised in modern thought.

Berkeley may be used as an Introduction to the ultimate problems of Modern Philosophy for the following among other reasons :—

1. His philosophical writings, although only philosophical fragments, are English classics inspired by metaphysical genius, which present subtle thought in graceful and transparent language.

2. Their principal doctrine, about the ultimate nature and powerlessness of Matter, suggests some of the chief questions at the root of our spiritual life. Spiritual Realism versus Materialism is the pervading note.

3. Berkeley is an important factor in the history of modern philosophy, especially British, during the period inaugurated by Locke's 'Essay', which includes the last two hundred years. The sceptical crisis of this Era, represented by Hume, was precipitated by the new questions about Matter and the Visible World that Berkeley had raised. An intellectual revolution followed, in which, largely through the direct and indirect influence of Berkeley's Principles, Locke was gradually exchanged either (*a*) for the Idealism of Kant

and Hegel, (*b*) for constructive Association psychology in its development from Hume and Hartley to the present day, or (*c*) for Reid's appeal to the Common Sense of Mankind.

The intrinsic freshness of Berkeley's thought, the literary charm of its expression, the romantic interest of his Spiritual Realism, its intellectual reach when it is carried into its issues, his historical importance, and the present urgency of the final questions concerning God and the Universe, all unite in recommending him as a stimulating companion for a student of philosophy. His new conception of Matter raises the fundamental questions of philosophy and theology.

This estimate of the educational value of Berkeley does not of course oblige the student to accept fully his (often misunderstood) conception of what the reality of the world presented to the senses consists in.

Berkeley's personal history is full of human interest. The early years are shrouded in a mystery that is in keeping with the halo of romance in which his life is enveloped. It is certain that he was born in the county of Kilkenny, in March, 1685, and that in March, 1700, he entered Trinity College, Dublin, where his next thirteen years were spent. Peter Browne, afterwards the philosophical bishop of Cork, was then provost of Trinity, and the seeds of modern thought were finding their way into the Irish College. Through the influence of Molyneux, Locke's *Essay concerning Human Understanding* had been introduced, and Malebranche too, the French philosophical contemporary of Locke, was not unknown in Dublin. The spirit of Descartes and of Bacon, the early operations of the Royal Society, and the discoveries of Newton and Leibniz, were also influences then and there at work. Berkeley's writings show early familiarity with Locke and Newton, Descartes and Malebranche.

When Berkeley was in Dublin, and before he had reached his thirtieth year, he had given to the world the three small philosophical classics which state and defend his new conception of Matter and consequent refutation of Materialism. In 1709 the *Essay towards a New Theory of Vision* appeared, to open the way for the other two. It was followed in 1710 by the *Principles of Human Knowledge*—a reasoned exposition of the spiritual ground and office of the material world. In 1713 they were further explained and illustrated, in a more popular form, in *Three Dialogues between Hylas and Philonous*. Like Descartes, Spinoza, and Hume, and in contrast to Locke, Kant, and Reid, Berkeley presented his leading thought to the world in early life—a fact in keeping with the fervid impetuosity of his temperament.

His intellectual growth at Trinity College, during the years which preceded the publication of these three classics, may be traced in his *Commonplace Book*. This is an interesting record of the awakening struggles of philosophical genius. It was first published in 1871, in the Oxford edition of his Works and Life. There he appears under the fervid inspiration of a new thought;—labouring to find fit expression for Principles which he was resolved to present to the world in as conciliatory a way as he could; but determined to employ them in sustaining spiritual faith, and in showing the limits of physical science.

In 1713 Berkeley visited London. His next twenty years were spent chiefly in France and Italy, and in America. His personal charm, as well as the novelty and boldness of his conceptions, made him an object of attention to eminent contemporaries. In 1724, after his return from Italy to Ireland, he was made Dean of Derry. Ardent philanthropy led him soon to resign this preferment, and carried him to North America, at the age of forty-five, where he meant to devote the remainder of his life to spreading Christian civilisation in the Western World, by founding a missionary

College at the Bermudas. But after three years of inevitable delay in Rhode Island, on his way to Bermuda, withdrawal of the public support on which the enterprise depended obliged him to return to Ireland.

The last twenty years of his life were spent in comparative retirement as Bishop of Cloyne in the south of Ireland.

Neither in the twenty years of movement, nor in the closing twenty years of retirement, was philosophy forgotten by Berkeley. A Latin tract on the cause of Motion in the world of sense, the fruit of studies in Italy, appeared in 1721, on his return from the Continent. *Alciphron or the Minute Philosopher*, a book of Dialogues, directed against sceptical free-thinkers, and unfolding the rationale of faith in God as God speaks to us in the Visible World, was a result of recluse life in Rhode Island. It was published in 1732, on his return from America, and was followed, a year later, by a *Further Vindication* of the spiritual meaning and purpose of the World we see. The latest issue of this ever-deepening course of philosophical thought appeared in 1744, under the quaint title of *Siris, or a Chain of Philosophical Reflections*—more from the point of view of Plato than of Locke, and more immediately in relation to God than to Matter.

Berkeley spent the evening of his days in philanthropy and in meditative quiet. For Cloyne he had a particular fondness. Its remoteness had a contemplative charm. But at last, when declining health needed change, his love for academical retirement carried him to Oxford, which for years had been before him in imagination as the ideal home of his old age. He enjoyed Oxford only for a few months. In January, 1753, death suddenly closed this beautiful life, devoted to reasoned exposition of the dependence of Nature upon Omnipresent Intelligence.

That the things we see and touch, and their supposed

inherent powers, are neither more nor less than appearances in the five senses, presented in a continuous natural order by the power of God; and further, that the material world thus presented by Supreme Active Reason is dependent for its reality on living mind being percipient of orderly sensuous phenomena;—this was the new conception of the universe presented by Berkeley. It arose in his youth under the influence of Locke; it was enlarged in later life by sympathy with Plato. Its consequences justify us in regarding it as one of the conceptions that mark epochs, and become springs of spiritual progress.

The state of Modern Philosophy before and after Berkeley illustrates this. An outline of the history, with Berkeley in the centre, may prepare the reader for the *Selections*.

DESCARTES (1596-1650) was the father of modern metaphysics. It originated in his endeavour to explode Prejudice by means of tentative Doubt. As the first step in philosophy Descartes refused to accept without support in reason **any** belief which, on trial, he might find it possible to suspend. He announced this as the means he had found effectual for delivering his own mind from irrational prejudices; for finding the genuine necessities of reason; and for correction of fallacies—chief ends of metaphysical inquiry. He recommended it as the way to transform a life of blind faith in inherited dogmas into the philosophic life of reasoned faith.

In trying the mental experiment of temporarily suspending *all* his beliefs, Descartes found doubt arrested by one irresistible conviction, namely, that of his own existence. This conviction he could not even for a moment hold in suspense. He expressed this intellectual necessity in the celebrated formula—*cogito ergo sum*, or *ego sum cogitans*—'I am conscious of existing.' This means that the changing conscious life so necessarily presupposes an unchanging *ego* or self.

that consciousness cannot arise without finding this conviction involved in it. From this starting-point—not adequately recognised in the ancient world—the philosophy of modern Europe has pursued its free course.

One who imbibed Cartesianism was accordingly ready to begin the life of reflection by being more sure of his own existence as a conscious person than of anything else. We know the *Self* involved in our own conscious life with the most perfect assurance that is conceivable: we know our own bodies even, and all things external to them, only through our Self being conscious. For if I ceased to be conscious, the things of sense would cease to be real, as far as I was concerned. And if all conscious life in the universe were to die, the dead Matter which remained would be as good as non-existent. Extended things are unconscious of existence: only conscious beings realise themselves and things around them: *they* contribute even to unconscious things their only intelligible reality, in feeling and knowing them. The conscious person, revealed to himself in the acts and states of which he is conscious, is therefore the primary reality. The existence of visible and tangible things, external to his own felt sensations or ideas, was with Descartes only an inference, not a primary datum —an inference which he vindicated on the ground of the trust we necessarily place in our own conscious experience as rooted in God. For this divine trust seemed to justify the assumption that we cannot be deceived regarding whatever we have a clear and distinct conviction of, which we find we have of the existence of a world outside our individual consciousness.

Descartes thus found *two* finite beings—one conscious and unextended, and the other extended and unconscious— and perfect Being or God, on whom the two depend. This ultimate duality of opposed dependent beings in the universe—the one invisible and the other visible—the one conscious and the other unconscious—was a difficulty in early modern philosophy. How were the *conscious* and *extended* being—*living thought* and *dead matter*—to be reconciled in a coherent philosophy? This, in its different phases, became for a time the question of questions. The extended world was so opposed by the Cartesian to the unextended ego or self of which he was conscious, that the possibility of science of the former by the latter, or of intercourse between the two, seemed impossible. Extended things and conscious life seemed to be mutually exclusive. How can they be *mixed*, either in our perceptions or in our voluntary movements? How can extended things become perceptions, and how can our invisible volitions produce changes in visible things?

Yet it was not denied that we do in fact perceive extended things; or that changes in things are referred to our volitions as their cause. The explanation offered by Cartesianism was, that the two dependent but mutually exclusive substances are perpetually dependent on and harmonised by God. All changes in extended things, and our perceptions of them, were viewed as effects of which the will of God must be the originating cause. Matter existed that it might be occasion for, and an interpretable sign of, Divine action and intention. On occasion of an impression produced by God in a human organism, God caused a corresponding perception in the human mind that animated the organism : when one exerted one's will to move, God caused the bodily motion that followed the volition. This conception of physical causation, as divinely ordered succession only, not real efficiency in the things of Sense, was further developed by two Cartesians, Geulinx and Malebranche. According to Malebranche (1638-1715) matter, because extended, could not become an immediate object of perception : and being in itself powerless and unintelligent, it could not be the active cause of our perception of its existence. So he was led to think that, while passive *sensations* of taste, smell, sound, and so on, are produced by Divine power, our conceptions of things as extended, or under mathematical relations, are our participations in Divine intelligence, so that we know the external world 'in God'. This monist tendency of later Cartesianism reached its extreme in SPINOZA (1632–77), who discarded the supposed duality, and treated self and matter as *correlative modes* of The One Being—still called by him God.

It was in this way that the material world was conceived by those leading thinkers in the seventeenth century, through whom Cartesianism was at last transformed into Spinozism.

But other intellectual influences were simultaneously contributing to form modern thought. BACON (1561-1626) in his *Novum Organum*, before Descartes, had urged the need for purifying the human mind from the prejudices apt to be generated by dependence on tradition. He too recommended free inquiry, which presupposes temporary doubt, as essential to the philosophic spirit, and an indispensable first step in the critical examination of our experience. Bacon was the English prophet of modern physical science; which men were then trying to construct, by better calculated observation of the qualities of things, and of the orderly sequence of events. His favourite lesson of man's dependence upon experience for real knowledge, and his warnings against empty verbal reasonings and dogmas unverified by facts, represented the spirit and method which Locke was soon after to apply, in his endeavour to find the origin and limits of human knowledge—the problem to which modern philosophy next addressed itself.

LOCKE (1632-1704) inaugurated the philosophical discussions of the eighteenth and nineteenth centuries by investigating mind experimentally. He applied himself, in Bacon's spirit, to study human understanding, in and through which we attain our ideas, our knowledge, and our beliefs, regarding the ego, the world, and God. What he called 'ideas' were for him facts important beyond all others, for by their means the external world was made known to us. He studied them in his own consciousness;—not in order to construct an imposing theory of the universe, but modestly to mark the growth, and take the measure of that limited understanding of ourselves and our surroundings which human beings have within their reach. By investigating this, in a plain matter-of-fact way, he hoped to discover the inevitable boundary of human certainty; as well as the ground of reasonable assent to what is only probable.[1]

The result of Locke's research, pursued for nearly twenty years, with this design in view, appeared in 1690, in his *Essay concerning Human Understanding*. The *Essay* contains, first an account of the ideas that are presented in human experience; next of the certainties, and the judgments of probability to which the ideas give rise. Locke argues, after a patient study of the facts, that all that man can know is constructed of simple or unanalysable ideas, some of them presented to our five senses, and others which arise when we reflect upon our mental operations. He concludes that nothing can be conceived that has not been given in one or other of these two ways.

In the last of the four books into which the *Essay* is divided, Locke discusses human certainties, and also our judgments of probability. Our gradual acquisitions through the five senses, and through reflection on our inner life are, according to him, the *materials* out of which we form certain knowledge and estimate probability. With a semblance of inconsistency, he tacitly assumes, as data prior to experience, fundamental principles, the *intellectual necessity* of which his theory of the origin of all ideas in experience,

---

[1] See Introduction to Locke's *Essay*.

strictly interpreted, inadequately recognises. Here is his account of the three primary certainties—The Ego, God, and Matter.

(*a*) Man's knowledge of his own existence as a self-conscious being, he resolved, like Descartes, into irresistible conviction. 'If I doubt of all other things, that very doubt makes me perceive my own existence, and will not suffer me to doubt of that.'—(*b*) The existence of God, or Eternal Mind, he treats as a consequence of the demand of reason for a sufficient Cause of his own existence, and 'as certainly evident to a man who thinks as any conclusion in mathematics.' In this argument he presupposes the necessity and universality of the principle of causation, but without explaining how 'experience' can make it universal and necessary.—(*c*) Our knowledge of Matter, or 'things that move in space,' we have, he says, 'only by sensation.' Here too he proceeds upon the principle of causation; for 'no man can know the existence of any being, except himself and God, but only when, 'by its actual operating upon him,' that being 'makes itself felt by him.' The ideas or appearances which are presented to us in our five senses, make us believe that '*something*' exists without us, at the time we have them, which causes us to have them; and we believe in the existence of this external cause of their appearance with 'a certainty as great as human nature is capable of conceiving the existence of anything but a man's self alone and God [1].'

Locke found two sorts of qualities or powers in that Something called Matter, which he supposed to be the cause of the ideas we perceive in sense. One sort was assumed by him to be like what we perceive; these were called its *primary*, *real*, or *mathematical* qualities: the other,

---

[1] See *Essay*, b. IV. ch. 9, 10, 11, for Locke's explanation of our knowledge of ourselves, God, and external things—the three existing certainties.

unlike what we perceive, were called its *secondary* or *imputed* qualities. Of the former sort are the sizes, figures, motions, impenetrability, and divisibility attributed to things;—qualities (or rather modes of quantity) which we cannot imagine any particle of matter to be destitute of. They belong to matter: they would be what we perceive them to be, even if there were no living being in the universe to perceive them. The secondary qualities, on the other hand,—the colours, sounds, tastes, and odours of things—are, so far as we directly perceive them, only sensations of which we are conscious. The heat we feel cannot be felt by the matter which forms the fire, nor can our feeling of taste exist in the orange. What these sensations correspond to in the 'something' without us, Locke cannot even imagine, if not to modifications of its primary qualities—atoms and their motions—that are unperceived by us. For, like the atomists of old, he conjectured that the secondary qualities might exist in the outward thing in the form of unperceived motions of its constituent atoms, connected by natural law with our sensations of colours, sounds, tastes, odours, heat and cold, to which they give rise. Colour or sound *as perceived* would thus be a kind of *feeling*, while *in itself* it is a mode of *motion*. But even if we could perceive these unperceivable atoms, and their supposed motions, Locke insisted that we could never without experience predict the sensations to which they would give rise in us, or anticipate their natural order. It is therefore fundamental in the *Essay*, that *absolutely demonstrable* physical science is impossible, consistently with the limits of human knowledge: the laws of nature, as discoverable by us, are in this respect arbitrary: that is to say, they might have been different from what they are: they are contingent on divine will, not eternally necessary.

Locke's 'something' or 'substance,' called Matter, external to, and the cause of, what is presented to our senses, was connected with what he taught about 'abstract' ideas. 'Idea' was the name applied by him to 'whatever we are conscious or percipient of, when viewed without respect to truth or falsehood, or to the relations in which certainty and probability consist. It corresponds so far to the 'simple apprehension' of logicians. The word in this wide meaning was naturally of frequent occurrence in an *Essay concerning human understanding*[1]. The second and third books of the *Essay* contain an analysis of our ideas, and conclude that they *all* depend upon experience. One class of ideas Locke signalises. He found, he says, in his scrutiny of human understanding, that men, especially philosophers, have not only ideas of *individual* things, as when they use their five senses, or when they exercise imagination: they have also ideas that are not ideas of individual things, that in consequence are not pictureable, and are therefore difficult to apprehend. He calls ideas of this sort *abstract*. The idea of a *triangle* is an example. It is an idea of a figure 'neither oblique nor rectangle, neither equilateral, equicrural, nor scalenon, but all and none of these at once; something imperfect that cannot exist; an idea "wherein some parts of different and inconsistent ideas are put together."' Another example is the abstract idea of *substance*. He describes it as made by abstraction—as the idea of a something which we accustom ourselves to suppose,

---

[1] Students of the present day are apt to misconceive the psychology of the seventeenth century from want of due regard to the special meaning of the word *idea*, as then much in use. By Plato it was used to express the archetypal essence of things. Through the Aristotelian distinction of form and matter, it came gradually to lose its high Platonic meaning, until with Descartes and Locke it was applied indiscriminately to all *phenomena* which we apprehend—in sense or otherwise. Berkeley, in his earlier writings, uses 'idea' for objects presented to our senses, and for representations of the same, which arise in memory, or are formed in imagination. In *Siris* he restores the term to its Platonic meaning, and prefers *phenomenon* as the name for what we perceive when we exercise our senses.

in which the qualities of things subsist, and from which they result—something related as a support or centre to the individual or concrete appearances that are presented to our senses and are regarded as qualities of things.

Locke describes his abstract idea of substance in terms which prepare for Berkeley's rejection of independent substance in Matter. 'The mind,' Locke says, 'being furnished with a great number of the simple ideas conveyed in by the senses as they are found in exterior things, or by reflection on its own operations, takes notice also that a certain number of these ideas *go constantly together*; which, being presumed to belong to *one* thing, are called, so united in one subject, by one name ; which, by inadvertency, we are apt afterward to talk of and consider as one simple idea, which indeed is a complication of many ideas together ; because, not imagining how these simple ideas *can* subsist by themselves, we accustom ourselves to suppose some *substratum* wherein they do subsist, and from which they do result ; which therefore we call Substance. So that if any one will examine himself concerning his notion of pure substance in general, he will find he has no other idea of it at all, but only a supposition of *he knows not what support* of qualities which affect our senses [1].'

Locke refers to other parts of his *Essay* for an answer to the question, whether the mere fact 'that we are *accustomed* to suppose' material substance is all that can be said on behalf of its reality. We want to know whether this 'custom' is grounded upon reason. So when treating of abstraction, he tries to show that the 'general idea of substance' is formed 'by abstracting'; that our idea of body or matter is thus an idea of 'an extended solid substance'; and our idea of mind or spirit that of 'a sub-

---

[1] Locke's *Essay*, b. II. ch. 23. §§ 1, 2.

stance that thinks or is conscious.' But in none of these mental experiences does he profess to find a 'clear and distinct' idea; he only finds that we are *somehow obliged* to suppose 'we know not what.' 'We have no other idea or notion of Matter than as *something* wherein sensible qualities which affect our senses do subsist.' In like manner, 'by supposing a substance wherein thinking, knowing, doubting, and a power of moving do subsist,' we have as clear a notion of Spirit as we can have of Body, —the one being supposed to be what he calls the *substratum* of those simple ideas that are presented to our senses; and the other supposed (in like ignorance of what *substratum* means) to be the *substratum* of the 'operations we experiment in ourselves within.' 'It is plain that the idea of corporeal substance is as remote from our conceptions and apprehensions as that of spiritual substance or spirit; and therefore from our not having any notion of the substance of spirit, we can no more conclude its non-existence than we can for the same reason deny the existence of body.' It is 'as rational to affirm there is no body, because we have no clear and distinct idea of the substance of matter, as to say there is no spirit, because we have no clear and distinct idea of the substance of a spirit.' But 'whatever be the secret *abstract* nature of substance in general, all the ideas we have of *particular* distinct substances are nothing but several combinations of simple ideas or qualities, coexisting in such, though unknown, cause of their union, so as to make the whole subsist of itself. What we call their powers make a great part of our complex ideas of substances.' In the end Locke finds that we are as ignorant of spiritual substance as of material substance. Berkeley, as we shall see, retains self or the internal substance of which we are conscious, while he rejects external substance.

The *Essay* of Locke[1], with its constant refrain, that real knowledge is never attained by the human mind 'without experience,' was coming into vogue when Berkeley was beginning to think. It seems to have awakened his eager and acute intelligence more than any other philosophical book. But Locke failed to satisfy him about an *unperceived* reality of Matter; and also about *abstract* ideas, especially the 'obscure' abstract idea of Matter.

Contemporary tendencies increased Berkeley's dissatisfaction with the opinions of Locke about Matter. His age, like our own, encouraged Materialism. The rise of the mixed mathematical sciences, and the habits formed by exclusive attention to external nature, were leading scientific men to attribute conscious life itself—that conscious life in which Descartes found the basis of knowledge, and among the facts of which Locke searched for certainties—to supposed power in Matter, that substance or 'something' without us, which Locke said was the cause of our ideas of sense. Power in Matter, it was suggested, might even cause conscious life, as well as all that happens in the material world. To Locke himself it had appeared possible that God might lend to organised matter the power of being conscious. 'It is not,' he says, 'much more remote from our comprehension to conceive this than to conceive that God should *superadd* to matter *another substance with a faculty of thinking*; since we know not in what thinking consists; nor to what sort of substances the first eternal thinking Being has been pleased to give that

---

[1] For interpretation and criticism of Locke's *Essay* as a whole, and not merely in its relation to Berkeley, I may refer to my annotated edition of the *Essay*, with the Prolegomena, published by the Oxford Clarendon Press in 1894; also to *Locke* in 'Philosophical Classics' (Blackwood, 1899).

power¹.' Locke here suggests only a subordinate, not an atheistic or universal materialism, for he presupposes *ultimate* dependence of matter, with its possible power of thinking, on God.

Such were some of the early issues of the endeavour of modern thought to explain conscious life and our perception of Matter. In Descartes and still more in Spinoza it was unwilling to accept perception and moral agency as inexplicable facts; and it was coming more and more to see that extended things could not exist as we find them in our experience, unless there were percipient beings alive, to realise their qualities. The tendency of Descartes and Malebranche was to explain perception by the agency of God—to find power *only* in Spirit—to take for granted the powerlessness of Matter. Hobbes, Gassendi, and the materialists, at the opposite philosophical extreme, recognised power *only* in Matter; and thus held that what is blind and unconscious is deeper and more explanatory than conscious reason. Spinoza, in his speculative flight, emptied visible things and finite spirits of real substance and power, and accordingly emptied God, or the *Unica Substantia*, of moral government. Locke, satisfied to report facts, offers no explanation of what is ultimately meant by Matter.

It was at this juncture that it occurred to Berkeley to discuss a question which had not been put, from the point of view at which he put it, by any ancient or modern. He found dogmas about Matter making men materialists. He pressed upon the world, with all the fervour of his Irish temperament, this New Question, to be answered before men could rest in Materialism:—What in reason should we mean when, with Locke, we assume the *reality*

---

[1] See *Essay*, b. IV. ch. 7. § 9; also b. I. ch. 4. § 18; b. II. ch. 23; b. III. ch. 10. § 15.

of 'matter'; and to *what power* should we refer the changing appearances presented to our senses? Let us, in the spirit of Locke, be faithful to facts, and to the ascertained limits of man's knowledge. A fuller and more faithful analysis of experience than that of Locke might perhaps show that the philosophers had been making an irrational assumption, in supposing that what we see and touch involves the existence of *unconscious substance*, endowed with *unknown powers*; or that we are obliged to accept this dogma, when, with the mass of mankind, we affirm the real existence of a material world.

To transform our conception of Matter, the existence of which mankind takes for granted, into an *intelligible* conception, and to show the *instrumental* and *subordinate* function of the material world in the spiritual economy of the universe, was what Berkeley attempted. His contemporaries and predecessors had been taking for granted that the things presented to sense exist as abstract substances; some had even thought that those substances explained self-conscious life and intelligence. He entreated them to reconsider their dogma, and to cease to suppose that Unreason could be the Supreme Power in the universe. Let them first make sure that Matter could really explain anything, or, indeed, that its independent reality was an intelligible dogma. Instead of blindly accepting propositions about the real existence and efficiency of Matter, he would first ask what 'existing,' and being 'real,' 'external,' 'substantial,' and 'powerful,' *mean*, when asserted of the things we are daily seeing and touching.

What Berkeley tried to do was to get this—as a previous question—put in place of the traditional dogmas about Matter, and Space, and Power. He wanted to find *the true philosophical meaning of Matter*; he did not doubt the reality of the material world, or the value of physical science. He wanted above all to settle the *true philosophical meaning of Causation*; he did not doubt that there was a subordinate sense in which outward things might be called causes.

Berkeley's place in history cannot be understood by those who do not see that what he wanted was to change the questions about the material world, with which his philosophical predecessors had been busy, into what he believed to be a deeper and more significant question. With this new question settled, in a fresh interpretation of the dogma that Matter exists, he hoped that thinking men might be relieved from perplexities about the things we see and touch, which retarded the physical sciences; and that they might also discover the irrationality of referring life, whether manifested in sense-perception or in any other intelligent way, to an unintelligible Something called 'matter' as its cause. Find out what Matter must mean, when we are faithful to facts and are not misled by empty abstract words, and by traditional dogmas about its nature and powers. This was his fervid entreaty. His promise was that when we have found this, we shall see that we do not need to search for proofs of its 'reality'; and that there is no reason for the materialistic assumption that Matter is endowed with powers which explain the universe—because in truth the things we see and touch, being all only caused causes, not originating causes, can in reason have only a subordinate sort of reality and power, and can afford no final explanation of anything.

But what are the facts to which we must be faithful when we are trying to find what we should mean by 'matter' and its 'powers'? In his *Principles of Human Knowledge*, Berkeley started with Locke's ambiguous thesis—that human knowledge is the gradual issue of ideas or appearances given in human experience [1].

[1] See Berkeley's metaphysical *Commonplace Book, passim*, in the Oxford edition of his *Works*. Compare *Principles of Human Knowledge*, §§ 1, 2.

When he reflected upon his experience in the five senses, he said that he could not find in experienced Matter either independent substance or originating power. Moreover, material substance, except as given in a living perception of concrete phenomena, seemed to him meaningless and unreal. But he found in abundance concrete sights and touches and sounds and tastes and smells. He found also *himself*, actually conscious of sights and touches and sounds and tastes and smells—conscious too of his own (continued) identity through all changes, and of his power to produce (to some extent) changes in what he saw and touched. But when he reflected upon his experience of what is called *matter*, he found only sights, touches, and other ideas or appearances, presented according to natural laws, and all dependent for their reality on a person percipient of them.

So Berkeley melted the material world into what is actually presented or presentable to our senses. The existence of *this* world was incapable even of Cartesian doubt. When we say that we see or touch a material object, all that we ought to mean is, that we perceive appearances in sense which have a practical meaning, inasmuch as our pleasures and pains largely depend upon them. When we are actually percipient, we have as much evidence of *their* reality as we have of our own. In being percipient we are conscious of our selves, and, simultaneously with this, of the passive and dependent appearances which our senses reveal. Strictly speaking we are *conscious* of the former and *percipient* of the latter. There is as little room for doubt and problematical inference in the one case as in the other. Human knowledge begins with these two *irreducible* facts—(*a*) self-consciousness, and (*b*) perceived appearances that in themselves are unsubstantial and powerless.

But Berkeley found more than this when he further considered the solid and extended bodies placed in space, composed of sense-presented appearances. For all sane persons believe that things around them and their own bodies exist independently of their own perceptions. But the sights, sounds, and other appearances presented to my senses are only transitory. I am not always perceiving them. So *they* cannot be the solid and extended things that do not pass away. We find moreover in Matter more than a mere succession of presented appearances. We find *clusters* of these, which we distinguish as *things*; and we speak of the appearances as *qualities* of the *things*. Into what facts of experience is this knowledge of *qualified things* to be resolved? If the things exist only while the actual perceptions last, what is meant by the *permanence* which seems to be implied in the *reality* of outward things?

If the material world were reduced to my passing perceptions, the existence of Matter would be only intermittent and fragmentary. The tree that I am looking at exists, as an object perceived by me, *only while I am looking at it*. And even then it so exists only in its *visible* qualities; for, being at a distance, the *invisible* qualities, which at the same time I attribute to it, are not, under these conditions, my actual perceptions. Do *they* all the while exist? If not, the greater part of what is meant by the tree is not existing, even at the very time that I see the tree. If external matter means only *actual* perception, all visible qualities of things must relapse into non-entity when things are left in the dark; and their tangible ones too, in the light as well, unless a percipient is *always* touching every part of them. The material world could not have existed millions of ages before men or other sentient beings began to be percipient, if *only this* is what is meant by its real existence [1].

---

[1] This question is raised by Locke (*Essay*, b. IV. ch. 11), when he says that the things of sense are certainly known to exist only while

Here Berkeley brings in what he calls our 'judgments of suggestion,' but without a vindication of their validity. *Suggestion* is the term he uses to express our tendency to expect the reappearance of the ideas or phenomena of sense in the order in which they have always been found connected. Perception through suggestion is indirect or acquired perception. It presupposes memory and imagination, and above all permanent rational order in the world of sense, the ever-changing appearances, which we call the material world. Suggestion rises at last into science of nature and scientific prevision, and affords room for scientific experiment and verification. The mere sight of the tree 'suggests' the sensation of resistance. This is so connected with what is seen, in the steady order of sense-presented appearances, that we *expect* to *feel resistance*, after going through the locomotive experience required to bring our bodies into collision with the tree. The one sense-appearance is the *suggesting sign* of the other. The connexion, somehow established between them, gives rise to what Berkeley calls 'language.' But the significance and interpretability of sensuous ideas is not confined to visible ones. All presented appearances in all the senses are significant and interpretable. Physical science is the interpretation. Each sense can thus do duty for the others. So the material world is found to consist not of *mere* phenomena, but of *significant* and *interpretable* phenomena. It is a cosmos, not a chaos.

While the most striking examples of the supreme fact that sense-presented ideas or phenomena constitute an interpretable language are those presented by Sight, one must never forget that the Symbolism of Nature is illustrated in our whole experience: we are continually trans-

---

they are actually present to our senses—their existence when by me unperceived being only taken for granted by me.

lating the language of each sense into data of some other sense, above all into those of Touch. The inductive inferences of science are only *elaborate* translations of this sort, founded ultimately, like those of sense-perception, on rational suggestion. The whole material world is a system of sensible signs. Every appearance of which we are percipient in our senses is significant of other appearances, of which at the time we are not actually percipient. The scientific significations of phenomena are not directly perceived in the transitory phenomena, nor can they be discovered by abstract reasoning. Our interpretations of nature are the gradual result of custom and intelligent comparison of instances; but it is a custom on the part of external nature which is found to involve reason: what in its scientific form is inductive reasoning, commences in the *habit* produced by the steady order latent among natural phenomena.

The connexion between a felt or a visible perception in sense and the expected phenomenon which it signifies, is said by Berkeley to be 'arbitrary.' He enlarges on its *arbitrariness*, and founds on this his favourite analogy of a language of natural signs—connexion between names and their meanings being in like manner arbitrary. This may seem to imply that the natural laws which govern the material world are capricious, and so not to be depended on. But what he intends is, that there is no *a priori* or eternal reason in things why, for example, a tree seen from a distance must 'suggest' the particular tactual phenomena which it does suggest; nor why any of the other constant connexions among phenomena which form the web of physical science might not have been other than it is in fact. Natural causation is natural symbolism, dependent on, and expressive of, the perfect reason and will of God. At our point of view it is not *necessary*, more than the connexion between a word and the meaning which men have agreed to connect with the word. In both cases the connexion is arbitrary. God, or perfect Will, constantly maintains sensible things and their natural laws.

Faith in divinely established connexion—that is to say in scientific connexion—among the ideas presented to our senses is Berkeley's explanation of belief in natural law. The consequent permanence in the relation between the *present* and the *expected*, in and among the different clusters of sense-phenomena—assumed as a judgment of common sense—is (so far) his explanation of belief in the 'permanence' of sensible things, *during the intervals in which they are not actually perceived*. To illustrate the fact that our expectations are at first suggested by habit, and that the reason latent in this habit is unfolded in physical science, is a result of his investigation of Vision, making it an important contribution to psychology. There is neither contradiction nor meaninglessness, he would say, in a material world that is composed of *significant sense-phenomena*, which we can all to some extent interpret and then make use of: there must be either meaninglessness or contradiction in the material world of the philosophers, which consists of *abstract material substances and powers*.

But Berkeley finds in our experience of the material world more than momentary sense-phenomena, and more than the scientific prevision which the fixed order and consequent significance of those phenomena makes possible. *Causation*, in its deepest meaning, is more than sense-symbolism. Indeed it is quite other than this. It is not constant connexion of certain phenomena with certain other phenomena. It is something that is found only in personal Volition, or in the assertion 'I *can* do this or that.' At least the germ of this deeper philosophy is found in Berkeley.

Besides the *present* perceptions of sense and the *suggested* or *expected* perceptions of sense, he finds that human experience necessarily involves the *notion* (not idea) of the percipient active being, or self-conscious person, that each individual calls *himself*, expressed by Ego—the personal pronoun 'I.' I cannot be percipient of my invisible conscious self in the way I am percipient of the sights or sounds or other phenomena of sense to which the term *idea* is confined by Berkeley. Still, I can use the personal pronoun with *meaning*; I can speak *intelligibly* about my continued identity and agency. So it may be said that we have a 'notion' of it, although not an idea or phenomenon. I must also believe in my own voluntary activity, or that I am the originating cause of all acts for which I am morally responsible; and I practically understand, through this moral experience, what *power* means. It is from moral experience that the word power gathers its deepest meaning; for the 'power' popularly attributed to things of sense is only constancy of sequence maintained by God. My conviction of *my own power* is as certain as my conviction of my own existence, to the extent to which I acknowledge my moral responsibility.

But there must be Power in the universe other than man's personal power: we find that *we* are not able to create the phenomena of which we are percipient in our senses, or to change the natural laws of their occurrence. We overcome the material world only by submission to the established order in which its ideas or phenomena appear; which therefore we regard as established by the Universal Power, not by us. Sometimes we find *ourselves* able, and therefore responsible—yet oftener unable, and therefore in this irresponsible; sometimes *we can* and sometimes *we cannot*; and our ability is small indeed in its range compared to our inability. It is in this experience of his own limited and resisted power that each one finds *himself*; we have in the same experience our one signal example of what the word *power* ultimately means. That which is done, but not by man, must have been done (so Berkeley might argue) by power which experience gives us examples of: it must be due to the moral agency of Spirit, not to anything in Matter.

It is thus necessary in reason that the universe presented in sense—unsubstantial and powerless in the highest meanings of substance and power—should be sustained and regulated by the moral agency of the Universal Power. This power is what we mean by God. We cannot go deeper. The Divine Active Reason is continuously presenting to us the phenomena of which we are percipient in the senses. God regulates, and suggests, in and through custom based on reason, the events which we have reason to expect. All the natural laws of the universe are simply manifestations of the Active Reason which the universe implies. This is the Efficient Cause at work in those metamorphoses of things with which alone the physical sciences are concerned; this is the cause of the natural order which yields science; and its final cause too is this same omnipresent rational Will. In and through God, or Active Reason, the material world becomes an intelligible world. Its constant order amidst constant change of its constituent phenomena, is accounted for. Its qualities, as well as the propositions of science concerning the qualified things, which, under the new conception of Matter, at first seemed dissolved in a chaos of perishable sensations, in the end present permanence and order, through the eternally operative Divine Rational Providence.

This, I think, is implied, though not fully realised, by Berkeley, in the explanation of what the *reality* of the material world means. The explanation virtually connects the three primary data of metaphysics—conscious Self, the material World, and God. It comprehends the two contrasted and dependent substances, and the one Supreme Substance and Power, according to Descartes,—the three ontological certainties of Locke. But this is not worked into system by Berkeley. What he did was done, he modestly says, 'with a view to giving hints to thinking men who have leisure and curiosity to go to the bottom of things, and pursue them in their own minds.' One result of his new conception of Matter was the substitution of GOD for unintelligible substance and power in Matter. The report he made, after he had reflected upon the relevant facts—freed from the bondage of empty abstract words—might be in effect this:—We in this mortal life reach practical knowledge of *ourselves* and of *God*, in and through interpretation of the significant phenomena of sense, commonly called *matter*; one end of whose significant and interpretable presence in the universe seems to be,—to enable us who interpret them to become conscious of ourselves, capable of fruitful intercourse with one another, all in the faith that we live and move and have our being in Omnipotent Goodness.

Berkeley, as we have seen, starts from Locke's ambiguous formula, which reduces complex human knowledge, in its last analysis, to human experience. But Locke and Berkeley, without critical analysis of what experience inevitably presupposes, proceed upon the assumption that there is in it *more* than isolated sensations. Locke's employment of the principle of causality in his explanation of our knowledge of God, for instance, is a virtual acknowledgment of more than sense-presented appearances in the constitution of knowledge. Clarke (1675-1729), the philosophical theologian of Locke's school, worked out, more elaborately than Locke, a 'demonstration' of the rational necessity for God. And the phenomena presented to the senses, with their interpretation by suggestion, do not exhaust the philosophy of Berkeley. Custom-induced suggestion was in the end *contrasted* with inference of reason. 'To perceive,' he tells us in one of his later works, 'to perceive[1], is one thing: to judge is another. So likewise to be suggested is one thing, and to be inferred another. Things are suggested and perceived by *sense*. We make judgments and inferences by the *intellect*[2].'

In *Siris* he puts the ideas or appearances presented in Sense and Suggestion more in the background. God and Divine Ideas are in the foreground. When he attributes to Aristotle the doctrine 'that the mind of man is without innate ideas,' in contrast to Plato, who found in the mind 'notions which never were nor can be in the sense,' he reveals his Platonic sympathies. 'Some,' he says, 'may think the truth to be this:—that there are properly no *ideas*, or passive objects, in the mind but what were derived from sense; but that there are also besides these her own acts or operations: such are *notions*.' Again: 'The perceptions of sense are gross: but even in the senses there is a difference..... By experiments of some we become acquainted with the lower faculties of the soul; and from them, whether by a gradual evolution or ascent, we arrive at the highest. Sense supplies images to memory. These become subjects for fancy to work upon. Reason considers and judges of the imaginations. And these acts of reason become new objects to the understanding. In this scale each lower faculty is a step that leads to one above it. And the uppermost naturally leads to the Deity; which is rather the object of intellectual knowledge than even of the discursive faculty, not to mention the sensitive[3].'

If Berkeley in his youth seems to resolve Experience into Sensation, the pervading tendency of *Siris* is to find the root of the universe and the foundation of experience

---

[1] 'to perceive,' i.e. to have ideas or phenomena present to our senses.
[2] *Vindication of New Theory of Vision*, sect. 42.
[3] See *Siris*, sect. 308, 303.

in Omnipresent Reason, and to see in the things of sense opportunity provided, through physical research and science, for useful education of the mind of man.

Such in outline was Berkeley's philosophical conception of the material world, as that conception appears, first in the fervid reasonings of his youth, awakened by Locke, and then in *Siris*, modified by the Platonic studies of later life. Let us now look at some of its issues in the period which followed.

Six years before *Siris* appeared, Locke's formula regarding the dependence of our limited knowledge on our limited 'experience,' had been understood by DAVID HUME (1711–76) to signify, that this experience includes only ideas presented in sense—called by Hume 'impressions.' Impressions of external and internal sense, blindly connected by custom—this was in the end his 'solution of sceptical doubt[1].' The universe was therefore at last 'a riddle, an ænigma, an inexplicable mystery.'

By his agnostic doubt, Hume obliged the sincere thinker to search further for the roots of knowledge, if indeed it was rooted at all.

Hume's paralysis of human intelligence was the chief event in the epoch of philosophy that was inaugurated by Locke, in which we are living. A critical exposure of the impossibility of interpreting human life, if knowledge at last means only sensuous experience, and if experience at last can mean only blindly suggested appearances, without root in reason—was the next act in the philosophical drama, after Berkeley's exhibition of the ultimate dependence of the material world for its qualities and utilities on percipient and active Mind. Materialism seemed, in Berkeley's theory, to be impossible. It was replaced by a spiritually-constituted

---

[1] See Hume's *Inquiry concerning Human Understanding*, ch. 2–8.

Universe, in which all extended things, including our own bodies, are supposed to exist only as groups of dependent and powerless sense-appearances; perceived and changed so far by finite persons; in subordination to omnipresent and ever active Divine Reason. But Berkeley's spiritually-constituted Universe, it was argued by Hume, involved assumptions which—on the hypothesis with which Hume started, namely, that experience is merely external and internal data of sense connected by blind custom—might be proved (if proof were possible in a total paralysis of reason) to be as absurd as Berkeley found an independent material world to be.

Hume's attempt to show that, on those Principles, mind or spirit is as sensuous as matter—as unsubstantial and powerless—is what gives him his conspicuous place in the history of modern theology and philosophy. His sceptical analysis of experience into customary connexion of presented appearances was first proposed, without qualification, in his *Treatise on Human Nature*, in 1739; then, less intrepidly, in 1748, in his *Inquiry concerning Human Understanding*. In both he referred to Berkeley's rejection of abstractions, and analysis of matter into orderly sensations, as memorable discoveries in philosophy. *Looking only at the negative part of what Berkeley taught*, he claimed for him a place among sceptics; adding, as evidence of this, that his 'arguments admit of no answer, and yet produce no conviction; their only effect being to produce that momentary amazement, irresolution, and confusion, which is the result of scepticism [1].'

The way in which Hume would bar as incompetent Berkeley's ascent, from the 'gross perceptions of sense' with which he starts, to 'the intellectual knowledge of Deity' in *Siris*, is argued throughout Hume's *Treatise of Human Nature*. The salient points of the argument should be studied:—

---

[1] *Inquiry concerning Human Understanding*, sect. xii. pt. i. note.

(a) A significant one is that in which Hume deals with Berkeley's 'notion' of Self. Berkeley takes for granted that I cannot help being conscious that I exist. Apart from the 'notion' of Self, found by reflection, his spiritually-constituted universe dissolves into transitory unconnected appearances. 'There are some philosophers,' Hume argues, 'who imagine we are every moment *conscious* of what we call our SELF; that we *feel* its existence and its continuance in existence; and so are certain, beyond the evidence of a demonstration, both of its perfect identity and simplicity. . . . Unluckily all these positive assertions are contrary to that very experience which is pleaded for them. . . . For my part, when I enter most intimately into what I call *myself*, I always stumble on some particular perception or other—of heat or cold, light or shade, love or hatred, pain or pleasure. I never can catch *myself* at any time without a perception, and never can observe anything but the perception. When my perceptions are removed for any time—as by sound sleep—so long am I insensible of *myself*, and may truly be said not to exist. And were all my perceptions removed by death, and I could neither think, nor feel, nor see, nor love, nor hate, after the dissolution of my body, I should be entirely annihilated; nor do I conceive what is farther requisite to make me a perfect nonentity [1].'

We have Berkeley's answer to this (by anticipation) in the third of his *Three Dialogues between Hylas and Philonous*. 'It seems to me,' Hylas objects, 'that, according to your own way of thinking, and in consequence of your own principles, it should follow that *you* are only a system of floating ideas, without any substance to support them. Words, you say, are not to be used without a meaning;

---

[1] See Hume's *Treatise on Human Nature, being an attempt to introduce the Experimental Method of reasoning into Moral Subjects*, b. I. pt. iv. sect 6.

and as there is no more meaning in *spiritual substance* than in *material substance*, the one ought to be exploded as well as the other.' 'How often,' replies Philonous (representing Berkeley), 'must I repeat that *I know or am conscious of my own being*, and that *I myself* am not my ideas, but somewhat else—a thinking active principle that perceives, knows, wills, and operates about ideas. I *know* that I—the same self—perceive both colours and sounds: that a colour cannot perceive a sound, nor a sound a colour: that I am therefore one individual principle, distinct from colour and sound: and, for the same reason, from all other sensible things and inert ideas. But I am not in like manner conscious either of the existence or essence of Matter.'

(*b*) Take, next, Hume's demand for *evidence* of that continual dependence on God, or omnipresent Reason, on the part of the material world, which Berkeley had maintained. —'It seems to me,' Hume argues, 'that this theory of the universal energy and operation of the Supreme Being is too bold ever to carry conviction with it, to a man sufficiently apprised of the weakness of human reason, and the narrow limits to which it is confined in its operations. . . . Our line is too short to fathom such immense abysses. And however we may flatter ourselves that we are guided in every step we take by a kind of verisimilitude and experience, we may be assured that this fancied experience has no authority, when we thus apply it to subjects that lie entirely out of the reach of experience. . . . We are ignorant, it is true, of the manner in which *bodies* operate on each other: *their* "force" or "energy" is entirely incomprehensible. But are we not equally ignorant of the manner or force in which the Supreme Mind operates either on itself or on body? Whence, I beseech you, do we acquire any idea of this? We have no sentiment or consciousness of this power in ourselves. We have no idea of the Supreme Being but what we learn by reflection upon our own faculties. Were our ignorance therefore a good reason for rejecting anything, we should be led into denying all energy in the Supreme Being as much as in the grossest matter. We surely comprehend as little the operations of the one as of the other. Is it more difficult to conceive that motion may arise from *impulse* than that it may arise from *volition*? All we know is our profound ignorance in both cases[1].'

(*c*) Berkeley's favourite doctrine of the *arbitrariness* of natural laws is by Hume translated into an arbitrariness in which anything might *a priori* be the 'cause' of anything else. *Total inexplicableness* is substituted by Hume for the Rational Will believed by Berkeley to connect phenomena and their changes in the order we find in nature Reason at the root of the Universe is not recognised by the sceptic: only blind change. All so-called knowledge is only opinion, produced physically by custom. Take the following:—' Whatever is *may* not continue to be. No negation of a fact can involve a contradiction. The non-existence of any being is as clear and distinct an idea as its existence. The proposition which affirms it not to be, however false, is no less conceivable and intelligible than that which affirms it to be. The case is different with the sciences, properly so called[2]. Every proposition which is not true is there unintelligible. That the cube of sixty-four is equal to the half of ten is a false proposition, and can never be distinctly conceived. But that Caesar, or the angel Gabriel, or any beings, never existed, may be a false proposition, but still is perfectly conceivable, and implies no contradiction. The existence, therefore, of *any concrete being* can only be proved by arguments from its cause or its effect; and these arguments are founded entirely on experience. If we reason *a priori*, anything may appear able

---

[1] See Hume's *Inquiry concerning Human Understanding*, sect. vii.

[2] The demonstrable sciences, e.g. mathematics.

to produce anything. The falling of a pebble may, for aught we know, extinguish the sun; or the wish of a man controul the planets in their orbits. It is only experience which teaches us the nature and bounds of cause and effect, and enables us to infer the existence of one object, in the world either of matter or of spirits, from that of another. Not only the Will of the Supreme Being may create matter, but, for aught we know *a priori*, the will of any other being might create it; or any other cause that the most whimsical imagination can assign [1].'

Thus in the sceptical nescience of Hume, what we call *reason* in nature resolves into inexplicable order, according to which events have hitherto followed one another. Reason in man is only habit. 'For, wherever repetition of any particular act or operation produces in us a propensity to renew the act or operation, without being impelled by any reasoning or process of the understanding, we always say that this *propensity* is the *effect* of Custom. By employing that word, we pretend not to have given the ultimate reason of such propensity. We only point out a principle of human nature, which is universally acknowledged, and which is well known by its effects. *Perhaps we can push our inquiries no farther* [2].'

[1] See *Inquiry*, § xii. pt. iii.—There are three divergent views about Nescience. They correspond severally to two extreme positions — Empirical Nescience, Absolute Idealism, and the intermediate 'broken system,' which, acknowledging final incomprehensibility, is satisfied with Faith in irreducible *credenda*, latent in our higher nature, which may by reflection be more or less transformed into *intelligenda* in philosophy. It is implied in the first that anything may *a priori* be the cause of anything; so that it is presumptuous to speak of an alleged cause as 'sufficient' or 'insufficient': this is Hume's account of the matter. According to the opposite view, each event must be determined according to universal rational necessity: this is the outcome of the ontological philosophy of Spinoza. The third finds the only true and 'sufficient' cause at last in active Reason and moral Agency—exemplified in our experience of our own moral agency, which presents man as an 'image of God.'

[2] See Hume's *Inquiry*, § v. p. 1.

Berkeley's method of disposing of Materialism, in his spiritual explanation of the words Matter and Reality, was thus followed, in the next movement in European thought, not by a fuller development of his Spiritual Philosophy, but by the Scepticism or Agnosticism which professes inability to find more in 'experience' than external and internal sensations, which inexplicably issue in beliefs that are ultimately non-rational. To this Berkeley was conducted, when he was interpreted by Hume, who surrendered all that is due to other elements in knowledge than sensations blindly connected by custom,—thus dissolving Berkeley's conception of a divinely-constituted universe.

Under this interpretation, in the middle of the eighteenth century, Locke's proposed analysis of human knowledge was paralysed. The empirical philosophy to which it had given rise, represented in Britain by Hume, had no further word to say—unless, contemporaneously, through Hartley and his school, to repeat the word 'association' as a universal solvent; and, in the nineteenth century, in Herbert Spencer and Darwin, to expand the associative tendency in the individual, by the principle of heredity, under the law of organic evolution, so as to connect it with the history of the race and with the whole economy of the universe. In France, Locke's philosophy, inadequately interpreted, was transformed into materialism in the latter part of the eighteenth century. On the other hand, metaphysics, long represented in Germany by LEIBNIZ (1646–1716), seemed to expire in the arid reasonings of the German school of Wolff, as the eighteenth century advanced.

Thus modern philosophy, due to the original Cartesian impulse, and the more particular direction given to it by Locke, issued in the constructive spiritualism of Berkeley, and then in the destructive nescience of Hume.

But man's disposition to rise out of ignorance, and if possible to attain certain knowledge, is permanent. Despair of philosophy was not the final result of the sceptical speculation of Hume, which the spiritually-constituted universe conceived by Berkeley, even when looked at only on its negative side, did not justify. For Hume's scepticism led to a deeper consideration of the foundations of knowledge in the light (*a*) of the actual constitution of the human mind, by Reid, and (*b*) of the principles presupposed in the very possibility of experience, by Kant.

The earliest immediate and direct effect of Hume was the attempt of REID (1710-96), by patient reflection, to awaken in human consciousness fundamental convictions that are incapable of logical proof, but are tacitly accepted by all sane persons. These he called Principles of the Common Sense, with which all men are divinely inspired. That we are thus inspired with faith in the external existence of the material world, is argued for and illustrated in Reid's *Inquiry into the Human Mind on the Principles of Common Sense* (1764). This and other inspired Convictions—in particular our conviction of our own personality and free personal agency—are defended in his *Essays on the Intellectual Powers* (1785) and *On the Active Powers* (1788)[1].

The other reaction against Hume was the attempt of KANT (1724-1804), by critical analysis, to show that constructive activity of reason is necessarily involved in the very constitution of experience. Kant was the contemporary of Reid. Without mutual concert, they unconsciously co-operated as early leaders in this movement towards constructive philosophy, which followed the total disintegration of human knowledge and faith by the Scottish sceptic. Kant's critical analysis of Pure Reason appeared in 1781, followed by an examination of Practical or Moral Reason, in 1788.

[1] I have discussed this philosophy in *Thomas Reid*, 'Famous Scots Series (1898).

Perhaps the secret intention of Hume was to illustrate defects in the philosophy proposed by Locke, with a view to its amendment, rather than finally to dissolve all human belief and thus extinguish human life. If so, the design succeeded; for a step in advance was taken by Reid and Kant, and more by their successors, in disclosing the ultimate basis of Science and Religion. Reid candidly recognises the sceptics as 'men whose business it is to pick holes in the fabric of knowledge, where it is weak and faulty; and when these places are properly repaired, the whole building becomes more firm and solid.' He says that at first he accepted Berkeley's account of Matter, till, imagining sceptical consequences to follow from it which gave him 'more uneasiness than the want of a material world,' it occurred to him to reconsider what he believed to be its source, in the pervading assumption of philosophers—that we are percipient, not of external realities but only of our own inward impressions, which we suppose to be faithful representations of reality. Kant found the source of scepticism in Hume's inadequate account of our belief in causation.

It is beyond the design of this Introduction to trace modern philosophy further in its revival after Hume. In this revival Reid and Kant hold a place analogous to that of Descartes in its first period. The philosophy of experience offered in Locke's *Essay* was insufficient: it overlooked the implicates necessarily presupposed in experience. Hence a scepticism, which confesses that, if experience is only transitory data of sense, somehow associated, there can be no knowledge. Reid and Kant gave expression to the need for recognising principles which are tacitly presupposed in the physical and moral experience of mankind, inasmuch as without them it would all dissolve. These underlying *credenda*, as Reid conceived them, or categories, in Kant's nomenclature, had been unconsciously proceeded upon by philosophers who, like Locke, vaguely referred all knowledge to 'experience.' For a profounder investigation of the constitution of experience we are indebted to the reaction from Hume.

The issue in the nineteenth century of this return to the spiritual constitution of experience, by Reid and by Kant, presents analogies to the issue, in the seventeenth century, of the more tentative philosophy of Descartes; before an investigation of the nature and limits of human knowledge had been initiated by Locke, and then pursued in two opposite directions—constructively by Berkeley, sceptically by Hume. The more recent issue has the advantage of its later development. In no philosophy do we find the full realisation of the philosophical ideal—only an approach to this; but we look for a nearer approach in later than in earlier speculations, because assisted by the extremes and collisions of the earlier thought. In the later or post-Kantian period, Kantism led to Hegelianism, as Cartesianism in the seventeenth century led to Spinozism. But the influence of Kant, through the negative side of his philosophy, appears even in Comte and Positivism, and in modern Agnosticism, as that of Descartes appears in Hume.

In an examination of philosophical opinions and systems we assume that true philosophy must at least not be self-contradictory. It must also be in harmony with the universal judgments of the common sense, or common reason, which science and morality can be shown to involve. It may further be granted that it ought not to reject practical beliefs, beneficially operative in human life (though often dormant in individual minds), which cannot be *proved* to be inconsistent with the necessities of reason.

To awaken a sympathetic response in individual minds to the spiritual convictions on which human life ought to rest, and with which man is, as it were, sub-consciously inspired, is the chief aim of philosophical education. From Socrates onwards this has been recognised by its true teachers. The regulative principles in the constitution of man, especially those which are characteristic of his higher life, are often not recognised consciously. Some of them are in many cases dormant; they are acted on without distinct consciousness. They are 'universal and necessary' potentially rather than intelligently. Thus the conviction that we are free rational beings, and therefore morally responsible, is often weak; or it is acted on without due recognition of what it implies. The same is true of those convictions of God and the higher life that belong to our moral experience. 'The natural man receiveth not the things of the spirit of God.' It is the office of religion and of philosophical education to assist in making the student aware of what is latent in his spiritual constitution, and implied in the Divine Reason in which we all share sub-consciously.

History is full of the records of reactions on behalf of principles, dormant in individuals and communities, which have, in consequence, lost influence for a time. Reason is eternal; our individual consciousness of the moral reason that is latent in the universe fluctuates and may be paralysed. The unpractical recluse, by habitual introspection, weakens his latent conviction of external reality. One who is exclusively devoted to observation of the visible world loses power of apprehending the invisible facts of spiritual experience, so that what cannot be seen or touched seems illusion.

In the twentieth century, the things of sense, and the means of making ourselves comfortable through skilful applications of the laws of the material world, occupy people's imagination as perhaps they never did before— not even at the time when Berkeley was led to inquire what Matter means, and what its true place and office is, in relation to self-conscious beings. In this way faith in moral agency and in God are lost in doubt, because they do not admit of verification by the senses, being implicates of our spiritual experience. That scientific certainty which is reached through verification by the senses—*although it involves faith*—is held paramount; the certainty that is reached without an appeal to the material world of the senses, *because it involves faith*, is rejected as illusory. That is to say, faith in physical order, which in the end is moral trust in God—the basis of our inferences in the sciences of nature—is strong. Faith in inferences which expressly presume ethical or spiritual postulates—not less lawfully rested on those implicates of moral experience—is weak.

Materialism, as it has done before, must disappear, when it contradicts what are found to be constituents of divine reason in man—though often dormant, or existing semi-consciously, in individual minds. Philosophy may even swing to the opposite extreme. For its history has been a succession of oscillations between one-sided physics and one-sided metaphysics—between Materialism which explains consciousness by motions of molecules, and the Idealism which explains the concrete things of sense and their motions by abstract Reason. These two opposites have repeatedly been refuted by the *reductio ad absurdum* of total Scepticism to which each has given rise. But the Sceptical Nescience of a philosophy emptied of God, thus induced, passes away in its turn, when the root-principles of divinely-inspired human nature have been revived in conscious life,—insight of them even deepened by the preceding collision of the two extremes and its sceptical issue. We are in this way better prepared to pass through the ordeal of another but more enlightened collision of extreme Materialism with extreme Idealism. It is thus that man advances through successive sceptical crises, consequent upon his own one-sided systems. What is permanent in our higher nature becomes enlightened and strengthened in the end, as the issue of the succession of philosophical controversies.

These *Selections from Berkeley* are meant to incite and prepare for this further reflection, in the light of later philosophy. They are so arranged as to carry the reader upwards through Berkeley's reasoned account of Matter, which makes it mean interpretable appearances in sense-phenomena, necessarily dependent on percipient and active Mind; followed by an analysis of the interpretation, reached at first through habit and suggestion, then rising into physical science; all ending in meditation about the ultimate unity of the universe in God, in whom we live and move and have our being.

FIRST PART

PHILOSOPHICAL PRINCIPLES

CONCERNING

MATTER AND SPIRIT

SELECTIONS FROM

BERKELEY'S 'TREATISE CONCERNING THE PRINCIPLES OF HUMAN KNOWLEDGE,' AND HIS 'DIALOGUES BETWEEN HYLAS AND PHILONOUS'

The same Principles which, at first view, lead to Scepticism, pursued to a certain point, bring men back to Common Sense.—BERKELEY.

EDITOR'S PREFATORY NOTE

BERKELEY'S *Treatise on the Principles of Human Knowledge*, as the one systematic exposition and defence of his subtle argument against Materialism, deserves to be explained in its systematic connexion.

The Introduction points to abuse of Language, even by philosophers, as the chief cause of the slow progress of human knowledge. Language had long been a cover for empty abstractions. The key to Berkeley's philosophical point of view is found in his attack on 'abstract ideas' in the Introduction—resumed in other places. The principle here unfolded is—that real knowledge deals with what is concrete; that there can be no concrete reality in the things of sense, commonly called the material world, apart from the perceptions of a living mind, in which alone Matter is realised; and that to test the meaning of terms, especially such terms as Matter and Mind, we must exemplify what we mean in individual examples.

Not to pretend to look for real substances or causes in abstractions which cannot be individualised, and always to verify words concerning Matter by what is actually presented in living perceptions of sense, is the lesson of the Introduction.

In the *Treatise* which follows, this lesson is applied, to show the meaninglessness of Matter, when it is supposed to be something that exists independently of living percipient mind. We cannot have an *abstract* idea of Matter, or an idea of it other than what is derived from the concrete manifestations given in our perceptions. The material world must consist of the perceptions of persons.

This central Principle about Matter is expounded, defended, and applied as follows :—

I. (Sect. 1–33.) These sections contain a reasoned exposition of what is meant by the real existence of Matter, which is resolved into concrete data of sense, instead of the meaningless abstract substance which philosophers had assumed it to be. Analysis of the reasons for adopting this conception affords abundant intellectual exercise for the student.

II. (Sect. 34–84.) We have in these sections a refutation of Objections to the Principles.

Other and graver objections, not suggested by Berkeley, and partly arising out of later philosophical thought, might be sought for, and critically examined by the student. Some of them are proposed in the *Annotations*.

III. (Sect. 85–156.) In the remainder of the *Treatise* the new conception of Matter, as consisting of data of sense that are necessarily dependent on mind for their intelligible existence, is applied to refute Scepticism and restore Belief: as well as to clear the way to progress in science. It is applied :—

(*a*) To restore, in an improved form, Beliefs which were dissolving in Scepticism (Sect. 85–96);

(*b*) To get rid of unmeaning abstractions (Sect. 97–100);

(*c*) To advance Sciences which had been impeded by empty conceptions of Matter, Causation, Space, Time, and Motion (Sect. 101–116);

(*d*) To relieve perplexities in mathematical reasonings (Sect. 117–134);

(*e*) To explain and sustain faith in human Immortality (Sect. 135–144);

(*f*) To explain the belief which each man has in the existence of other men (Sect. 145);

(*g*) To explain and sustain faith in the existence of God (Sect. 146–156).

I have appended to the First Part of the Selections portions of the *Dialogues between Hylas and Philonous*, in which the New Principles are discussed in an easy familiar manner, Hylas arguing for the old abstract conception of Matter, and Philonous vindicating Berkeley's conception. The lucidity of thought, the play of fancy, and the ardent enthusiasm with which difficulties involved in the book of Principles are disentangled in the *Dialogues*, may serve as a relief to the more systematic and didactic style of the preceding Selections.

In dealing with this short method with Materialists, the student may find some of his best philosophical education in critically testing the New Principles and the conclusions drawn from them.

I

BERKELEY'S INTRODUCTION TO THE PRINCIPLES

1. PHILOSOPHY being nothing else but *the study of wisdom and truth*[1], it may with reason be expected that those who have spent most time and pains in it should enjoy a greater calm and serenity of mind, a greater clearness and evidence of knowledge, and be less disturbed with doubts and difficulties than other men. Yet so it is, we see the illiterate bulk of mankind, that walk the high-road of plain common sense, and are governed by the dictates of nature, for the

---

[1] Philosophy seeks for the deepest or most real insight attainable by man into the meaning of his experience. Its aim, as distinguished from ordinary knowledge and the special sciences, is to exhibit knowledge in an all-comprehensive unity.

Is this aim attainable? Can human experience be reduced to a unity in which faith is entirely converted into articulate knowledge? Philosophy, as 'the study of wisdom and truth,' seems to find when it tries that this is inconsistent with a due recognition of the infinite and therefore finally mysterious Reality. Bacon thus puts it as regards the data, for instance, of religion:—'As for perfection or completeness in divinity it is not to be sought. For he that will reduce a knowledge into an art will make it round and uniform; but in divinity many things must be left abrupt' (*Advancement of Learning*). So too in the end many things must by us be left 'abrupt', in our finally incomplete philosophical science. The imaginative ardour of Berkeley was at first apt to encourage the expectation that philosophy could solve all difficulties, transforming our final faith into perfect science. We find him less sanguine in his later years.

most part easy and undisturbed. To them nothing that is familiar appears unaccountable or difficult to comprehend [1]. They complain not of any want of evidence in their senses, and are out of all danger of becoming Sceptics. But no sooner do we depart from Sense and Instinct to follow the light of a superior Principle—to reason, meditate, and reflect on the nature of things, but a thousand scruples spring up in our minds concerning those things which before we seemed fully to comprehend. Prejudices and errors of sense do from all parts discover themselves to our view; and, endeavouring to correct these by reason, we are insensibly drawn into uncouth paradoxes, difficulties, and inconsistencies, which multiply and grow upon us as we advance in speculation, till at length, having wandered through many intricate mazes, we find ourselves just where we were, or, which is worse, sit down in a forlorn Scepticism [2].

2. The cause of this is thought to be the obscurity of things, or the natural weakness and imperfection of our understandings. It is said, 'the faculties we have are few, and those designed by nature for the support and pleasure of life, and not to penetrate into the inward essence and constitution of things. Besides, the mind of man being finite, when it treats of things which partake of infinity, it is not to be wondered at if it run into absurdities and contradictions, out of which it is impossible it should ever extricate itself; it being of the nature of infinite not to be comprehended by that which is finite [3].'

---

[1] Custom dulls apprehension, till it is awakened by fresh philosophical reflection. 'Truths of all others the most awful and interesting are often considered as so true that they lose all the power of truth.'

[2] The aim of Berkeley was, by reflection, to make us aware of the final meaning that is otherwise dormant in the data of the senses.

[3] Cf. Descartes' Third Meditation; also Locke's *Essay*, Introduction, §§ 4–7. Locke attributes the perplexities of Philosophy to rash application of our narrow understanding; which is meant to regulate our lives—not to make the universe perfectly intelligible to us.

3. But, perhaps, we may be too partial to ourselves in placing the fault originally in our faculties, and not rather in the wrong use we make of them. It is a hard thing to suppose that right deductions from true principles should ever end in consequences which cannot be maintained or made consistent. We should believe that God has dealt more bountifully with the sons of men than to give them a strong desire for that knowledge which he had placed quite out of their reach. This were not agreeable to the wonted indulgent methods of Providence, which, whatever appetites it may have implanted in the creatures, doth usually furnish them with such means as, if rightly made use of, will not fail to satisfy them [1]. Upon the whole, I am inclined to think that the far greater part, if not all, of those difficulties which have hitherto amused philosophers, and blocked up the way to knowledge, are entirely owing to ourselves—that we have first raised a dust and then complain we cannot see.

4. My purpose therefore is, to try if I can discover what those Principles are which have introduced all that doubtfulness and uncertainty, those absurdities and contradictions, into the several Sects of Philosophy; insomuch that the wisest men have thought our ignorance incurable, conceiving it to arise from the natural dulness and limitation of our faculties. And surely it is a work well deserving our pains to make a strict inquiry concerning the First Principles of Human Knowledge, to sift and examine them

---

[1] Have we reason to assume that the data of our moral and physical experience can be (by us) resolvable into perfect science? Does philosophy not at last issue in the faith that the realities of existence are *capable* of solution, though not fully by us, whose necessarily finite knowledge of things is under relations of time and change? To take the universe as we find it, after we have exhausted reflection upon it, is 'wisdom,' even if we find that it consists at last of irreducible facts. We are not to imagine that the attainable end of human science and philosophy is Omniscience, which makes no demand upon faith, i.e. trust.

on all sides; especially since there may be some grounds to suspect that those lets and difficulties, which stay and embarrass the mind in its search after truth, do not spring from any darkness and intricacy in the objects, or natural defect in the understanding, so much as from False Principles which have been insisted on, and might have been avoided [1].

5. How difficult and discouraging soever this attempt may seem, when I consider what a number of very great and extraordinary men have gone before me in the like designs, yet I am not without some hopes—upon the consideration that the largest views are not always the clearest, and that he who is short-sighted will be obliged to draw the object nearer, and may, perhaps, by a close and narrow survey, discern that which had escaped far better eyes.

6. In order to prepare the mind of the reader for the easier conceiving what follows, it is proper to premise somewhat, by way of Introduction, concerning the Nature and Abuse of Language [2]. But the unravelling this matter leads me in some measure to anticipate my design, by taking notice of what seems to have had a chief part in rendering speculation intricate and perplexed, and to have occasioned innumerable errors and difficulties in almost all parts of

---

[1] Berkeley explains the anarchy of Philosophy by the meaningless 'principles,' to which,—under cover of empty abstract terms,—it had helped to give currency. Men put words in place of concrete ideas, and then call the empty words ·abstract ideas.'

[2] 'The inadequacy of the words of ordinary language for the purposes of Philosophy,' as Sir J. Mackintosh remarks, 'is an ancient and frequent complaint. The philosopher alone is doomed to use the rudest tools for the most refined purposes. He must reason in words of which the looseness and vagueness are suitable in the ordinary intercourse of life, but which are almost as remote from the extreme exactness and precision required in philosophy as the hammer and axe would be unfit for the finest exertions of skilful handiwork.'

knowledge. *And that is the opinion that the mind hath a power of framing abstract ideas or notions*[1] *of things.* He who is not a perfect stranger to the writings and disputes of philosophers must needs acknowledge that no small part of them are spent about *abstract ideas*[2]. These are in a more especial manner thought to be the object of those sciences which go by the name of Logic and Metaphysics, and of all that which passes under the notion of the most abstracted and sublime learning, in all which one shall scarce find any question handled in such a manner as does not suppose their existence in the mind, and that it is well acquainted with them[3].

7. It is agreed on all hands that the qualities or modes of things do never *really exist* each of them apart by itself, and separated from all others, but are mixed, as it were,

---

[1] 'Idea' and 'notion' seem here to be taken as synonymes; afterwards Berkeley makes them represent an important distinction.

[2] With Berkeley 'idea' means—an appearance presented to the senses, or represented in imagination. For him 'abstract idea' would be abstract image, which is impossible.

[3] Compare with what follows against *abstract ideas* (as Berkeley understands idea), §§ 97-100, 118-132, 143; *New Theory of Vision*, §§ 122-125. See also *Alciphron*, Dial. vii. 5-7, and *Defence of Free Thinking in Mathematics*, §§ 45-48, in *Works*, vols. ii. iii. But in the end compare all this with *Siris*, § 335, and the sections which follow on the 'Ideas' of Plato, to which Berkeley's intellectual 'notions' are nearer than *his* ideas or sensuous phenomena.

In the following sections, on the misuse and right use of words, Berkeley has Locke much in view. What is said of 'abstract ideas' in Locke's *Essay* may be studied, with the commentary in my edition of the *Essay* (Clarendon Press, 1894). See §§ 11-13 which follow. Hume refers to Berkeley (*Treatise of Human Nature*, b. I. part 1. chap. 7) as having produced 'one of the greatest and most valuable discoveries that has been made of late years in the republic of letters,' in bringing to light the absurdity of abstract ideas. So also J. S. Mill, in *Fortnightly Review* for Nov. 1871, extols Berkeley's 'discovery' of the legitimate office of abstraction in the formation of human knowledge, as distinguished from the illusion that it can be a factor of perceptions of sense and mental images that are not individual but abstract.

and blended together, several in the same object. But, we are told, the mind being able to *consider* each quality singly, or abstracted from those other qualities with which it is united, does by that means frame to itself abstract ideas. For example, there is perceived by sight an object extended, coloured, and moved: this mixed or compound idea the mind resolving into its simple, constituent parts, and viewing each by itself, exclusive of the rest, does frame the abstract ideas of extension, colour, and motion. Not that it is possible for colour or motion to exist without extension; but only that the mind can frame to itself by *abstraction* the *idea* of colour exclusive of extension, and of motion exclusive of both colour and extension.

8. Again, the mind having observed that in the particular extensions perceived by sense there is something common and alike in all, and some other things peculiar, as this or that figure or magnitude, which distinguish them one from another; it considers apart or singles out by itself that which is common, making thereof a most abstract idea of extension, which is neither line, surface, nor solid, nor has any figure or magnitude, but is an idea entirely prescinded from all these[1]. So likewise the mind, by leaving out of the particular colours perceived by sense that which distinguishes them one from another, and retaining that only which is common to all, makes an idea of colour in abstract which is neither red, nor blue, nor white, nor any other determinate colour. And, in like manner, by considering motion abstractedly not only from the body moved, but likewise from the figure it describes, and all particular directions and velocities, the abstract idea of motion is framed; which equally corresponds to all particular motions whatsoever that may be perceived by sense.

---

[1] 'Prescinded,' i.e. exclusively attended to. To *prescind* an object is to attend to it—to the exclusion of other objects.

9. And as the mind frames to itself abstract ideas of qualities or modes, so does it, by the same *precision* or mental separation, attain abstract ideas of the more compounded beings which include several co-existent qualities. For example, the mind having observed that Peter, James, and John resemble each other in certain common agreements of shape and other qualities, leaves out of the complex or compounded idea it has of Peter, James and any other particular man, that which is peculiar to each, retaining only what is common to all, and so makes an abstract idea wherein all the particulars equally partake—abstracting entirely from and cutting off all those circumstances and differences which might determine it to any particular existence. And after this manner it is said we come by the abstract idea of *man*, or, if you please, *humanity*, or *human nature*; wherein it is true there is included colour, because there is no man but has some colour, but then it can be neither white, nor black, nor any particular colour, because there is no one particular colour wherein all men partake. So likewise there is included stature, but then it is neither tall stature, nor low stature, nor yet middle stature, but something abstracted from all these. And so of the rest. Moreover, there being a great variety of other creatures that partake in some parts, but not all, of the complex idea of man, the mind, leaving out those parts which are peculiar to men, and retaining those only which are common to all the living creatures, frames the idea of *animal*, which abstracts not only from all particular men, but also all birds, beasts, fishes, and insects. The constituent parts of the abstract idea of animal are body, life, sense, and spontaneous motion. By *body* is meant body without any particular shape or figure, there being no one shape or figure common to all animals, without covering, either of hair, or feathers, or scales, &c., nor yet naked: hair, feathers, scales, and nakedness being the distinguishing properties of particular animals,

and for that reason left out of the *abstract idea*. Upon the same account the spontaneous motion must be neither walking, nor flying, nor creeping; it is nevertheless a motion, but what that motion is it is not easy to conceive.

10. Whether others have this wonderful faculty of abstracting their ideas, they best can tell. For myself, I find I have indeed a faculty of imagining, or representing to myself, the idea of those *particular* things I have perceived, and of variously compounding and dividing them. I can imagine a man with two heads, or the upper parts of a man joined to the body of a horse. I can consider the hand, the eye, the nose, each by itself abstracted or separated from the rest of the body.—But then whatever hand or eye I imagine, it must have some particular shape and colour. Likewise the idea of man that I frame to myself must be either of a white, or a black, or a tawny, a straight, or a crooked, a tall, or a low, or a middle-sized man. I cannot by any effort of thought conceive [1] the *abstract* idea above described.—And it is equally impossible for me to form the abstract idea of motion distinct from the body moving, and which is neither swift nor slow, curvilinear nor rectilinear; and the like may be said of all other abstract general ideas whatsoever. To be plain, I own myself able to abstract *in one sense*, as when I consider some particular parts or qualities separated from others, with which, though they are united in some object, yet it is possible they may really exist without them. But I deny that I can abstract from one another, or conceive separately, those qualities which it is impossible should exist so separated; or that I can frame a general notion, by abstracting from particulars in the manner aforesaid—which last are the two proper acceptations of *abstraction*. And there is

---

[1] 'Conceive' here means *realise in imagination*. Only concrete objects can be so realised.

ground to think most men will acknowledge themselves to be in my case. The generality of men which are simple and illiterate never pretend to *abstract notions*[1]. It is said they are difficult and not to be attained without pains and study; we may therefore reasonably conclude that, if such there be, they are confined only to the learned.

11. I proceed to examine what can be alleged in defence of the doctrine of abstraction, and try if I can discover what it is that inclines the men of speculation to embrace an opinion so remote from Common Sense as that seems to be. There has been a late deservedly esteemed philosopher[2] who, no doubt, has given it very much countenance, by seeming to think the having abstract general ideas is what puts the widest difference in point of understanding betwixt man and beast. 'The having of general ideas,' saith he, 'is that which puts a perfect distinction betwixt man and brutes, and is an excellency which the faculties of brutes do by no means attain unto. For, it is evident we observe no footsteps in them of making use of general signs for universal ideas; from which we have reason to imagine that they have not the faculty of abstracting, or making general ideas, since they have no use of words or any other general signs.' And a little after: 'Therefore, I think, we may suppose that it is in this that the species of brutes are discriminated from men, and it is that proper difference wherein they are wholly separated, and which at last widens to so wide a distance. For, if they have any ideas at all, and are not bare machines (as some[3] would have them), we cannot

[1] Here 'abstract notion' = abstract idea, abstract phenomenon.
[2] Locke. Consider whether Locke really means by 'abstract ideas' what Berkeley supposes he does. Study the relative passages in Locke's *Essay*. The objections in the text are due partly to Locke's confused expression, and partly to Berkeley's limitation of 'idea' to phenomenon.
[3] The Cartesians, rejecting one of the alternatives open in their philosophy—that brutes are self-conscious, preferred the other—that they are mere organisms.

deny them to have some reason. It seems as evident to me that they do, some of them, in certain instances reason as that they have sense; but it is only in particular ideas, just as they receive them from their senses. They are the best of them tied up within those narrow bounds, and have not (as I think) the faculty to enlarge them by any kind of abstraction.'—*Essay on Human Understanding*, b. II. ch. 11. §§ 10 and 11. I readily agree with this learned author, that the faculties of brutes can by no means attain to abstraction. But then if this be made the distinguishing property of that sort of animals, I fear a great many of those that pass for men must be reckoned into their number. The reason that is here assigned why we have no grounds to think brutes have abstract general ideas is, that we observe in them no use of words or any other general signs; which is built on this supposition— that the making use of words implies the having general ideas. From which it follows that men who use language are able to abstract or generalise their ideas. That this is the sense and arguing of the author will further appear by his answering the question he in another place puts: 'Since all things that exist are only particulars, how come we by general terms?' His answer is: 'Words become general by being made the signs of general ideas.'—*Essay on Human Understanding*, b. III. ch. 3. § 6.—But it seems that a word becomes general by being made the sign, not of an abstract general idea, but of several particular ideas, any one of which it indifferently suggests to the mind. For example, when it is said 'the change of motion is proportional to the impressed force,' or that 'whatever has extension is divisible,' these propositions are to be understood of motion and extension in general; and nevertheless it will not follow that they suggest to my thoughts an idea of motion without a body moved, or any determinate direction and velocity, or that I must conceive an abstract general idea of extension, which is neither line, surface, nor solid, neither great nor small, black, white, nor red, nor of any other determinate colour. It is only implied that whatever *particular* motion I consider, whether it be swift or slow, perpendicular, horizontal, or oblique, or in whatever object, the axiom concerning it holds equally true. As does the other of every *particular* extension, it matters not whether line, surface, or solid, whether of this or that magnitude or figure [1].

12. By observing how ideas become general, we may the better judge how words are made so. And here it is to be noted that I do not deny absolutely there are general ideas, but only that there are any *abstract* general ideas; for, in the passages we have quoted wherein there is mention of general ideas, it is always supposed that they are formed by abstraction, after the manner set forth in sections 8 and 9. Now, if we will annex a meaning to our words, and speak only of what we can conceive, I believe we shall acknowledge that an idea which, considered in itself, is particular, becomes general by being made to represent or stand for all other particular ideas of the same sort.—To make this plain by an example, suppose a geometrician is demonstrating the method of cutting a line in two equal parts. He draws, for instance, a black line of an inch in length: this, which in

---

[1] What are now called *concepts* were probably intended by advocates of so-called *abstract ideas*. Berkeley seems to recognise them sometimes, under the name of 'notions.' 'A concept cannot *as such* be presented as an individual thing; but it must contain no attribute incompatible with the individual presentation of the objects that are united under it. It is not itself individual, but it can comprehend only such attributes as are capable of individualisation. ... Yet the rule *individualise your concepts* does not mean *sensationalise them*, unless the senses are the only sources of presentation.' (Mansel; see *Proleg. Logica*, pp. 23, 33.) When a mathematician *exemplifies* in perception or imagination what a triangle is, he will have an individual triangle before him; but he can form propositions about triangles which do not depend upon *this* or *that* individual, or upon their being right-angled or acute-angled or obtuse-angled.

itself is a particular line, is nevertheless with regard to its signification general, since, as it is there used, it represents all particular lines whatsoever; so that what is demonstrated of it is demonstrated of all lines, or, in other words, of a line in general. And, as *that particular line* becomes general by being made a sign, so the *name* 'line,' which taken absolutely is particular, by being a sign is made general. And as the former owes its generality not to its being the sign of an abstract or general line, but of all particular right lines that may possibly exist, so the latter must be thought to derive its generality from the same cause, namely, the various particular lines which it indifferently denotes[1].

13. To give the reader a yet clearer view of the nature of abstract ideas, and the uses they are thought necessary to, I shall add one more passage out of the *Essay on Human Understanding*, which is as follows:—'Abstract ideas are not so obvious or easy to children or the yet unexercised mind as particular ones. If they seem so to grown men it is only because by constant and familiar use they are made so. For, when we nicely reflect upon them, we shall find that general ideas are fictions and contrivances of the mind, that carry difficulty with them, and do not so easily offer themselves as we are apt to imagine. For example,

---

[1] Berkeley does not go so far as to say, with extreme Nominalists, that an individual object becomes general by the accident of it and other objects being denoted by the same name; or that 'generality' consists in this name, apart from its concept, being applied to an indefinite number of individuals. He here explains *how* a particular object may represent an indefinite number of particular objects, each individualising the concept which connects them. It may be added that their common name, *itself a particular thing*, is connected with their concept in the mind by an *arbitrary* tie; for the name—spoken or written—is not *itself* an example of the concept which it is employed to signify, and may vary, as it does, in different languages. It is an *arbitrary* sign of qualities common to many individual objects, each of which exemplifies the concept.

does it not require some pains and skill to form the general idea of a triangle (which is yet none of the most abstract, comprehensive, and difficult); for it must be neither oblique nor rectangle, neither equilateral, equicrural, nor scalenon, but all and none of these at once? In effect, it is something imperfect that cannot exist, an idea wherein some parts of several different and inconsistent ideas are put together. It is true the mind in this imperfect state has need of such ideas, and makes all the haste to them it can, for the conveniency of communication and enlargement of knowledge, to both which it is naturally very much inclined. But yet one has reason to suspect such ideas are marks of our imperfection. At least this is enough to shew that the most abstract and general ideas are not those that the mind is first and most easily acquainted with, nor such as its earliest knowledge is conversant about.'—B. IV. ch. 7. § 9. If any man has the faculty of framing in his mind such an idea of a triangle as is here described, it is in vain to pretend to dispute him out of it, nor would I go about it. All I desire is that the reader would fully and certainly inform himself whether he has such an idea or no. And this, methinks, can be no hard task for any one to perform. What more easy than for any one to look a little into his own thoughts, and there try whether he has, or can attain to have, an idea that shall correspond with the description that is here given of the general idea of a triangle—which is neither oblique nor rectangle, equilateral, equicrural nor scalenon, but all and none of these at once [1]?

---

[1] The language of Locke is awkward. Does it mean more than that the concept of a triangle *may* be individualised in *any one* of its many possible applications—oblique, equilateral, &c.—in all of which it is as it were latent? No concept can, *as such*, be pictured. It belongs to the intellectual constitution, not to the variable matter, of human thought, and so neither in perception nor in imagination can we realise universal relations. Only in the concrete example are they thus realisable.

14. Much is here said of the difficulty that abstract ideas carry with them, and the pains and skill requisite to the forming them. And it is on all hands agreed that there is need of great toil and labour of the mind, to emancipate our thoughts from particular objects, and raise them to those sublime speculations that are conversant about abstract ideas. From all which the natural consequence should seem to be, that so difficult a thing as the forming abstract ideas was not necessary for *communication*, which is so easy and familiar to all sorts of men. But, we are told, if they seem obvious and easy to grown men, it is only because by constant and familiar use they are made so. Now, I would fain know at what time it is men are employed in surmounting that difficulty, and furnishing themselves with those necessary helps for discourse. It cannot be when they are grown up, for then it seems they are not conscious of any such painstaking; it remains therefore to be the business of their childhood. And surely the great and multiplied labour of framing abstract notions will be found a hard task for that tender age. Is it not a hard thing to imagine that a couple of children cannot prate together of their sugar-plums and rattles and the rest of their little trinkets, till they have first tacked together numberless inconsistencies, and so framed in their minds abstract general ideas, and annexed them to every common name they make use of?

15. Nor do I think them a wit more needful for the *enlargement of knowledge* than for communication. It is, I know, a point much insisted on, that all knowledge and demonstration are about universal notions, to which I fully agree: but then it does not appear to me that those notions are formed by abstraction in the manner premised—*universality*, so far as I can comprehend, not consisting in the absolute, positive nature or conception of anything, but in the *relation* it bears to the particulars signified or represented

by it; by virtue whereof it is that things, names, or notions [1], being in their own nature *particular*, are rendered *universal*. Thus, when I demonstrate any proposition concerning triangles, it is to be supposed that I have in view the universal idea of a triangle; which ought not to be understood as if I could frame an idea of a triangle which was neither equilateral, nor scalenon, nor equicrural; but only that the particular triangle I consider, whether of this or that sort it matters not, doth equally stand for and represent all rectilinear triangles whatsoever, and is *in that sense universal*. All which seems very plain and not to include any difficulty in it [2].

16. But here it will be demanded, how we can know any proposition to be true of all particular triangles, except we have first seen it demonstrated of the abstract idea of a triangle which equally agrees to all? For, because a property may be demonstrated to agree to some one particular triangle, it will not thence follow that it equally belongs to any other triangle, which in all respects is not the same with it. For example, having demonstrated that the three angles of an isosceles rectangular triangle are equal to two right ones, I cannot therefore conclude this affection agrees to all other triangles which have neither a right angle nor two equal sides. It seems therefore that, to be certain this proposition is universally true, we must either make a particular demonstration for every particular triangle, which is impossible, or once for all demonstrate it of the abstract

---

[1] 'Notion' is here again synonymous with individual perceptions and imaginations,—not confined, as afterwards by Berkeley, to νοήματα and διανοήματα.

[2] This and the next are important sections. They touch the penetrating question—*what that is in the constitution of things* which enables us to extend our knowledge beyond the immediate data of sense, as in our inductive inferences. Is it not the omnipresence of reason, order, or law in the universe? Unless the universe were divinely constituted, it could not be reasoned about.

idea of a triangle, in which all the particulars do indifferently partake and by which they are all equally represented.—To which I answer, that, though the idea I have in view whilst I make the demonstration be, for instance, that of an isosceles rectangular triangle whose sides are of a determinate length, I may nevertheless be certain it extends to all other rectilinear triangles, of what sort or bigness soever. And that because neither the right angle, nor the equality, nor determinate length of the sides, are at all concerned in the demonstration. It is true the diagram I have in view includes all these particulars, but then there is not the least mention made of them in the proof of the proposition. It is not said the three angles are equal to two right ones, because one of them is a right angle, or because the sides comprehending it are of the same length. Which sufficiently shews that the right angle might have been oblique, and the sides unequal, and for all that the demonstration have held good. And for this reason it is that I conclude that to be true of any obliquangular or scalenon which I had demonstrated of a particular right-angled equicrural triangle, and not because I demonstrated the proposition of the abstract idea of a triangle. [¹And here it must be acknowledged that a man may consider a figure merely as triangular, without attending to the particular qualities of the angles, or relations of the sides. So far he may abstract²; but this will never prove that he can frame an abstract, general, inconsistent idea of a triangle. In like manner we may consider Peter so far forth as man, or so far forth as animal, without framing the forementioned

---

[1] What follows to the end of this section was added in Berkeley's third edition.

[2] Here Berkeley grants that without abstraction in one sense of the term, there can be no scientific or philosophic knowledge of things. But this abstraction means *exclusive attention* to the *common attributes*, or *connecting relations*, of *individual* things.

abstract idea, either of man or of animal, inasmuch as all that is perceived is not considered.]

17. It were an endless as well as an useless thing to trace the Schoolmen, those great masters of abstraction, through all the manifold inextricable labyrinths of error and dispute which their doctrine of abstract natures and notions seems to have led them into. What bickerings and controversies, and what a learned dust have been raised about those matters, and what mighty advantage has been from thence derived to mankind, are things at this day too clearly known to need being insisted on. And it had been well if the ill effects of that doctrine were confined to those only who make the most avowed profession of it. When men consider the great pains, industry, and parts that have for so many ages been laid out on the cultivation and advancement of the sciences, and that notwithstanding all this the far greater part of them remain full of darkness and uncertainty and disputes that are like never to have an end, and even those that are thought to be supported by the most clear and cogent demonstrations contain in them paradoxes which are perfectly irreconcilable to the understandings of men, and that, taking all together, a very small proportion of them does supply any real benefit to mankind, otherwise than by being an innocent diversion and amusement—I say, the consideration of all this is apt to throw them into a despondency and perfect contempt of all study. But this may perhaps cease upon a view of the False Principles that have obtained in the world, amongst all which there is none, methinks, hath a more wide and extended sway over the thoughts of speculative men than this of *abstract* general ideas [1].

---

[1] To say that the sort of *abstraction* against which Berkeley argues is impossible is simply to say that *substances abstracted from all qualities*, are unimaginable. But this does not prove that unrelated images, *per se*, can constitute science; or that they can become knowledge without their relations being involved in the knowledge; or that

18. I come now to continue the *source* of this prevailing notion, and that seems to me to be Language. And surely nothing of less extent than reason itself could have been the source of an opinion so universally received. The truth of this appears as from other reasons so also from the plain confession of the ablest patrons of abstract ideas, who acknowledge that they are made in order to naming; from which it is a clear consequence that if there had been no such thing as speech or *universal* signs there never had been any thought of abstraction. See b. III. ch. 6. § 39, and elsewhere of the *Essay on Human Understanding*. Let us examine the manner wherein Words have contributed to the origin of that mistake.—First then, it is thought that every name has, or ought to have, one only precise and settled signification; which inclines men to think there are certain abstract, determinate ideas that constitute the true and only immediate signification of each general name, and that it is by the mediation of these abstract ideas that a general name comes to signify any particular thing. Whereas, in truth, there is no such thing as one precise and definite signification annexed to any general name, they all signifying indifferently a great number of particular ideas [1]. All which does evidently follow from what has been already said, and will clearly appear to any one by a little reflection. To this it will be objected that every name that has a definition is thereby restrained to one certain signification. For example, a triangle is defined to be 'a plain surface comprehended by three right lines,' by which that name is limited to denote one certain idea and no other. To which I answer, that in the defini-

---

progress in science is other than an ever widening and deepening intellectual apprehension of the relations of individual things.

[1] The same concept or notion is found exemplified in any one of innumerable particular objects.

tion it is not said whether the surface be great or small, black or white, nor whether the sides are long or short, equal or unequal, nor with what angles they are inclined to each other; in all which there may be great variety, and consequently there is no one settled idea which limits the signification of the word triangle. It is one thing for to keep a name constantly to the same definition, and another to make it stand everywhere for the same idea; the one is necessary, the other useless and impracticable [1].

19. But, to give a farther account how words came to produce the doctrine of abstract ideas, it must be observed that it is a received opinion that language has no other end but the communicating our ideas, and that every significant name stands for an idea. This being so, and it being withal certain that names which yet are not thought altogether insignificant do not always mark out particular conceivable ideas, it is straightway concluded that they stand for abstract notions. That there are many names in use amongst speculative men which do not always suggest to others determinate particular ideas, or in truth anything at all, is what nobody will deny. And a little attention will discover that it is not necessary (even in the strictest reasonings) significant names which stand for ideas should, every time they are used, excite in the understanding the ideas they are made to stand for—in reading and discoursing, names being for the most part used as letters are in Algebra, in which, though a particular quantity be marked by each letter, yet to proceed right it is not requisite that in every step each letter suggest to your thoughts that particular quantity it was appointed to stand for [2].

---

[1] Yet definition can determine the individual objects to which a common name is applicable, although the *relations* which constitute the concept expressed by the name defined cannot, as such, be pictured in imagination. They are imaginable only in concrete examples.

[2] Compare with this the so-called 'symbolical knowledge' of Leibniz

20. Besides, the communicating of ideas marked by words is not the chief and only end of language, as is commonly supposed. There are other ends, as the raising of some passion, the exciting to or deterring from an action, the putting the mind in some particular disposition—to which the former is in many cases barely subservient, and sometimes entirely omitted, when these can be obtained without it, and I think does not unfrequently happen in the familiar use of language. I entreat the reader to reflect with himself, and see if it does not often happen, either in hearing or reading a discourse, that the passions of fear, love, hatred, admiration, and disdain, and the like, arise immediately in his mind upon the perception of certain words, without any ideas coming between [1]. At first, indeed, the words might have occasioned ideas that were fitting to produce those emotions; but, if I mistake not, it will be found that, when language is once grown familiar, the hearing of the sounds, or sight of the characters, is oft immediately attended with those passions which at first were wont to be produced by the intervention of ideas that are now quite omitted. May we not, for example, be affected with the promise of a *good thing*, though we have not an idea of what it is? Or is not the being threatened with *danger* sufficient to excite a dread, though we think not of any

(*Opera Philosophica*, pp. 79-80, Erdmann). See also Stewart on 'Abstraction' (*Elements*, vol. I. ch. 4. §§ 1 and 2)—where he treats of individual examples, or *resembling* signs, and of words, or *non-resembling* signs.

[1] That is to say, without any 'ideas' (particular examples) of the concepts signified by the words rising up in his imagination in the act of hearing or of reading—the *word* doing service instead. Language in this way more easily discharges its *practical* function, which is to evoke emotion and incite to action as much as to convey either intellectual notions or mental images; but we are apt, in consequence, unconsciously to accept words that are meaningless. To escape this disaster we should test our concepts by exemplifying them, dismissing **the names** till their meanings are thus recognised.

particular evil likely to befall us, nor yet frame to ourselves an idea of danger in abstract? If any one shall join ever so little reflection of his own to what has been said, I believe that it will evidently appear to him that general names are often used in the propriety of language without the speaker's designing them for marks of ideas in his own, which he would have them raise in the mind of the hearer. Even proper names themselves do not seem always spoken with a design to bring into our view the ideas of those individuals that are supposed to be marked by them. For example, when a schoolman tells me 'Aristotle hath said it,' all I conceive he means by it is to dispose me to embrace his opinion with the deference and submission which custom has annexed to that name. And this effect is often so instantly produced in the minds of those who are accustomed to resign their judgment to authority of that philosopher, as it is impossible any idea either of his person, writings, or reputation should go before. So close and immediate a connexion may custom establish betwixt the very *word* Aristotle and the motions of assent and reverence in the minds of some men. Innumerable examples of this kind may be given, but why should I insist on those things which every one's experience will, I doubt not, plentifully suggest unto him[1]?

21. We have, I think, shewn the impossibility of Abstract Ideas. We have considered what has been said for them by their ablest patrons; and endeavoured to shew they are of no use for those ends to which they are thought neces-

---

[1] Compare *Alciphron*, Dial. VII. §§ 8-10. Berkeley here shows how words—especially in politics, theology, and metaphysics—impose upon the uneducated and half-educated—determining their feelings and conduct independently of their intelligence; and why uneducated persons are annoyed by exactness e. g. in philosophical discussion. History records theological controversies and social revolutions which were largely due to the influence on the unreflecting of verbal shibboleths without meaning, at least without meaning for such minds.

sary. And lastly, we have traced them to the source from whence they flow, which appears evidently to be language. —It cannot be denied that words are of excellent use, in that by their means all that stock of knowledge which has been purchased by the joint labours of inquisitive men in all ages and nations may be drawn into the view and made the possession of one single person. But most parts of knowledge have been strangely perplexed and darkened by the *abuse* of words and general ways of speech wherein they are delivered. Since therefore words are so apt to impose on the understanding, whatever *ideas* I consider, I shall endeavour to take *them* bare and naked into my view, keeping out of my thoughts, so far as I am able, those *names* which long and constant use hath so strictly united with them; from which I may expect to derive the following advantages :—

22. *First*, I shall be sure to get clear of all controversies purely verbal—the springing up of which weeds in almost all the sciences has been a main hindrance to the growth of true and sound knowledge. *Secondly*, this seems to be a sure way to extricate myself out of that fine and subtle net of *abstract ideas* which has so miserably perplexed and entangled the minds of men; and that with this peculiar circumstance, that by how much the finer and more curious was the wit of any man, by so much the deeper was he likely to be ensnared and faster held therein. *Thirdly*, so long as I confine my thoughts to my own ideas divested of words, I do not see how I can easily be mistaken. The objects I consider, I clearly and adequately know. I cannot be deceived in thinking I have an idea which I have not. It is not possible for me to imagine that any of my own ideas are alike or unlike that are not truly so. To discern the agreements or disagreements there are between my ideas, to see what ideas are included in any compound idea and what not, there is nothing more requi-

site than an attentive perception of what passes in my own understanding[1].

23. But the attainment of all these advantages does presuppose an entire deliverance from the deception of words which I dare hardly promise myself; so difficult a thing it is to dissolve an union so early begun, and confirmed by so long a habit as that betwixt words and ideas. Which difficulty seems to have been very much increased by the doctrine of *abstraction*. For, so long as men thought abstract ideas were annexed to their words, it does not seem strange that they should use words for ideas—it being found an impracticable thing to lay aside the word, and retain the *abstract* idea in the mind, which in itself was perfectly inconceivable.

This seems to me the principal cause why those who have so emphatically recommended to others the laying aside all use of words in their meditations, and contemplating their bare ideas, have yet failed to perform it themselves. Of late many have been very sensible of the absurd opinions and insignificant disputes which grow out of the abuse of words. And, in order to remedy these evils, they advise well, that we attend to the ideas signified, and draw off our attention from the words which signify them[2]. But, how good soever this advice may be they have given others, it is plain they could not have a due regard to it themselves, so long as they thought the only immediate use of words was to signify ideas, and that the immediate signification of every general name was a determinate abstract idea.

---

[1] Berkeley appeals throughout to this test. He everywhere entreats the student to *try* whether he can conceive clearly and distinctly the meanings of his words, through individual examples.

[2] See Locke, *Essay*, b. II. ch. 13. §§ 18, 28; also b. III. ch. 10. The drift of Berkeley's exhortation is good so far as it is fitted to guard us against the dangerous tendency to accept empty words instead of legitimate concepts, a lesson which it was a chief purpose of Locke's *Essay* to insist upon.

24. But, these being known to be mistakes, a man may with greater ease prevent his being imposed on by words. He that knows he has no other than *particular* ideas, will not puzzle himself in vain to find out and conceive [1] the *abstract* idea annexed to any name. And he that knows names do not always stand for ideas will spare himself the labour of looking for ideas where there are none to be had. It were, therefore, to be wished that every one would use his utmost endeavours to obtain a clear view of the ideas he would consider, separating from them all that dress and incumbrance of words which so much contribute to blind the judgment and divide the attention [2]. In vain do we extend our view into the heavens and pry into the entrails of the earth, in vain do we consult the writings of learned men and trace the dark footsteps of antiquity—we need only draw the curtain of words, to behold the fairest tree of knowledge, whose fruit is excellent, and within the reach of our hand.

25. Unless we take care to clear the First Principles of Knowledge from the embarras and delusion of words, we may make infinite reasonings upon them to no purpose; we may draw consequences from consequences, and be never the wiser. The farther we go, we shall only lose ourselves the more irrecoverably, and be the deeper entangled in difficulties and mistakes. Whoever therefore designs to read the following sheets, I entreat him that he

---

[1] To 'conceive' here means to form a mental *image*, e.g. of a triangle that is neither right-angled, acute-angled, nor obtuse-angled; which of course, on trial, is found impossible.

[2] Here the student may perhaps ask what he is expected to do when his words signify διανοήματα and νοήματα—what Berkeley sometimes called *notions*, in contrast to *ideas* (αἰσθήματα and φαντάσματα),—if it be true that *all* words must *at bottom* signify only what is presentable in sense, or representable in imagination. Did he, even in the imperfect philosophy of his youth, intend to limit human understanding to sense and sensuous imagination, overlooking intellectual implicates indispensable to intelligent experience?

would make my words the occasion of his own thinking, and endeavour to attain the same train of thoughts in reading that I had in writing them. By this means it will be easy for him to discover the truth or falsity of what I say. He will be out of all danger of being deceived by my words, and I do not see how he can be led into an error by considering his own naked, undisguised ideas.

II

RATIONALE OF THE PRINCIPLES

1. IT is evident to any one who takes a survey of the *objects* of human knowledge, that they are either (*a*) *ideas* actually imprinted on the senses; or else (*b*) *ideas* perceived by attending to the passions and operations of the mind; or lastly (*c*) *ideas* formed by help of memory and imagination, either compounding, dividing, or barely representing those originally perceived in the aforesaid ways[1].—By sight I have the ideas of light and colours, with their several degrees and variations. By touch I perceive hard and soft, heat and cold, motion and resistance; and of all these more and less either as to quantity or degree. Smelling furnishes me with odours; the palate with tastes; and hearing conveys sounds to the mind in all their variety of tone and composition.

And as several of these are observed to accompany each other, they come to be marked by one name, and so to be reputed as one THING[2]. Thus, for example, a cer-

---

[1] All phenomena, including those of human nature, whether actually perceived, remembered, or imagined, are called *ideas* by Berkeley in his early philosophical works. In *Siris* the perceptions of sense are called *phenomena*, according to our present usage. The thesis is ambiguous as expressed both by Locke and by Berkeley; and Berkeley even more than Locke fails, in his earlier writings, to recognise theoretically what is necessarily presupposed in the experience upon which he proceeds in subsequent reasonings.

[2] Is 'observation' alone enough to account for this synthesis, in which

tain colour, taste, smell, figure and consistence having been observed to go together, are accounted one distinct thing, signified by the name *apple*; other collections of ideas constitute a stone, a tree, a book, and the like sensible things—which as they are pleasing or disagreeable excite the passions of love, hatred, joy, grief, and so forth.

2. But besides all that endless variety of ideas or objects of knowledge, there is likewise *something which knows or perceives them, and exercises divers operations*,—as willing, imagining, remembering,—about them. This perceiving, active being is what I call MIND, SPIRIT, SOUL, or MYSELF [1]. By which words I do not denote any one of my ideas, but a thing entirely distinct from them, wherein they exist, or, which is the same thing, whereby they are perceived—for the existence of an idea consists in being perceived.

3. That neither our thoughts nor passions, nor ideas formed by the imagination, exist without the mind [2], is what everybody will allow.

And to me it is no less evident that the various SENSATIONS, or *ideas imprinted on the sense*, however blended or combined together (that is, whatever *objects* [3] they compose),

---

sense-presented phenomena (by him called ideas) are conceived as *qualities* of *things*? 'I own the word *idea*, not being commonly used for *thing*, sounds something out of the way,' he says elsewhere. 'My reason for so using it is because a necessary relation to mind is implied by the term *idea*.'

[1] This unique element necessarily involved in experience is usually signified by the personal pronoun 'I'—*Ego*,—in contrast to the changing ideas or phenomena of which we are percipient.

[2] 'Without the mind,' i.e. unperceived—after total withdrawal of conscious or percipient life. Ideas in memory and imagination, by consent of all, could not exist *per se*, or in a totally dead universe. This raises his chief question:—Can a totally dead universe exist? Are natural phenomena, as presented to our senses, independent of a knowing, feeling, and active *Ego*, in which they can be realised? Must not all phenomena depend for their reality upon *Egos*? Must not all *things* depend upon persons? Is not personal consciousness the root of reality? He begins to answer this question in the next sentence.

[3] 'Objects' = 'things,' i.e. *aggregates* of ideas or phenomena, recognised

cannot exist otherwise than in a mind perceiving them. I
think an intuitive knowledge may be obtained of this by
any one that shall attend to *what is meant by the term
EXIST when applied to sensible things.* The table I write
on I say exists, that is, I see and feel it; and if I were out
of my study I should say it existed—meaning thereby that
if I was in my study I might perceive it, or that some other
spirit actually does perceive it. There was an odour, that
is, it was smelt; there was a sound, that is, it was heard; a
colour or figure, and it was perceived by sight or touch.
This is all that I can understand by these and the like
expressions. For as to what is said of *the absolute existence
of unthinking things without any relation to their being
perceived,* that is to me *perfectly unintelligible.* Their *esse*
is *percipi*; nor is it possible they should have any existence out of the minds or thinking things which perceive
them[1].

as 'qualities' of the aggregates, and of which the 'material world'
consists.

[1] The characteristic question of Berkeley's philosophy might be thus
expressed :—Do the phenomena presented to the five senses—the
individual things of sense—which seem to be *only* aggregates of
ideas—really exist as things totally independent of percipient mind?
Are solid things that move in space—the things we actually touch and
see—independent of the sentient and intelligent life that exists in the
universe, in a way that feelings and fancies are not? His answer is,
that the things we touch and see cannot be real otherwise than as
appearances of which *a* (not necessarily *my*) mind is percipient: their
esse is *percipi*. The reason for this is, that the supposition of phenomena
existing when no one is percipient of them, is an unintelligible, if not
a self-contradictory, supposition. To say 'this table *exists*,' or is
'something real,' means, if it has any meaning, that it is seen or felt by
some one. Out of all perception, or imagination, of the phenomena
(called its qualities), the word 'table' is an empty abstraction. Let all
life in the universe be annihilated, and what becomes of the data now
realised in the five senses? (He has still to explain the transformation
of 'sensations' into 'qualities' of things moving in space—the transformation of momentary sensation into what is believed to be permanent
quality.)

Ueberweg charges Berkeley with begging his principal question,

4. [1] It is indeed an opinion strangely prevailing amongst men, that houses, mountains, rivers, and in a word all sensible objects, have an existence, natural or real, distinct from their being perceived by the understanding. But, with how great an assurance and acquiescence soever this principle may be entertained in the world, yet whoever shall find in his heart to call it in question may, if I mistake not, perceive it to involve a manifest contradiction. For, what are the forementioned objects but the things we perceive by sense? and what do we perceive besides our own ideas or sensations? and is it not plainly repugnant that any one of *these*, or any combination of them, should exist unperceived [2]?

5. If we throughly examine this tenet it will, perhaps, be found at bottom to depend on the doctrine of *abstract ideas*. For can there be a nicer strain of abstraction than to distinguish the *existence* of sensible objects from their *being perceived*, so as to conceive [3] them existing unperceived? Light and colours, heat and cold, extension and figures—in a word the things we see and feel—what are they but so

---

because he sets out by *naming* the things of sense *sensations* or *ideas*—thus implying in the connotation of their name, that they have only a mind-dependent existence. But Berkeley need not, at setting out, be required to mean more than that all that we are percipient of in sense is perceived, and must therefore be, *so far*, dependent on mind—leaving it still open to inquire whether existence in absolute independence of all perception is intelligible.

[1] §§ 4-24 contain the *rationale* of his answer to the question about the relation of Matter to Mind that was raised in § 3. That unperceived Matter must be meaningless seems to him hardly to require proof, being self-evident to any one who attends to what must be meant by 'exist' and 'real.' That the unthinking are notwithstanding disposed to give a different answer, he attributes (§ 5) to that tendency to employ empty verbal abstractions which he had ridiculed in the Introduction.

[2] How does Berkeley, in thus limiting my 'perceptions' to the phenomena of which I am percipient in sense—'our own ideas'—not subside into Panegoism?

[3] Does 'conceive' here mean imagine—have a mental picture of?

many sensations, notions, ideas, or impressions on the sense[1]? and is it possible to separate, even in thought, any of these from perception? For my part, I might as easily divide a thing from itself. I may, indeed, divide in my thoughts, or conceive apart from each other, those things which, perhaps, I never perceived by sense so divided. Thus, I imagine the trunk of a human body without the limbs, or conceive the smell of a rose without thinking on the rose itself. So far, I will not deny, I can abstract—if that may properly be called *abstraction* which extends only to the conceiving separately such objects as it is possible may really exist or be actually perceived asunder. But my conceiving or imagining power does not extend beyond the possibility of real existence or perception[2]. Hence, as it is impossible for me to see or feel anything without an actual sensation of that thing, so is it impossible for me to conceive in my thoughts any sensible thing or object distinct from the sensation or perception of it. In truth, the object and the sensation are the same thing and cannot therefore be abstracted from each other.

6. Some truths there are so near and obvious to the mind that a man need only open his eyes to see them. Such I take this important one to be, viz. that all the choir of heaven and furniture of the earth, in a word all those bodies which compose the mighty frame of the world, have not any subsistence without a mind—that their *being* is *to be perceived or known*; that consequently so long as they are not actually perceived by me, or do not exist in my mind or that of any other created spirit, they must either have no exist-

---

[1] Here the 'things of sense' are vaguely called 'notions'—a term in this passage synonymous with sensation, idea, phenomenon. Berkeley has not defined what he means, here and elsewhere, by the metaphor 'impressions on sense,' which, taken literally, makes 'perception' *motion in the bodily organ*, instead of *state of conscious life*.

[2] 'Real existence or perception,' i. e. existence as realised in actual perception.

ence at all, or else subsist in the mind of some Eternal Spirit—it being perfectly unintelligible, and involving all the absurdity of abstraction, to attribute to any single part of them an existence independent of a spirit. To be convinced of which, the reader need only reflect, and try to separate in his own thoughts the *being* of a sensible thing from its *being perceived*[1].

7. From what has been said it is evident there is not any other substance[2] than SPIRIT, or *that which perceives*[3]. But, for the fuller demonstration of this point, let it be considered the sensible qualities are colour, figure, motion, smell, taste, &c., *i.e.* the ideas perceived by sense. Now, for an idea to exist in an unperceiving thing is a manifest contradiction; for to have an idea is all one as to perceive; that therefore wherein colour, figure, &c. exist must perceive them; hence

---

[1] Ueberweg accepts Berkeley's arguments as regards the necessary dependence of phenomena of sense, *as phenomena*, alike severally and in aggregates, on percipient mind: he denies that he has *proved* that they may not *also* be external things, existing in space independently of being perceived, and which may so operate on our senses that the spirit which animates our organism is able to perceive them.

Berkeley has not here given reason for adopting the alternative—that sensible things do subsist continuously in the perception of the Eternal Spirit, during intervals in which they are not perceived by any finite spirit—instead of the counter alternative of their ceasing to exist during such intervals. He does not even ask *why* we are obliged to believe in their continuity. Still less does he explain *how* things would exist in the Eternal Mind during intervals of finite perception. Is this more intelligible than abstract or unperceived existence? Do they exist as perceptions of sense in the mind of God?

[2] He does not say distinctly what he means by 'substance.' He seems (like Descartes) to distinguish finite and relative from infinite substance—the infinite substance being God.

[3] Does this imply that each spirit or ego must be *always* percipient of phenomena—that mind must always be conscious? Otherwise should we not in an *unconscious spirit* (on Berkeley's premises) still have an empty abstraction, open to his objection against *unperceived things?* Indeed he says in his *Commonplace Book*, that the essence of mind is conscious activity;—an 'unthinking substance or substratum of ideas' being a 'manifest contradiction.'

it is clear there can be no unthinking substance or *substratum* of those ideas.

8. But, say you, though the ideas themselves do not exist without the mind, yet there may be things like them, whereof they are copies or resemblances, which things exist without the mind in an unthinking substance [1]. I answer, an idea can be nothing but an idea; a colour or figure can be like nothing but another colour or figure [2]. If we look but never so little into our own thoughts, we shall find it impossible for us to conceive a likeness except only between our ideas. Again, I ask whether those supposed originals or external things, of which our ideas are the pictures or representations, be themselves perceivable or no? If they are, then they are ideas and we have gained our point; but if you say they are not, I appeal to any one whether it be sense to assert a colour is like something which is invisible; hard or soft, like something which is intangible; and so of the rest.

9. Some there are who make a distinction betwixt *primary* and *secondary* qualities [3]. By the former they mean

---

[1] As those seem to say who, in contrast with Berkeley, hold that our perception of the material world is *not* immediate, but reached through representative ideas. With Berkeley ideas which appear in sense are not representative: they are the *presented* phenomena of which his world is composed.

[2] The reader should ponder this assumption, illustrating it to himself and examining its reason. Compare it with Locke's assumption, *Essay*, II. 8, that our ideas of *some* of the qualities of matter *are resemblances* of what really exists in things.

[3] Locke is here in his view. See *Essay*, b. II. ch. 8. In this and the seven following sections we have Berkeley's criticism of Locke's account of the Qualities of Matter. That account implies that some of them are independent of sensations. For Locke took for granted that those qualities commonly called *primary* do not need to be perceived in order to be real. Those called *secondary*, on the other hand, are manifested only subjectively, in the sensations on which they depend. So we *know* the primary, and we only *feel* the secondary. But Berkeley tries, in what follows, to melt down the primary into phenomena like

extension, figure, motion, rest, solidity, impenetrability, and *number*; by the latter they denote *all other sensible qualities*,—as colours, sounds, tastes, and so forth. The ideas we have of these last they acknowledge not to be the resemblances of anything existing without the mind, or unperceived; but they will have our ideas of the primary qualities to be patterns or images of things which exist without the mind—in an unthinking substance which they call Matter.—By Matter, therefore, we are to understand *an inert* [1], *senseless substance, in which extension, figure and motion do actually subsist*. But it is evident, from what we have already shewn, that extension, figure, and motion are only ideas existing in the mind; and that an idea can be like nothing but another idea; and that consequently neither they nor their archetypes [2] can exist in an unperceiving substance. *Hence, it is plain that the very notion of what is called Matter or corporeal substance involves a contradiction in it* [3].

10. They who assert that *figure*, *motion*, and the rest of the primary or original qualities do exist without the mind, in unthinking substances, do at the same time acknowledge that colours, sounds, heat, cold, and suchlike secondary

---

the secondary, affirming at the same time the reality of both, as realised in their perceptions.

[1] The *necessary powerlessness* of Matter, with the consequent absurdity of all materialistic explanations of the universe, is of the essence of Berkeley's philosophy.

[2] 'Their archetypes,' i. e. the independent things, movable in space, which the ideas or phenomena presented in sense were supposed to symbolise.

[3] In this section Berkeley has defined the 'Matter' against which his reasoning is directed. It is inert, unperceiving, and unperceived: yet extension, figure, and motion are attributed to it: it is *per se* extended, figured, and movable. He argues that this is unintelligible, and that even the mathematical qualities of things must be melted down into sensations, which of course can exist only when perceived. Movement in space cannot survive the withdrawal of the percipient activity which is needed for realising it.

qualities, do not—which they tell us are sensations existing in the mind alone, that depend on and are occasioned by the different size, texture, and motion of the minute particles of matter[1]. This they take for an undoubted truth, which they can demonstrate beyond all exception. Now, if it be certain that those original qualities are inseparably united with the other sensible qualities, and not, even in thought, capable of being abstracted from them, it plainly follows that they exist only in the mind. But I desire any one to reflect and try whether he can, by any abstraction of thought, conceive the extension and motion of a body without all other sensible qualities[2]. For my own part, I see evidently that it is not in my power to frame an idea of a body extended and moving, but I must withal give it some colour or other sensible quality which is acknowledged to exist only in the mind. In short, extension, figure, and motion, abstracted from all other qualities, are inconceivable. Where therefore the other sensible qualities are, there must these be also, to wit, in the mind and nowhere else.

11. Again, *great* and *small*, *swift* and *slow*, are allowed to exist nowhere without the mind, being entirely relative, and changing as the frame or position of the organs of sense varies. The extension therefore which exists without the mind[3] is neither great nor small, the motion neither swift nor

---

[1] See Locke's *Essay*, b. II. ch. 8. §§ 16-18; ch. 23. § 11; b. IV. ch. 3. §§ 24-26, for his theory of the *relation* of the secondary to the primary qualities of matter—the former being the supposed natural issue of (by us) unperceivable modifications of the primary atoms. Locke consequently denies the possibility of strictly demonstrative science of nature, holding that physical science must ultimately rest on probable presumptions. Berkeley puts all qualities—secondary and primary—on the same sensuous footing. Their essence is *percipi*. There is only one way in which they can be real, i. e. in the conscious life of spirit. If this ceases they cease.

[2] That we cannot perceive extensions and motions unless as blended with sensations may be granted. Does it follow that extension and motion are only transitory sensations?

[3] 'Without the mind,' i. e. unperceived.

slow, that is, they are nothing at all. But, say you, they are extension in general, and motion in general: thus we see how much the tenet of extended moveable substances existing without the mind depends on that strange doctrine of *abstract ideas*[1]. And here I cannot but remark how nearly the vague and indeterminate description of Matter or corporeal substance, which the modern philosophers are run into by their own principles, resembles that antiquated and so much ridiculed notion of *materia prima*, to be met with in Aristotle and his followers[2]. Without extension solidity cannot be conceived; since therefore it has been shewn that extension exists not in an unthinking substance, the same must also be true of solidity.

12. That *number* is entirely the creature of the mind[3], even though the other qualities be allowed to exist without, will be evident to whoever considers that the same thing bears a different denomination of number as the mind views it with different respects. Thus, the same extension is one, or three, or thirty-six, according as the mind considers it with reference to a yard, a foot, or an inch. Number is so visibly relative, and dependent on men's understanding, that it is strange to think how any one should give it an absolute existence without the mind. We say one book, one page, one line, &c.; all these are equally units, though some contain several of the others. And in each instance, it is plain, the unit relates to some particular combination of ideas arbitrarily put together by the mind.

---

[1] Does it follow that if Extension, viewed apart from the perceptions of individuals, is 'neither great nor small'; or that Motion, so abstracted, is 'neither swift nor slow,' they must, after conscious mind is withdrawn, be 'nothing at all'?

[2] For Aristotle's πρώτη ὕλη, see his *Phys.* I. 9; also *Metaph.* VII. 3.

[3] If Number is entirely a 'creature of the mind,' how does Berkeley reconcile this with what he says elsewhere about *plurality* of finite spirits?

13. *Unity* I know some[1] will have to be a simple or uncompounded idea, accompanying all other ideas into the mind. That I have any such idea answering the word *unity* I do not find; and if I had, methinks I could not miss finding it: on the contrary, it should be the most familiar to my understanding, since it is said to accompany all other ideas, and to be perceived by all the ways of sensation and reflexion. To say no more, it is an *abstract* idea[2].

14. I shall further add, that, after the same manner as modern philosophers prove certain sensible qualities to have no existence in Matter, or without the mind, the same thing may be likewise proved of all other sensible qualities whatsoever. Thus, for instance, it is said that heat and cold are affections only of the mind, and not at all patterns of real beings existing in the corporeal substances which excite them, for that the same body which appears cold to one hand seems warm to another[3]. Now, why may we not as well argue that figure and extension are not patterns or resemblances of qualities existing in Matter, because to the same eye at different stations, or eyes of a different texture at the same station, they appear various, and cannot therefore be the images of anything settled and determinate without the mind? Again, it is proved that sweetness is not really in the sapid thing, because the thing remaining unaltered the sweetness is changed into bitter, as in case of a fever or otherwise vitiated palate. Is it not as reasonable to say that motion is not without the mind, since if the

---

[1] Locke for instance. See *Essay*, b. II. ch. 7. § 7.
[2] Cf. Locke's *Essay*, b. II. ch. 7. § 7; ch. 13. § 26; ch. 16. § 1, where 'number' is said to be 'the most universal idea we have,' applicable to everything real or imaginary.
[3] Yet we find a standard in the thermometer, in which *motion* (a primary quality) is substituted for *sensations* of heat and cold (secondary qualities), which are thus interpreted in terms of motion. Berkeley argues that the *motion* equally with the *feeling of heat* is dependent on being realised in living perception.

succession of ideas in the mind become swifter the motion, it is acknowledged, shall appear slower without any alteration in any external object?

15. In short, let any one consider those arguments which are thought manifestly to prove that colours and tastes exist *only* in the mind, and he shall find they may with equal force be brought to prove the same thing of extension, figure, and motion.—Though it must be confessed this method of arguing does not so much prove that there is no extension or colour in an outward object, as that *we* do not know by *sense* which is the *true* extension or colour of the object. But the arguments foregoing [1] plainly shew it to be impossible that any colour or extension at all, or other sensible quality whatsoever, should exist in an unthinking subject without the mind; or in truth, that there should be any such thing as an outward object [2].

16. But let us examine a little the received opinion.—It is said extension is a mode or accident of Matter, and that Matter is the *substratum* that supports it. Now I desire that you would explain to me what is meant by Matter's *supporting* extension. Say you, I have no idea of Matter and therefore cannot explain it. I answer, though you have no positive, yet, if you have any meaning at all, you must at least have a relative idea of Matter; though you know

---

[1] See §§ 5-9, which argue that if all conscious mind were withdrawn from the universe, the words which now signify sensible things must become meaningless.

[2] His conclusion, in this part of the argument against Matter as an independent factor in the universe of existence—which turns on the mind-dependent character of the *qualities* of Matter—is that *all* of them—the primary as much as the secondary—resolve into phenomena which presuppose a living percipient, and therefore cannot be real in the absence of all sentient intelligence. In its absence they cease to be actual; and supposed 'Matter' becomes an unintelligible abstraction. All its qualities, including its motions, are dependent for their reality on percipient activity lifting them into it: and this holds good of our organism itself as well as of extra-organic bodies.

not what it is, yet you must be supposed to know what relation it bears to accidents, and what is meant by its supporting them. It is evident 'support' cannot here be taken in its usual or literal sense—as when we say that pillars support a building; in what sense therefore must it be taken?

17. If we inquire into what the most accurate philosophers declare themselves to mean by *material substance*[1], we shall find them acknowledge they have no other meaning annexed to those sounds but the idea of *being in general*, together with the relative notion of *its supporting accidents*. The general idea of Being appeareth to me the most abstract and incomprehensible of all other; and as for its supporting accidents, this, as we have just now observed, cannot be understood in the common sense of those words; it must therefore be taken in some other sense, but what that is they do not explain. So that when I consider the two parts or branches which make the signification of the words *material substance*, I am convinced there is no distinct meaning annexed to them. But why should we trouble ourselves any farther, in discussing this material *substratum* or 'support' of figure, and motion, and other sensible qualities? Does it not suppose *they* have an existence without the mind? And is not this a direct repugnancy, and altogether inconceivable[2]?

---

[1] He argues elsewhere that the meaninglessness applies exclusively to *material substance*, and not to *spiritual substance*. He accepts the *ego*, or spiritual substance, as an intelligible datum of consciousness. Personal pronouns, he argues, have meaning: unperceived phenomena have none.

[2] He seems to have Locke in view. Cf. Locke's *Essay*, b. I. ch. 4. § 18; b. II. ch. 12. §§ 3-6; ch. 13. § 19; ch. 23, where our idea of substance, as distinct from all perceived qualities, is said to be dark, confused, and of little use. Yet Locke hesitates to dismiss this abstract idea—as Hume afterwards did; or even to exclude it from the material world—as Berkeley is here doing. For Locke recognises it as something of which we are conscious, obscure though it be—the idea of ' one

18. But though it were possible that solid, figured, moveable *substances* may exist without the mind, *corresponding to* the ideas we have of bodies, yet how is it possible for us to know this? Either we must know it by Sense or by Reason.—As for our senses, by them we have the knowledge *only* of our sensations, ideas, or those things that are immediately perceived by sense, call them what you will: but they do not inform us that things exist without the mind, or unperceived, like to those which are perceived. This the Materialists themselves acknowledge[1].—It remains therefore that if we have any knowledge at all of external things, it must be by Reason inferring their existence from what is immediately perceived by sense. But what reason can induce us to believe the existence of bodies without the mind, from what we perceive, since the very patrons of Matter themselves do not pretend there is any *necessary* connexion betwixt them and our ideas? I say it is granted on all hands—and what happens in dreams, frenzies, and the like, puts it beyond dispute—that it is possible we might be affected with all the ideas we have now, though there were no bodies existing without resembling them. Hence, it is evident the supposition of external bodies is not necessary for the producing our ideas; since it is granted they are produced sometimes, and might possibly be produced always in the same order we see them in at present, without their concurrence.

knows not what *support* of the perceived qualities, 'which we are *somehow obliged* to presuppose.'

[1] 'Materialist' here includes all who maintain the reality of material substance neither percipient nor perceived; not limited, as it commonly is, to those who take Matter, or movable atoms, to be the only real existence. The hypothesis that God, by divinely-established law in nature, has made Matter able to be conscious, must be distinguished from the Universal Materialism which substitutes blind atomism for God. Locke while rejecting the latter suggests the possibility of the former.

19. But, though we might possibly have all our sensations without them, yet perhaps it may be thought easier to conceive and explain the manner of their production, by supposing external bodies in their likeness rather than otherwise; and so it might be at least probable there are such things as bodies that excite their ideas in our minds. But neither can this be said; for, though we give the materialists their external bodies, they by their own confession are never the nearer knowing *how* our ideas are produced; since they own themselves unable to comprehend in what manner body can act upon spirit, or how it is possible it should imprint any idea in the mind[1]. Hence it is evident the production of ideas or sensations in our minds can be no reason why we should suppose Matter or corporeal substances, since *that* is acknowledged to remain equally inexplicable with or without this supposition. If therefore it were possible for bodies to exist without the mind[2], yet to hold they do so must needs be a very precarious opinion; since it is to suppose, without any reason at all, that God has created innumerable beings that are entirely useless, and serve to no manner of purpose[3].

20. In short, if there were external bodies, it is impossible we should ever come to know it; and if there were not, we might have the very same reasons to think there were that we have now. Suppose—what no one can deny possible—an intelligence *without the help of external bodies,*

---

[1] So Locke, who professes inability to explain how the percipient act originates, although we may find by observation the organic conditions under which it manifests itself. Locke repudiates any final explanation of perception. He takes it as an inexplicable fact.

[2] 'Without the mind,' i.e. in the absence of all percipient life.

[3] Not 'useless' if it can be shown that the *independent* existence of sensible things is needed in order to (*a*) my knowledge of the existence of other men; (*b*) the existence of continuous order in nature; and (*c*) the recognition of my own existence as a person. Of all which afterwards.

to be affected with the same train of sensations or ideas that you are, imprinted in the same order, and with like vividness in his mind. I ask whether that intelligence hath not all the reason to believe the existence of corporeal substances, represented by his ideas, and exciting them in his mind, that you can possibly have for believing the same thing? Of this there can be no question; which one consideration were enough to make any reasonable person suspect the strength of whatever arguments he may think himself to have, for the existence of bodies without the mind[1].

21. Were it necessary to add any farther proof against the Existence of Matter[2], after what has been said, I could instance several of those errors and difficulties (not to mention impieties) which have sprung from that tenet. It has occasioned numberless controversies and disputes in philosophy, and not a few of far greater moment in religion. But I shall not enter into the detail of them in this place, as well because I think arguments *a posteriori* are unnecessary for confirming what has been, if I mistake not, sufficiently demonstrated *a priori*[3], as because I shall hereafter find occasion to speak somewhat of them.

22. I am afraid I have given cause to think I am need-

---

[1] Whether Berkeley's conception of the material world can be reconciled with *law in nature*, without presupposing covertly what it professedly rejects, is the question which here begins to suggest itself. If the reality of natural order among phenomena requires the *unperceived* or *independent* existence of what is manifested to us in sense, then Berkeley must not say that the independent matter is 'entirely useless,' and 'serves no manner of purpose.'

[2] i.e. its existence independently of realising Spirit.

[3] In its old meaning 'reasoning *a priori*' is from the presupposed essential nature (real definition) of a cause—prior to any experience of its effects; 'reasoning *a posteriori*' is based upon observation of its effects. The premises in the former case are abstract principles; those in the latter are facts of experience. The method of the former is deductive; that of the latter inductive.

lessly prolix in handling this subject. For, to what purpose is it to dilate on that which may be demonstrated with the utmost evidence in a line or two, to any one that is capable of the least reflection? It is but looking into your own thoughts, and so *trying whether you can conceive it possible* for a sound, or figure, or motion, or colour to exist without the mind or unperceived. This easy trial may perhaps make you see that what you contend for is a downright contradiction. Insomuch that I am content to put the whole upon this issue :—If you can but conceive it possible for one extended moveable substance, or, in general, for any one idea, or anything like an idea, to exist otherwise than in a mind perceiving it[1], I shall readily give up the cause. And, as for all that compages of external bodies you contend for, I shall grant you its existence, though you cannot either (*a*) give me any reason why you believe it exists, or (*b*) assign any use to it when it is supposed to exist. I say, the bare possibility of your opinions being true shall pass for an argument that it is so.

23. But, say you, surely there is nothing easier than for me to imagine trees, for instance, in a park, or books existing in a closet, and nobody by to perceive them. I answer, you may so, there is no difficulty in it; but what is all this, I beseech you, more than framing in *your* mind certain ideas which you call books and trees, and at the same time omitting to frame the idea of any one that may perceive them? *But do not you yourself perceive or think of them all the while?* This therefore is nothing to the purpose : it only shews you have the power of imagining or forming ideas in your mind; but it does not shew that you can conceive it possible the objects of your thought may exist without the mind. To make out this, *it is necessary that you conceive them existing unconceived or unthought*

---

[1] Is a universe empty of all percipient life, finite or Divine, conceivable?

of, which is a manifest repugnancy. When we do our utmost to conceive the existence of external bodies, we are all the while only contemplating our own ideas. But the mind, *taking no notice of itself*, is deluded to think it can and does conceive bodies existing unthought of or without the mind, though at the same time they are apprehended by or exist in itself[1]. A little attention will discover to any one the truth and evidence of what is here said, and make it unnecessary to insist on any other proofs against the existence of *material substance*[2].

24. It is very obvious, upon the least inquiry into our own thoughts, to know whether it be possible for us to *understand* what is meant by the *absolute* existence of sensible objects *in themselves*, or *without the mind*. To me it is evident those words mark out either a direct contradiction, or else nothing at all. And to convince others of this, I know no readier or fairer way than to entreat they would calmly attend to their own thoughts; and if by this attention the emptiness or repugnancy of those expressions does appear, surely nothing more is requisite for their conviction. It is on this therefore that I insist, to wit, that the absolute existence of unthinking things are words without a meaning, or which include a contradiction[3]. This is what I repeat

---

[1] It may be asked whether this argument does not equally apply to the existence of *other persons*; whose existence, as signified by material phenomena, it is one aim of Berkeley's philosophy to vindicate. Conscious life *external to his own*, is not, he would argue, *meaningless* in the way u: perceived matter is. This is an intelligible sort of externality, derived from our notion of our own self-conscious life. But what of persons in their intervals of apparent unconsciousness? Is the existence of an *unconscious* spirit more intelligible than the existence of unperceived matter?

[2] What we only imagine is so far real, but it is real subjectively or privately—not as part of the universal system of ordered things. Now, it is the *interrupted* existence of material things in living experience that Berkeley has to reconcile with faith in their permanence.

[3] (*a*) A 'contradiction,' if they mean that sensible objects are at

and inculcate, and earnestly recommend to the attentive thoughts of the reader.

25. All our ideas, sensations, notions, or the things which we perceive, by whatsoever names they may be distinguished, are visibly inactive—there is nothing of Power or Agency included in them. So that one idea or object of thought cannot produce or make any alteration in another. —To be satisfied of the truth of this, there is nothing else requisite but a bare observation of our ideas. For, since they and every part of them exist only in the mind, it follows that there is nothing in them but what is perceived: but whoever shall attend to his ideas, whether of sense or reflection, will not perceive in them any power or activity; there is, therefore, no such thing contained in them. A little attention will discover to us that the very being of an idea implies passiveness and inertness in it, insomuch that it is impossible for an idea to do anything, or, strictly speaking, to be the cause of anything: neither can it be the resemblance or pattern of any active being, as is evident from sect. 8. Whence it plainly follows that extension, figure, and motion cannot be the cause of our sensations. To say, therefore, that these are the effects of powers result-

---

once perceived and not perceived—phenomenal and yet not phenomenal. (*b*) 'Words without a meaning' if what is intended is, that Matter is 'something' other than natural phenomena. The argument rests on the assumption that what is not sense-presented is not merely unimaginable, but must be empty abstraction. But for Berkeley's recognition elsewhere that personal pronouns are not meaningless, this principle would involve the agnostic phenomenalism of Hume.

Berkeley rejects, as meaningless, a material world unrealised by any living percipient. He takes no account of the distinction between existence that is only *potential* and existence that is *actual*, i. e. realised in living experience. The function of x or mystery in human knowledge is a subject to be pondered, with the question whether philosophy can ever entirely eliminate x.

ing from the configuration, number, motion, and size of corpuscles, must certainly be false [1].

26. We perceive a continual *succession* of ideas; some are anew excited, others are changed or totally disappear. There is therefore some Cause of these ideas, whereon they depend, and which produces and changes them. That this cause cannot be any quality, or idea, or combination of ideas is clear from the preceding section. It must therefore be a substance; but it has been shewn that there is no corporeal or material substance: it remains therefore that the cause of ideas is an incorporeal active substance or Spirit [2].

---

[1] In this and the next section we have the rudiments of that conception of Causality and Power which it is the chief purpose of Berkeley's philosophy to unfold. It implies the *total powerlessness of Matter*. In § 25 he turns from Spirit giving reality to the material world, to Spirit as the *only real agent in existence*. Here his first position is, that there is no power or active causality in things of sense: 'bare observation' gives proof of their inactivity, he says. Customary sequence among things, maintained by God, is the only sort of 'causality' which Berkeley recognises in the *material* world; which is with him a divinely-established system of significant phenomena, in which *a priori* anything might by God have been made the sign or so-called natural cause of anything. This is like the physical conception of causality, afterwards professed by Hume, Brown, Comte, the Mills, and others, in harmony with Bacon's favourite conception of external nature as a system of interpretable signs, of which the natural sciences are the interpretation. With them, however, it was not, as with Berkeley, limited to the material world, and so with them agency proper is left out of account.

[2] Here Berkeley, like Locke, without an express analysis of the ambiguous term 'cause,' proceeds tacitly upon the assumption, that every change necessarily presupposes the existence of something out of which it issues. Power is with him more than antecedent phenomenon. He sees in phenomena only ordered signs, Spirit *alone* being the cause of their order and consequent significance or interpretability. The material world is thus emptied of power, and its supposed 'powers' are refunded into Spirit. All appearances in sense and the constant order in which they appear are passive or caused: only Spirit actively causes. Except metaphorically, he does not attribute efficacy to any sensible thing: the material world consists of aggregated phenomena,

27. A Spirit is one simple, undivided, active being—as it *perceives* ideas it is called the *Understanding*, and as it is *produces* or otherwise *operates* about them it is called the *Will*. Hence there can be no *idea* formed of a soul or spirit; for, all ideas whatever, being passive and inert, (vid. sect. 25,) cannot represent unto us, by way of image or likeness, that which acts. A little attention will make it plain to any one that to have an idea which shall be *like* that active principle of motion and change of ideas is absolutely impossible. Such is the nature of Spirit, or that which acts, that it cannot be of itself perceived, but only by the effects which it produceth.—If any man shall doubt of the truth of what is here delivered, let him but reflect and try if we can frame the idea of any Power or Active Being; and whether he has ideas of two principal powers, marked by the names *Will* and *Understanding*, distinct from each other, as well as from a third idea of Substance or Being in general, with a

uniform in their sequences. In recognising only a divinely arbitrary invariableness in the natural order of phenomena, he takes no explicit account of our justification in refunding effects into causes, and causes that are adequate to the effects.

In these sections Berkeley seems to found our notion of Power on our intuitive conviction of our own activity—akin to the solution adopted afterwards by Reid, Stewart, and Maine de Biran. Elsewhere (e.g. *Siris*, 257) he seems to trace it specially to agency for which one is responsible, and in which, therefore, he must be free to act or not to act. His views (more developed in the *Vindication* and in *Siris*) may be compared with those of Locke, *Essay*, b. II. ch. 21 and ch. 26; also with the reduction of the causal relation afterwards proposed by Hume; with the analysis of causation by Kant, as a 'category' constitutive of experience; or (turning to ancient speculation) with the Aristotelian Four Causes. Hume tries to show that *necessity* of connexion among phenomena is an illusion. Kant finds the notion of cause presupposed in the very possibility of an *intelligible* experience. According to Aristotle, everything presupposes (*a*) *matter* of which it is made; (*b*) *form* or *essence* by which it may be defined; (*c*) *force* or *efficiency* by which the matter and form have been united in its constitution; and (*d*) *end* or *purpose* which it is its function to fulfil;—so that a philosophical knowledge of an individual thing, or of the universe itself, would be a knowledge of it in all these four relations.

relative notion of its supporting or being the subject of the aforesaid powers—which is signified by the name Soul or Spirit[1]. This is what some hold; but, so far as I can see, the words *will, soul, spirit,* do not stand for different ideas, or, in truth, for any idea at all, but for something which is very different from ideas, and which, being an Agent, cannot be like unto, or represented by, any idea whatsoever. Though it must be owned at the same time that we have some *notion*[2] of soul, spirit, and the operations of the mind; such as willing, loving, hating—inasmuch as we know or understand the meaning of these words.

28. I find I can excite ideas in my mind at pleasure, and vary and shift the scene as oft as I think fit[3]. It is no more than willing, and straightway this or that idea arises in my fancy; and by the same power it is obliterated and makes way for another. This making and unmaking of ideas doth very properly denominate the mind active. This much is certain and grounded on experience: but when we talk of unthinking agents, or of exciting ideas exclusive of Volition, we only amuse ourselves with words[4].

[1] According to Locke we have no *positive* idea either of corporeal or of spiritual substance; yet he recognises an obscure *negative* idea of both. Berkeley accepts, *as given in consciousness of self*, the 'notion' (not idea or phenomenon) of *spiritual* substance. Hume afterwards rejected both, as neither can be traced to a sense-given phenomenon. Kant recalled the intellectual notion of substance, as necessarily involved in the intelligibility of experience.

[2] In short, according to Berkeley, the notions and judgments of substance and cause seem given to us empirically in our consciousness of continued personality and of moral agency, rather than as necessarily involved in experience. He says too that we have 'notions,' not 'ideas,' of them; for Spirit cannot be phenomenalised.

[3] In this and the five following sections we have Berkeley's account of the difference between the original data or ideas of cause, and our subjective imagination of those data.

[4] The *impotence* of Matter rather than its *unreality*, when it is not perceived, is the lesson of spiritual philosophy.

29. But, whatever power I may have over my own thoughts, I find the ideas actually perceived by Sense have not a like dependence on my will. When in broad daylight I open my eyes, it is not in my power to choose whether I shall see or no, or to determine what particular objects shall present themselves to my view; and so likewise as to the hearing and other senses, the ideas imprinted on them are not creatures of my will. There is therefore some *other* Will or Spirit that produces them.

30. The ideas of Sense are more strong, lively, and distinct than those of the Imagination; they have likewise a steadiness, order, and coherence, and are not excited at random, as those which are the effects of human wills often are, but in a regular train or series—the admirable connexion whereof sufficiently testifies the wisdom and benevolence of its Author. Now the set rules or established methods wherein the Mind we depend on excites in us the ideas of sense, are called the *laws of nature*; and these we learn by experience[1], which teaches us that such and such ideas are attended with such and such other ideas, in the ordinary course of things.

31. This gives us a sort of foresight which enables us to regulate our actions for the benefit of life. And without this we should be eternally at a loss; we could not know how to act anything that might procure us the least pleasure, or remove the least pain of sense. That food nourishes, sleep refreshes, and fire warms us; that to sow in the seed-time is the way to reap in the harvest; and in general that to obtain such or such ends, such or such means are conducive—all this we know, not by discovering any *necessary*

---

[1] Something more than present phenomena is here tacitly presupposed in 'experience': otherwise, experience is only of what is at the moment, not of what will always be. How does experience give conviction of the *constancy* of order, if it is concerned only with ideas or phenomena of sense now present?

connexion between our ideas, but only by the *observation* of the settled laws of nature, without which we should be all in uncertainty and confusion, and a grown man no more know how to manage himself in the affairs of life than an infant just born [1].

32. And yet this consistent uniform working, which so evidently displays the goodness and wisdom of that Governing Spirit whose Will constitutes the laws of nature, is so far from leading our thoughts to Him, that it rather sends them wandering after second causes. For, when we perceive certain ideas of Sense constantly followed by other ideas, and we know this is not of our own doing, we forthwith attribute power and agency to the ideas themselves, and make one the cause of another, than which nothing can be more absurd and unintelligible. Thus, for example, having observed that when we perceive by sight a certain round luminous figure we at the same time perceive by touch the idea of sensation called heat, we do from thence conclude the sun to be the *cause* of heat. And in like manner perceiving the notion and collision of bodies to be attended with sound, we are inclined to think the latter the *effect* of the former.

33. The ideas imprinted on the Senses by the Author of nature are called *real things*: and those excited in the Imagination being less regular, vivid, and constant, are more properly termed *ideas*, or *images of things*, which they copy and represent. But then our sensations, be they never so vivid and distinct, are nevertheless ideas; that is, they exist in the mind [2], or are perceived by it, as truly as the ideas of

---

[1] Reduction of induction to present 'observation' is open to the difficulty suggested in the preceding note.

[2] 'in the mind' is here and elsewhere used figuratively for *being perceived*, not for being *locally* within mind,—to which terms of locality are foreign. We do not speak of the size or shape of a thought, or a feeling, or a volition, apart from their correlative organic conditions, with which physiology is concerned.

its own framing. The ideas of Sense are allowed to have more reality in them, that is, to be more strong, orderly, and coherent than the creatures of the mind; but this is no argument that they exist without the mind. They are also less dependent on the spirit, or thinking substance which perceives them, in that they are excited by the will of another and more powerful Spirit; yet still they are *ideas*, and certainly no idea, whether faint or strong, can exist otherwise than in a mind perceiving it[1].

---

[1] Such is Berkeley's account of the difference between perceived things and imagined things—between actual perception in sense and mere fancy. Things of which we are percipient, he says, (*a*) appear involuntarily, as far as the percipient is concerned, while fancies are our own creatures; (*b*) the former are more strong, lively, and distinct than the latter, thus differing from them in degree; (*c*) they are units in a fixed orderly system. The second of these three distinguishing marks was afterwards emphasised by Hume, in his contrast between *impressions* and their (representative) *ideas* (*Treatise of Human Nature*, b. I. pt. 1. §§ 1, 3; pt. 4. § 7: *Inquiry concerning Human Understanding* § 2). Hume explains all *belief* as the issue of the natural tendency of blind custom to *enliven* those ideas or phenomena that are found in constant connexion; thus transforming them from capricious fancies into beliefs. 'The memory, senses, and understanding are,' he says, 'all of them founded on the intensity or vivacity of our ideas.'—See Leibniz, *De modo distinguendi Phenomena Realia ab Imaginariis*, and Locke, *Essay*, b. IV. ch. 2. § 14; ch. 4; ch. 11, for opinions antecedent to Berkeley.

III

OBJECTIONS TO THE PRINCIPLES

34. Before we proceed any farther it is necessary we spend some time in answering Objections which may probably be made against the Principles we have hitherto laid down. In doing of which, if I seem too prolix to those of quick apprehensions, I desire I may be excused, since all men do not equally apprehend things of this nature, and I am willing to be understood by every one.

First, then, it will be *objected* that by the foregoing principles all that is real and substantial in nature is banished out of the world; and instead thereof a chimerical scheme of *ideas* takes place. All things that exist exist only in the mind, that is, they are purely notional[1]. What therefore becomes of the sun, moon, and stars? What must we think of houses, rivers, mountains, trees, stones; nay, even of our own bodies? Are all these but so many chimeras and illusions on the fancy?

To all which, and whatever else of the same sort may be objected, I *answer*, that by the principles premised we are not deprived of any one thing in nature. Whatever we see, feel, hear, or any wise conceive or understand, remains as secure as ever, and is as real as ever. There is a *rerum natura*, and the distinction between realities and chimeras retains its full force. This is evident from sect. 29, 30,

---

[1] 'notional.' Here *notion* is undistinguished from *idea* or *phenomenon*. Cf. § 27.

and 33, where we have shewn what is meant by *real things*, in opposition to *chimeras*, or ideas of our own framing [1]; but then they both equally exist in the mind, and in that sense are alike *ideas*.

35. I do not argue against the existence of any one thing that we can apprehend either by sense or reflection. That the things I see with my eyes and touch with my hands do exist, really exist, I make not the least question. The only thing whose existence we deny is that which *philosophers* call *matter* or *corporeal substance*. And in doing of this there is no damage done to the rest of mankind, who, I dare say, will never miss it. The atheist indeed will want the colour of an empty name to support his impiety; and the philosophers may possibly find they have lost a great handle for trifling and disputation.

36. If any man thinks this detracts from the existence or reality of things, he is very far from understanding what hath been premised in the plainest terms I could think of. Take here an abstract of what has been said:—There are spiritual substances, minds, or human souls, which excite ideas [2] in themselves at pleasure [3]: but these are faint, weak, and unsteady in respect of others they perceive by Sense, which, being impressed upon them according to certain Rules or Laws of Nature, speak themselves the effects of a Mind more powerful and wise than human spirits. These latter are said to have *more reality* [4] in them than the former;—by which is

---

[1] 'of our own framing,' whereas 'real things' are continuously presented by a power other than ours—the Divine Power universally operative in nature.

[2] 'ideas,' i.e. fancies, in contrast to the real ideas of which we are percipient in sense, and which enable us to interpret nature.

[3] Ideas thus raised we call fancies or dreams of imagination, in contrast with the real ideas or natural phenomena which are presented in our senses.

[4] 'more reality.' This implies that *reality admits of degrees*. Accordingly that is for *me* most real which enters most into relation

meant that they are more affecting, orderly, and distinct, and that they are not fictions [1] of the mind perceiving them. And in this sense the sun that I see by day is the real sun, and that which I imagine by night is the idea of the former [2]. In the sense here given of *reality*, it is evident that every vegetable, star, mineral, and in general each part of the mundane system, is as much a *real being* by our principles as by any other. Whether others mean anything by the term *reality* different from what I do, I entreat them to look into their own thoughts and see.

37. It will be urged that thus much at least is true, to wit, that we take away all corporeal *substances*. To this my answer is, that if the word 'substance' be taken in the vulgar sense—for a *combination* of sensible qualities, such as extension, solidity, weight, and the like—this we cannot be accused of taking away; but if it be taken in a philosophic sense— for the *support* of accidents or qualities *without the mind*, then indeed I acknowledge that we take it away, if one may be said to take away that which never had any existence, not even in the imagination.

38. But after all, say you, it sounds very harsh to say we eat and drink ideas, and are clothed with ideas. I acknowledge it does so—the word *idea* not being used in common

---

with my individual personality; for *man*, that which most fully satisfies the ideal man. Thus the appearances presented to the senses are more realised when interpreted scientifically than when looked at or felt unintelligently; and when also apprehended philosophically, or in their relation to God, they are realised in the highest degree. But do mere fancies differ from actual perceptions only in degree?

[1] The appearances or qualities of things, when actually presented to our senses, are 'not fictions': they are reality immediately present in sense. They cannot misrepresent, because they are not representative of reality, but are themselves the real thing: they constitute matter.

[2] Here again we have the signal difference between imagined matter and real matter insisted on, and sought to be reconciled with the already argued unsubstantiality and powerlessness of the material world, apart from percipient and active mind.

discourse to signify the several combinations of sensible qualities which are called *things*;—and it is certain that any expression which varies from the familiar use of language will seem harsh and ridiculous. But this doth not concern the truth of the proposition, which in other words is no more than to say, we are fed and clothed with those things which we perceive immediately by our senses. The hardness or softness, the colour, taste, warmth, figure, or suchlike qualities, which, combined together, constitute the several sorts of victuals and apparel, have been shewn to exist only in the mind that perceives them; and this is all that is meant by calling them *ideas*; which word, if it was as ordinarily used as *thing*, would sound no harsher nor more ridiculous than it. I am not for disputing about the propriety, but the truth of the expression. If therefore you agree with me that we eat and drink and are clad with *the immediate objects of sense, which cannot exist unperceived or without the mind*, I shall readily grant it is more proper or conformable to custom that they should be called *things* rather than *ideas*.

39. If it be demanded why I make use of the word *idea*, and do not rather in compliance with custom call them *things*, I answer, I do it for two reasons:—first, because the term *thing*, in contradistinction to *idea*, is generally supposed to denote somewhat existing without the mind[1]; secondly, because *thing* hath a more comprehensive signification than *idea*, including spirit or thinking things as well as ideas[2]. Since therefore the objects of sense exist only in the mind, and are withal thoughtless and inactive[3], I choose to mark them by the word *idea*[4], which implies those properties.

[1] i.e. unperceived—unrealised by any conscious being.
[2] Self-conscious agents are properly called *persons*, in contrast to *things*.
[3] He takes for granted that he has already demonstrated the wholly dependent substantiality and power attributable to matter.
[4] 'Sensation,' 'impression,' 'percept,' 'phenomenon,' might be sub-

40. But, say what we can, some one perhaps may be apt to reply, he will still believe his senses, and never suffer any arguments, how plausible soever, to prevail over the certainty of them. Be it so; assert the evidence of sense as high as you please; we are willing to do the same. That what I see, hear, and feel *doth exist*, that is to say, is perceived by me, I no more doubt than I do of my own being. But I do not see how the testimony of *sense* can be alleged as a proof for the existence of anything which is *not perceived by sense*. We are not for having any man turn sceptic and disbelieve his senses; on the contrary, we give them all the stress and assurance imaginable; nor are there any principles more opposite to Scepticism than those we have laid down, as shall be hereafter clearly shewn [1].

41. *Secondly*, it will be *objected* that there is a great difference betwixt real fire, for instance, and the idea of fire, betwixt dreaming or imagining oneself burnt, and actually being so: if you suspect it to be only the idea of fire which you see, do but put your hand into it and you will be convinced with a witness [2]. This and the like may be urged in opposition to our tenets.—To all which the *answer* is evident from what hath been already said; and I shall only add in this place, that if real fire be very different from the idea of fire, so also is the real pain that it occasions very different from the idea of the same pain; and yet nobody will pretend that real pain either is, or can possibly be, in an

stituted, though objections are open to them all. In *Siris* he prefers *phenomenon* to *idea*, as the name for appearances presented in the senses.

[1] Berkeley argues that to suppose sensible things which are not perceived by *any* mind is as absurd as to suppose perception without perception. But to resolve *things* wholly into isolated ideas or phenomena leaves the material world without any principle connecting its present with its absent phenomena, and therefore unintelligible. This is the essence of Scepticism.

[2] So Locke, *Essay*, b. IV. ch. 11. §§ 7, 8.

unperceiving thing, or without the mind, any more than its idea[1].

42. *Thirdly*, it will be *objected* that we *see* things actually without, or at a distance from us; and which consequently do not exist in the mind; it being absurd that those things which are seen at the distance of several miles should be as near to us as our own thoughts.—In *answer* to this, I desire it may be considered that in a dream we do oft perceive things as existing at a great distance off, and yet for all that, those things are acknowledged to have their existence only in the mind.

43. But, for the fuller clearing of this point, it may be worth while to consider *how it is that we perceive distance and things placed at a distance by sight*. For, that we should in truth see external space, and bodies actually existing in it—some nearer, and others farther off—seems to carry with it some opposition to what hath been said of bodies existing nowhere without the mind. The consideration of this difficulty it was that gave birth to my *Essay towards a New Theory of Vision*, which was published not long since—wherein it is shewn that *distance* or *outness* is neither immediately of itself perceived by sight, nor yet apprehended or judged of by lines and angles, or anything that hath a necessary connexion with it; but that it is only suggested[2] to our thoughts by certain visible ideas and sensations attending vision, which in their own nature have no manner of similitude or relation either with distance or things placed

---

[1] But is there no more outness and independence of percipient mind in the solid things of sense than there is in transitory pains and pleasures—though both, it is granted, are different from the bare imagination of either?

[2] The term *suggestion*, so significant in Berkeley, here makes its first appearance in the *Principles*. See *Theory of Vision*, § 16, *note*.—'Suggestion'—simple suggestion and relative—was employed long afterwards, as a synonym for mental association, in the psychology of Thomas Brown.

at a distance; but, by a connexion taught us by experience [1], they come to signify and suggest them to us—after the same manner that words of any language suggest the ideas they are made to stand for; insomuch that a man born blind and afterwards made to see, would not, at first sight, think the things he saw to be without his mind, or at any distance from him. See sect. 41 of the forementioned treatise.

44. The ideas of sight and touch make two species entirely distinct and heterogeneous. *The former are marks and prognostics of the latter.* That the proper objects of sight neither exist without the mind, nor are the images of external things, was shewn even in that treatise. Though throughout the same the contrary be supposed true of tangible objects—not that to suppose that vulgar error was necessary for establishing the notion therein laid down, but because it was beside my purpose to examine and refute it in a discourse concerning *Vision*. So that in strict truth the ideas of sight, when we apprehend by them distance and things placed at a distance, do not suggest or mark out to us things actually existing at a distance, but only admonish us what ideas of touch [2] will be imprinted in our minds at such and such distances of time, and in consequence of such and such actions. It is, I say, evident from what has been said in the foregoing parts of this *Treatise*, and in sect. 147 and elsewhere of the *Essay* concerning Vision, that visible ideas are the Language whereby the Governing Spirit on whom we depend informs us what tangible ideas he is about to imprint upon us, in case we excite this or that motion in our own bodies. But for a fuller information in this point I refer to the *Essay* itself [3].

---

[1] 'Suggestion' is here rested upon 'experience,' or customary connexion, and is then made the constructive influence in the formation of visual perception, if not ultimately of physical science.

[2] Under 'touch' and 'tangible ideas,' he includes what is now called muscular sense, and also our sense of locomotive activity.

[3] *Visual expectation* develops into *universal sense symbolism*.

45. *Fourthly*, it will be *objected* that from the foregoing principles it follows things are every moment annihilated and created anew. The objects of sense exist only when they are perceived; the trees therefore are in the garden, or the chairs in the parlour, no longer than while there is somebody by to perceive them. Upon shutting my eyes all the furniture in the room is reduced to nothing, and barely upon opening them it is again created.—In *answer* to all which, I refer the reader to what has been said in sect. 3, 4, &c., and desire he will consider whether he means anything by the actual existence of an idea distinct from its being perceived. For my part, after the nicest inquiry I could make, I am not able to discover that anything else is meant by those words; and I once more entreat the reader to sound his own thoughts, and not suffer himself to be imposed on by words. If he can conceive it possible either for his ideas or their archetypes to exist without being perceived, then I give up the cause; but if he cannot, he will acknowledge it is unreasonable for him to stand up in defence of he knows not what, and pretend to charge on me as an absurdity the not assenting to those propositions which at bottom have no meaning in them[1].

46. It will not be amiss to observe how far the received principles of philosophy are themselves chargeable with those pretended absurdities. It is thought strangely absurd that upon closing my eyelids all the visible objects around me should be reduced to nothing; and yet is not this what philosophers commonly acknowledge, when they agree on all hands that light and colours, which alone are the proper and immediate objects of sight, are mere sensations[2] that

---

[1] This repeats the warning against empty abstractions with which he introduced us to philosophy; for such, according to his argument, are material substances and powers unperceived by any mind.

[2] It is the want of *permanence* in things, which seems to follow Berkeley's conception of matter, that is objected to; but this objection equally applies also to that providence, or 'constant creation,' held by

exist no longer than they are perceived? Again, it may to some perhaps seem very incredible that things should be every moment creating, yet this very notion is commonly taught in the schools. For the Schoolmen, though they acknowledge the existence of matter, and that the whole mundane fabric is framed out of it, are nevertheless of opinion that it cannot subsist without the divine conservation, which by them is expounded to be a continual creation.

47. Farther, a little thought will discover to us that though we allow the existence of Matter, or corporeal substance, yet it will unavoidably follow, from the principles which are now generally admitted, that the *particular bodies*, of what kind soever, do none of them exist whilst they are not perceived. For, it is evident, from sect. 11 and the following sections, that the Matter philosophers contend for is *an incomprehensible somewhat*, which hath none of those particular qualities whereby the bodies falling under our senses are distinguished one from another. But, to make this more plain, it must be remarked that the infinite divisibility of Matter is now universally allowed, at least by the most approved and considerable philosophers, who, on the received principles, demonstrate it beyond all exception. Hence, it follows there is an infinite number of parts in each particle of Matter, which are not perceived by sense[1]. The reason therefore that any particular body seems to be of a finite magnitude, or exhibits only a finite number of parts to sense, is, not because it contains no more, since in itself it contains an infinite number of parts, but because the sense is not

many long before Berkeley argued that *percipi* was the essence of the 'constantly created' material object.

Berkeley's limitation of power to Spirit substitutes for substance and power in the 'extended thing,' the constant creative activity of God (§§ 6, 48, &c.).

[1] It is of the essence of infinite division that it can never be completed, because every actual division must be carried further.

acute enough to discern them. In proportion therefore as the sense is rendered more acute, it perceives a greater number of parts in the object; that is, the object appears greater, and its figure varies, those parts in its extremities which were before unperceivable appearing now to bound it in very different lines and angles from those perceived by an obtuser sense. And at length, after various changes of size and shape, when the sense becomes infinitely acute the body shall seem infinite. During all which there is no alteration in the body, but only in the sense. Each body therefore, considered in itself, is infinitely extended, and consequently void of all shape and figure [1]. From which it follows that, though we should grant the existence of Matter to be never so certain, yet it is withal as certain, the Materialists themselves are by their own principles forced to acknowledge, that neither the particular bodies perceived by sense, nor anything like them, exists without the mind. Matter, I say, and each particle thereof, is according to them infinite and shapeless; and it is the mind that frames all that variety of bodies which compose the visible world, any one whereof does not exist longer than it is perceived.

48. But, after all, if we consider it, the objection proposed in sect. 45 will not be found reasonably charged on the principles we have premised, so as in truth to make any objection at all against our notions. For, though we hold indeed the objects of sense to be nothing else but ideas which cannot exist unperceived, yet we may not hence conclude they have no existence except only while they are perceived by *us*; since there may be some other Spirit that perceives them though we do not. Wherever bodies are said to have no existence without the mind, I would not be understood to mean this or that particular mind, but *all minds whatsoever*. It does not therefore follow from the foregoing

---

[1] The infinite in quantity is wholly unimaginable as an idea or sensuous phenomenon.

principles that bodies are annihilated and created every moment, or exist not at all during the intervals between *our* perception of them[1].

49. *Fifthly*, it may perhaps be *objected* that if extension and figure exist only in the mind, it follows that the mind is extended and figured; since extension is a mode or attribute which (to speak with the schools) is predicated of the *subject* in which it exists.—I answer, those qualities are *in the mind* only as they are perceived by it—that is, not by way of *mode* or *attribute*, but only by way of *idea*; and it no more follows the soul or mind is extended, because extension exists in it alone, than it does that it is red or blue, because those colours are on all hands acknowledged to exist in it, and nowhere else. As to what philosophers say of 'subject' and 'mode,' that seems very groundless and unintelligible.

---

[1] To explain our confidence in the *continued identity* of the things we see and touch, notwithstanding their constant flux in our perceptions; and to show *how* they exist during intervals in which there might be no sense-perception of them by any mind, is Berkeley's difficulty.

With reference to Berkeley's reply to the fourth objection, it has been urged that if sensible things exist only supernaturally in God's will and thought, when unperceived by us; and if, as realised, they are dependent on our (often interrupted) sense-perceptions,—then, what we call the *same* thing is *many* things, each of them annihilated and created anew with every opening and closing of our senses.—Did the Herculanean manuscripts, some one asks, not really exist during the centuries in which they were buried; and shall we say that when they were discovered God created them anew? Is this restoration explained by the assumption that all things are divinely governed according to natural laws? Is law in nature possible except on the supposition that things *exist in space*, independently of realisation in percipient life? That there may be inhabitants in Mars, though no man on earth has ever seen them, must be admitted; but this means only that in the progress of our knowledge we may realise them for ourselves. That which is related to present perception according to the natural laws which regulate experience is physically real.

Perfect similarity in the sense-phenomena manifested, not objective numerical identity, constitutes 'sameness' in sensible things, according to Berkeley. As to *personal* identity he is obscure.

For instance, in this proposition—'a die is hard, extended, and square,' they will have it that the word *die* denotes a subject or substance, distinct from the hardness, extension, and figure which are predicated of it, and in which they exist. This I cannot comprehend: to me a die seems to be nothing distinct from those things which are termed its modes or accidents. And, to say 'a die is hard, extended, and square' is not to attribute those qualities to a subject distinct from and supporting them, but only an explication of the meaning of the word *die* [1].

50. *Sixthly*, you will *object* there have been a great many things explained by matter and motion: take away these and you destroy the whole corpuscular philosophy, and undermine those mechanical principles which have been applied with so much success to account for the phenomena. In short, whatever advances have been made, either by ancient or modern philosophers, in the study of Nature do all proceed on the supposition that corporeal substance or Matter doth really exist.—To this I *answer* that there is not any one phenomenon explained on that supposition which may not as well be explained without it, as might easily be made appear by an induction of particulars [2]. To

---

[1] If Space and extended things exist only in and through percipient mind, it may seem that mind must be extended; so that after all we are landed in Materialism.—Berkeley's reply throws light on his conception of the relation between sense and the phenomenon of extension—between the percipient and the interpretable appearances. Percipient mind is related to extension, figure, and what else is given in sense in the *unique* relation of percipient to what is perceived, with whatever 'otherness' that altogether unique relation may involve. It is not *so* related as that the extended phenomenon or idea is an *attribute* of the ego.

[2] It has been further objected—that all physico-mathematical explanations of events in nature presuppose that the things of sense and their changes are absolutely independent of percipient mind, and also that Berkeley's conception of what 'reality' of the material world means is inconsistent with the 'conservation of force.'

explain the phenomena, is all one as to shew why, upon such and such occasions, we are affected with such and such ideas. But how Matter should operate on a Spirit, or produce any idea in it, is what no philosopher will pretend to explain; it is therefore evident there can be no use of Matter in Natural Philosophy [1]. Besides, they who attempt to account for things do it, not by corporeal substance, but by figure, motion, and other qualities; which are in truth no more than mere ideas [2], and therefore cannot be the *cause* of anything, as hath been already shewn. See sect. 25.

51. *Seventhly*, it will upon this be demanded whether it does not seem absurd to take away natural causes [3], and ascribe everything to the immediate operation of Spirits? We must no longer say upon these principles that fire heats, or water cools, but that a Spirit heats, and so forth. Would not a man be deservedly laughed at, who should talk after this manner?—I *answer*, he would so; in such things we ought to think with the learned, and speak with the vulgar. They who to demonstration are convinced of the truth of the Copernican system do nevertheless say

[1] The question for Materialism is—whether conscious life in man, in its rational and voluntary manifestations, must originate in (*a*) a power like itself, intellect being the only possible cause of what is intellectual,—or may be only (*b*) a natural sequence to changes in matter. With Berkeley the human body, in itself unsubstantial and impotent, is ultimately dependent on active Spirit; and the human ego is also conditioned by its own mind-dependent organism, as healthy or diseased. They are known as mutually dependent; but the dependence of the conscious ego differs in kind from the dependence of matter and the organism. Universal Materialism, moreover, differs from this modified Materialism, as remarked in a former note.

[2] 'ideas,' i.e. phenomena which succeed one another naturally in our sense-experience.

[3] 'take away natural causes,' i.e. empty natural causes of all inherent power, and refer their supposed powers to the constant agency of God.

'the sun rises,' 'the sun sets,' or 'comes to the meridian;' and if they affected a contrary style in common talk it would without doubt appear very ridiculous. A little reflection on what is here said will make it manifest that the common use of language would receive no manner of alteration or disturbance from the admission of our tenets.

52. In the ordinary affairs of life, any phrases may be retained, so long as they excite in us proper sentiments, or dispositions to act in such a manner as is necessary for our well-being, how false soever they may be if taken in a strict and speculative sense. Nay, this is unavoidable, since, propriety being regulated by custom, language is suited to the received opinions, which are not always the truest. Hence it is impossible—even in the most rigid, philosophic reasonings—so far to alter the bent and genius of the tongue we speak as never to give a handle for cavillers to pretend difficulties and inconsistencies. But a fair and ingenuous reader will collect the sense from the scope and tenor and connexion of a discourse, making allowances for those inaccurate modes of speech which use has made inevitable.

53. As to the opinion that there are no Corporeal Causes [1], this has been heretofore maintained by some of the Schoolmen, as it is of late by others among the modern philosophers; who, though they allow Matter to exist, yet will have God *alone* to be the immediate efficient cause of all things. These men saw that amongst all the objects of sense there was none which had any power or activity included in it; and that by consequence this was likewise true of whatever

---

[1] The essential principle is, that Matter cannot be the *active* cause of anything; so that physical change must itself in all cases presuppose spiritual agency. It thus reconciles the common-sense recognition of natural order, on which science of nature proceeds, with the constant causal regulation of the natural order by God.

bodies *they* supposed to exist without the mind, like unto the immediate objects of sense [1]. But then, that they should suppose an innumerable multitude of created beings, which they acknowledge are not capable of producing any one effect in nature, and which therefore are made to no manner of purpose, since God might have done everything as well without them—this I say, though we should allow it possible, must yet be a very unaccountable and extravagant supposition [2].

54. In the *eighth* place, the universal concurrent Assent of Mankind [3] may be thought by some an invincible argument in behalf of Matter, or the existence of external things. Must we suppose the whole world to be mistaken? And if so, what cause can be assigned of so widespread and predominant an error?—I *answer*, first, that, upon a narrow inquiry, it will not perhaps be found so many as is imagined do really believe the existence of Matter, or things without the mind. Strictly speaking, to believe that which involves a contradiction, or has no meaning in it, is impossible; and whether the foregoing expressions are not of that sort,

---

[1] 'bodies'—of which the *ideas*, or immediate objects of sense, were supposed by them (not by Berkeley nor by Reid) to be only representatives.

[2] The reference in this section is to Malebranche, Geulinx, and other so-called Occasionalists in the seventeenth century, who, while they maintained an independent existence of Matter, denied, like Berkeley, but on other grounds, its *efficiency*. They held that, on occasion of the affection of the organism, perception is evoked by God.

[3] This is like the argument from 'common sense' for the reality of the material world, as put by Reid. The point in question is not, however, whether the world, *in some sense of the term* '*real*,' really exists; it is what we should mean, if we are not to indulge in empty verbal abstraction, when we assert its reality. That the unreflecting part of mankind should have a confused view of what the external reality of matter means is not to be wondered at. It is the office of philosophical meditation to improve their conception, making it deeper and truer.

I refer it to the impartial examination of the reader. In one sense, indeed, men may be said to believe that Matter exists; that is, they act as if the immediate cause of their sensations, which affects them every moment, and is so nearly present to them, were some senseless, unthinking being. But, that they should clearly apprehend any meaning marked by those words, and form thereof a settled speculative opinion, is what I am not able to conceive. This is not the only instance wherein men impose upon themselves, by imagining they believe those propositions which they have often heard, though at bottom they have no meaning in them[1].

55. But secondly, though we should grant a notion to be never so universally and stedfastly adhered to, yet this is but a weak argument of its truth to whoever considers what a vast number of prejudices and false opinions are everywhere embraced with the utmost tenaciousness, by the unreflecting (which are the far greater) part of mankind. There was a time when the antipodes and motion of the earth were looked upon as monstrous absurdities even by men of learning: and if it be considered what a small proportion they bear to the rest of mankind, we shall find that at this day those notions have gained but a very inconsiderable footing in the world.

56. But *ninthly*, it is demanded that we assign a Cause of this Prejudice, and account for its obtaining in the world. —To this I *answer*, that men knowing they perceived several ideas, whereof *they themselves* were not the authors—as not being excited from within, nor depending on the operation of their wills—this made them maintain those ideas or objects of perception had an existence independent of and

---

[1] That our perceptions of the material world are only perceptions of mind-dependent phenomena is what Reid is supposed to refute.

without the mind, without ever dreaming that a contradiction was involved in those words. But, philosophers having plainly seen that *the immediate objects of perception* do not exist without the mind, they in some degree corrected the mistake of the vulgar; but at the same time run into another, which seems no less absurd, to wit, that there are certain objects really existing without the mind, or having a subsistence distinct from being perceived, of which our ideas are only images or resemblances, imprinted by those objects on the mind[1]. And this notion of the philosophers owes its origin to the same cause with the former, namely, their being conscious that *they* were not the authors of their own sensations, which they evidently knew were imprinted from without, and which therefore must have some cause distinct from the minds on which they are imprinted[2].

57. But why they should suppose the ideas of sense to be excited in us by *things in their likeness*, and not rather have recourse to *Spirit*, which alone can act, may be accounted for, first, because they were not aware of the repugnancy there is, as well in supposing things like unto our ideas existing without, as in attributing to them power or activity. Secondly, because the Supreme Spirit which excites those ideas in our minds, is not marked out and limited to our view by any particular finite collection of sensible ideas, as human agents are by their size, complexion, limbs, and motions. And thirdly, because His operations are regular and uniform. Whenever the course of nature is interrupted by a miracle, men are ready to own the presence of a Superior Agent. But, when we see things go on in the ordinary course, they do not excite in us any

---

[1] This is the hypothesis of a wholly representative perception in sense, against which Reid's philosophy was a protest.

[2] A 'representative' perception presupposes real but unperceived things—existing *behind* what is perceived.

reflection; their order and concatenation, though it be an argument of the greatest wisdom, power, and goodness in their creator, is yet so constant and familiar to us that we do not think them the immediate effects of a FREE SPIRIT; especially since inconsistency and mutability in acting, though it be an imperfection, is looked on as a mark of *freedom* [1].

58. *Tenthly*, it will be objected that the notions we advance are inconsistent with several sound truths in Philosophy and Mathematics. For example, the motion of the earth is now universally admitted by astronomers as a truth grounded on the clearest and most convincing reasons. But, on the foregoing principles, there can be no such thing. For, motion being only an idea, it follows that if it be not perceived it *exists* not: but the motion of the earth is not perceived by sense.—I *answer*, that tenet, if rightly understood, will be found to agree with the principles we have premised; for, the question whether the earth moves or no amounts in reality to no more than this, to wit, whether we have reason to conclude, from what has been observed by astronomers, that if we were placed in such and such circumstances, and such or such a position and distance both from the earth and sun, *we should perceive* the former to move among the choir of the planets, and appearing in all respects like one of them; and this, by the established rules of nature which

---

[1] But *divine* 'arbitrariness' is not caprice. Confusion about this occasions the difficulty of allowing that God originates and constantly maintains law in nature. Philosophy struggles to resolve seeming contingencies into the rational unity that is only in part revealed to our limited intelligence of the universe. *Sense* is confused thought, which the rational constitution latent in nature enables human intellect to convert into physical science. But the narrow intellectual power and experience of man can never entirely eliminate probability in the conversion. Locke, who may have suggested to Berkeley his favourite conception of arbitrariness in the constitution of the laws of nature, maintained that therefore *man* could form no *demonstrable* science of nature.

we have no reason to mistrust, is reasonably collected from the phenomena.

59. We may, from the experience we have had of the train and succession of ideas[1] in our minds, often make, I will not say uncertain conjectures, but sure and well-grounded predictions concerning the ideas we shall be affected with pursuant to a great train of actions, and be enabled to pass a right judgment of what would have appeared to us, in case we were placed in circumstances very different from those we are in at present. Herein consists the knowledge of nature, which may preserve its use and certainty very consistently with what hath been said. It will be easy to apply this to whatever objections of the like sort may be drawn from the magnitude of the stars, or any other discoveries in astronomy or nature.

60. In the *eleventh* place, it will be demanded to what purpose serves that curious organisation of plants, and the animal mechanism in the parts of animals; might not vegetables grow, and shoot forth leaves and blossoms, and animals perform all their motions, as well without as with all that variety of internal parts so elegantly contrived and put together; which, being ideas, have nothing powerful or operative in them, nor have any *necessary* connexion with the effects ascribed to them? If it be a Spirit that immediately produces every effect by a *fiat* or act of His will, we must think all that is fine and artificial in the works, whether of man or nature, to be made in vain. By this doctrine, though an artist has made the spring and wheels, and every movement of a watch, and adjusted them in such a manner as he knew would produce the motions he designed, yet he must think all this is done to no purpose, and that it is an

---

[1] Our sense-experience is here supposed to be constituted by divinely-established associations of natural phenomena or sense-presented ideas—not by what is commonly meant by 'association of ideas.'

Intelligence which directs the index, and points to the hour of the day. If so, why may not the Intelligence do it, without his being at the pains of making the movements and putting them together? Why does not an empty case serve as well as another? And how comes it to pass that whenever there is any fault in the going of a watch, there is some corresponding disorder to be found in the movements, which being mended by a skilful hand all is right again? The like may be said of all the Clockwork of Nature, great part whereof is so wonderfully fine and subtle as scarce to be discerned by the best microscope. In short, it will be asked, how, upon our principles, any tolerable account can be given, or any final cause assigned, of an innumerable multitude of bodies and machines, framed with the most exquisite art, which in the common philosophy have very apposite uses assigned them, and serve to explain abundance of phenomena?

61. To all which I *answer*, first, that though there were some difficulties relating to the administration of Providence, and the uses by it assigned to the several parts of nature, which I could not solve by the foregoing principles, yet this objection could be of small weight against the truth and certainty of those things which may be proved *a priori*, with the utmost evidence and rigour of demonstration. Secondly, but neither are the received principles free from the like difficulties; for, it may still be demanded to what end God should take those roundabout methods of effecting things, by instruments and machines, which no one can deny might have been effected by the mere command of His will, without all that apparatus: nay, if we narrowly consider it, we shall find the objection may be retorted with greater force on those who hold the existence of those machines without the mind; for it has been made evident that solidity, bulk, figure, motion, and the like have no *activity* or *efficacy* in them, so as to be capable of producing any one effect in nature. See

sect. 25. Whoever therefore supposes *them* to exist (allowing the supposition possible) when they are not perceived does it manifestly to no purpose; since the only use that is assigned to them, as they exist unperceived, is that they produce those perceivable effects, which in truth cannot be ascribed to anything but Spirit.

62. But, to come nigher the difficulty, it must be observed that though the fabrication of all those parts and organs be not absolutely necessary to the producing *any* effect, yet it is necessary to the producing of things *in a constant regular way according to the laws of nature*. There are certain general laws that run through the whole chain of natural effects: these are learned by the observation and study of nature, and are by men applied as well to the framing artificial things for the use and ornament of life as to the explaining the various phenomena;—which explanation consists only in shewing the conformity any particular phenomenon hath to the general laws of nature, or, which is the same thing, in discovering the *uniformity* there is in the production of natural effects; as will be evident to whoever shall attend to the several instances wherein philosophers pretend to account for appearances. That there is a great and conspicuous *use* in these regular constant methods of working observed by the Supreme Agent hath been shewn in sect. 31. And it is no less visible that a particular size, figure, motion, and disposition of parts are necessary, though not absolutely to the producing any effect, yet to the producing it according to the standing mechanical laws of nature. Thus, for instance, it cannot be denied that God, or the Intelligence that sustains and rules the ordinary course of things, might, if He were minded to produce a miracle, cause all the motions on the dial-plate of a watch, though nobody had ever made the movements and put them in it: but yet, if He will act agreeably to the rules of mechanism—by Him for wise ends established and maintained in the creation—

it is necessary that those actions of the watchmaker, whereby he makes the movements and rightly adjusts them, precede the production of the aforesaid motions; as also that any disorder in them be attended with the perception of some corresponding disorder in the movements, which being once corrected all is right again [1].

63. It may indeed on some occasions be necessary that the Author of nature display His overruling power in producing appearances out of the ordinary series of things. Such exceptions from the general rules of nature are proper *to surprise and awe men into an acknowledgment of the Divine Being;* but then they are to be used but seldom, otherwise there is a plain reason why they fail of that effect. Besides, God seems to choose the convincing our reason of His attributes by the works of nature, which discover so much harmony and contrivance in their make, and are such plain indications of wisdom and beneficence in their Author, rather than to astonish us into a belief of His Being by anomalous and surprising events [2].

---

[1] When Berkeley recognises rational order omnipresent in nature, his position, it has been urged, is untenable, because he can only *assume*, not *prove*, the continued conformity of the phenomena presented in sense to that order;—and because this very assumption implies that things exist independently of being perceived, scientific interpretation of things presupposing their independent existence. Between our perceptions in eating and our perceptions of the consequent growth of our bodies, for instance, many sequences are interposed, which exist unperceived by sentient mind; but these, as each term in the sequence is only a datum of sense, cannot, it is argued, *when thus unperceived,* be identified with the supersensible Ideas of God. So too with the existence of the planets anterior to *sentient* intelligence.—On the other hand, Berkeley might ask in reply, whether the qualities of the material world could maintain a conceivable existence after the extinction of all perception; also whether there is more difficulty in explaining (consistently with his conception of the material world) the unperceived growth of our bodies, or the early geological periods, than there is in explaining the existence of the *tangible* qualities of a house or a mountain when one is only *seeing* it.

[2] The nature and office of miracles is here touched. If the whole

64. To set this matter in a yet clearer light, I shall observe that what has been objected in sect. 60 amounts in reality to no more than this:—ideas are not anyhow and at random produced, there being a certain order and connexion between them, like to that of cause and effect: there are also several combinations of them made in a very regular and artificial manner, which seem like so many *instruments* in the hand of nature that, being hid as it were behind the scenes, have a secret operation in producing those appearances which are seen on the theatre of the world, being themselves discernible only to the curious eye of the philosopher. But, since one idea cannot be the *cause* of another, to what purpose is that connexion? And, since those instruments—being barely *inefficacious perceptions* in the mind—are not subservient to the production of natural effects, it is demanded why they are made; or, in other words, what reason can be assigned why God should make us, upon a close inspection into His works, behold so great variety of ideas so artfully laid together, and so much according to rule; it not being credible that He would be at the expense (if one may so speak) of all that art and regularity to no purpose?

65. To all which my answer is, first, that the connexion of ideas does not imply the relation of *cause* and *effect*, but only of a *mark* or *sign* with the *thing signified*[1]. The fire which I see is not the *cause* of the pain I suffer upon my approaching it, but the *mark* that forewarns me of it. In like

evolution of nature is always and immediately caused by God, where, it may be asked, is the room for miraculous interference with this divine order? Berkeley's answer to this may be gathered from § 62. Spiritual insight, although different in kind from sensuous perception, ordinary or miraculous, may be awakened by physical miracles.

[1] When it is objected that what exists unperceived by *me* must have existed independently of *my* perception, it should be remembered that the orderly sense-symbolism here supposed to constitute externality in nature is postulated by human minds in virtue of their faith in God.

manner the noise that I hear is not the *effect* of this or that motion or collision of the ambient bodies, but the *sign* thereof. Secondly, the reason why ideas are formed into machines, that is, artificial and regular combinations, is the same with that for combining letters into words. That a few original ideas may be made to signify a great number of effects and actions, it is necessary they be variously combined together. And, to the end their use be permanent and universal, these combinations must be made by *rule*, and with *wise contrivance*. By this means abundance of information is conveyed unto us, concerning what we are to expect from such and such actions, and what methods are proper to be taken for the exciting such and such ideas—which in effect is all that I conceive to be distinctly meant when it is said[1] that, by discerning the figure, texture, and mechanism of the inward parts of bodies, whether natural or artificial, we may attain to know the several uses and properties depending thereon, or the nature of the thing[2].

66. Hence, it is evident that those things which, under the notion of a cause co-operating or concurring to the production of effects, are altogether inexplicable, and run us into great absurdities, may be very naturally explained, and have a proper and obvious use assigned to them, when they are considered only as marks or signs for our information. And it is the searching after and endeavouring to understand this Language (if I may so call it) of the Author of Nature, that ought to be the employment of the natural philosopher[3]; and not the pretending to explain things by

---

[1] By Locke, for instance, in his hypothesis of the natural dependence of the secondary on the primary qualities of matter.

[2] This section expresses well the office of the orderly material world in occasioning mental activity, and educating us scientifically, which perhaps is partly the final cause of its existence and elaborate organization.

[3] Compare this with the 'homo naturae minister et interpres' of Bacon.

corporeal causes[1], which doctrine seems to have too much estranged the minds of men from that Active Principle, that supreme and wise Spirit 'in whom we live, move, and have our being[2].'

67. In the *twelfth* place, it may perhaps be *objected* that—though it be clear from what has been said that there can be no such thing as an inert, senseless, extended, solid, figured, moveable substance existing without the mind, such as philosophers describe Matter,—yet, if any man shall leave out of his idea of matter the positive ideas of extension, figure, solidity and motion, and say that he means only by that word an inert, senseless substance, that exists without the mind or unperceived, which is the *occasion* of our ideas, or at the presence whereof God is pleased to excite ideas in us—it doth not appear but that Matter taken in this sense may possibly exist.—In *answer* to which I say, first, that it seems no less absurd to suppose a substance without accidents, than it is to suppose accidents without a substance. But secondly, though we should grant this unknown substance may possibly exist, yet *where* can it be supposed to be? That it exists not in the *mind* is agreed; and that it exists not in *place* is no less certain—since all place or extension exists only in the mind, as hath been already proved. It remains therefore that it exists nowhere at all.

68. Let us examine a little the description that is here given us of Matter. It neither acts, nor perceives nor is perceived; for this is all that is meant by saying it is an

---

[1] 'Corporeal causes'—which Berkeley thinks he has already disposed of, in his 'proof' that *productive power* cannot be found in the material world, and that spiritual agency is the only efficient in nature.

[2] The search for physical 'causes' and natural laws thus becomes search for the meaning of the 'language' addressed to men in nature by the Universal Spirit. Does the causality that belongs to the things of sense mean no more than is signified by this metaphor of the natural order being virtually a Divine Language?

inert, senseless, unknown substance;—which is a definition entirely made up of negatives[1], excepting only the relative notion of its standing under or supporting. But then it must be observed that it supports nothing at all, and how nearly this comes to the description of a *nonentity* I desire may be considered. But, say you, it is the *unknown occasion*, at the presence of which ideas are excited in us by the will of God. Now, I would fain know how anything can be present to us, which is neither perceivable by sense nor reflection, nor capable of producing any idea in our minds, nor is at all extended, nor hath any form, nor exists in any place. The words 'to be present,' when thus applied, must needs be taken in some abstract and strange meaning, and which I am not able to comprehend.

69. Again, let us examine what is meant by *occasion*. So far as I can gather from the common use of language, that word signifies either the agent which produces any effect, or else something that is observed to accompany or go before it in the ordinary course of things. But when it is applied to Matter as above described, it can be taken in neither of those senses; for Matter is said to be passive and inert, and so cannot be an agent or efficient cause. It is also unperceivable, as being devoid of all sensible qualities, and so cannot be the occasion of our perceptions in the latter sense—as when the burning my finger is said to be the occasion of the pain that attends it. What therefore can be meant by calling Matter an *occasion*? This term is either used in no sense at all, or else in some very distant from its received signification.

70. You will perhaps say that Matter, though it be not perceived by us, is nevertheless perceived by God, to whom it is the *occasion* of exciting ideas in our minds. For, say you, since we observe our sensations to be imprinted in an

---

[1] This approaches Kant's 'thing in itself' (*ding an sich*), made up of negatives.

orderly and constant manner, it is but reasonable to suppose that there are certain constant and regular occasions of their being produced. That is to say, that there are certain permanent and distinct parcels of Matter, corresponding to our ideas, which, though they do not excite them in our minds, or anywise immediately affect us, *as being altogether passive and unperceivable to us,* they are nevertheless to God, *by whom they are perceived,* as it were so many occasions to remind Him when and what ideas to imprint on our minds—that so things may go on in a constant uniform manner.

71. In answer to this, I observe that, as the notion of Matter is here stated, the question is no longer concerning the existence of a thing distinct from *Spirit* and *idea*, from perceiving and being perceived; but whether there are not certain Ideas, of I know not what sort, in the mind of God, which are so many marks or notes that direct Him how to produce sensations in our minds in a constant and regular method—much after the same manner as a musician is directed by the notes of music to produce that harmonious strain and composition of sound which is called a tune, though they who hear the music do not perceive the notes, and may be entirely ignorant of them. But, this notion of Matter (which after all is the only intelligible one that I can pick from what is said of 'unknown occasions') seems too extravagant to deserve a confutation. Besides, it is in effect no objection against what we have advanced, viz. that there is no *senseless unperceived* substance.

72. If we follow the light of reason, we shall, from the constant uniform method of our sensations, collect the goodness and wisdom of the Spirit who excites them in our minds; but this is all that I can see reasonably concluded from thence. To me, I say, it is evident that the being of a Spirit infinitely wise, good, and powerful is abundantly

sufficient to explain all the appearances of nature. But, as for *inert, senseless Matter*, nothing that I perceive has any the least connexion with it, or leads to the thoughts of it. And I would fain see any one explain any the meanest phenomenon in nature by *it*, or shew any manner of reason, though in the lowest rank of probability, that he can have for its existence, or even make any tolerable sense or meaning of that supposition. For, as to its being an occasion, we have, I think, evidently shewn that with regard to *us* it is no occasion. It remains therefore that it must be, if at all, the occasion to *God* of exciting ideas in us; and what this amounts to we have just now seen.

73. It is worth while to reflect a little on the motives which induced men to suppose the existence of *material substance*; that so having observed the gradual ceasing and expiration of those motives or reasons, we may proportionably withdraw the assent that was grounded on them. First, therefore, it was thought that colour, figure, motion, and the rest of the sensible qualities or accidents, did really exist without the mind [1]; and for this reason it seemed needful to suppose some unthinking *substratum* or substance wherein they did exist—since they could not be conceived to exist by themselves [2]. Afterwards, in process of time, men being convinced that colours, sounds, and the rest of the *sensible secondary* qualities had no existence without the mind, they stripped this *substratum* or material substance of *those* qualities—leaving only the *primary* ones, figure, motion, and suchlike, which they still conceived to exist without the mind, and consequently to stand in need of a material

---

[1] This is the uneducated supposition, which assumes that the material world could be exactly what we now experience, if no one was experiencing—disregarding what is added by our sensations even in the case of the secondary qualities.

[2] He hardly explains *why* the appearances presented in sense may not, *per se*, be regarded as *Substances manifested*.

support. But, it having been shewn that none even of these can possibly exist otherwise than in a spirit or mind which perceives them, it follows that we have no longer any reason to suppose the being of Matter; nay, that it is utterly impossible that there should be any such thing—so long as that word is taken to denote an *unthinking substratum* of qualities or accidents, wherein they exist without the mind [1].

74. But—though it be allowed by the Materialists themselves that Matter was thought of only for the sake of supporting accidents, and, the reason entirely ceasing, one might expect the mind should naturally, and without any reluctance at all, quit the belief of what was solely grounded thereon—yet the prejudice is riveted so deeply in our thoughts, that we can scarce tell how to part with it, and are therefore inclined, since the *thing* itself is indefensible, at least to retain the *name*, which we apply to I know not what abstracted and indefinite notions of *being*, or *occasion*, though without any show of reason, at least so far as I can see. For, what is there on our part, or what do we perceive, amongst all the ideas, sensations, notions [2] which are imprinted on our minds, either by sense or reflection [2], from whence may be inferred the existence of an inert, thoughtless, unperceived *occasion?* and, on the other hand, on the part of an All-sufficient Spirit, what can there be that should make us believe or even suspect He is directed by an inert *occasion* to excite ideas in our minds?

75. It is a very extraordinary instance of the force of prejudice, and much to be lamented, that the mind of man

---

[1] It has been argued, in opposition to this, that although the sensible qualities themselves cannot exist *per se* as they are found in our experience, yet the steady order of the phenomena we perceive implies the existence of *something* independent of the perception. Berkeley finds in God this independent ' something.'

[2] Here he uses ' idea, sensation, and notion' as synonymous, and speaks of internal ' ideas of *reflection* ' even, as ' imprinted.'

retains so great a fondness, against all the evidence of reason, for a *stupid thoughtless Somewhat*; by the interposition whereof it would as it were screen itself from the Providence of God, and remove Him farther off from the affairs of the world. But, though we do the utmost we can to secure the belief of Matter; though, when reason forsakes us, we endeavour to support our opinion on the bare possibility of the thing; and though we indulge ourselves in the full scope of an imagination not regulated by reason to make out that poor possibility, yet the upshot of all is—that there are certain *unknown Ideas in the mind of God*; for this, if anything, is all that I conceive to be meant by *occasion* with regard to God. And this at the bottom is no longer contending for the thing, but for the name.

76. Whether there are such Ideas in the mind of God, and whether *they* may be called by the name *Matter*, I shall not dispute. But, if you stick to the notion of an unthinking substance or support of extension, motion, and other sensible qualities, then to me it is most evidently impossible there should be any such thing; since it is a plain repugnancy that those qualities should exist in or be supported by an unperceiving substance [1].

77. But, say you, though it be granted that there is no thoughtless support of extension and the other qualities or accidents which we perceive, yet there may perhaps be some

---

[1] Berkeley says years afterwards that he has 'no objection to calling the Ideas in the mind of God archetypes of ours,' and that he objects only to those [unthinking] archetypes supposed to exist *per se*, without any consciousness of them. (See my *Life of Berkeley*, ch. v.) And in truth his account of what the reality of the material world means presupposes divine Ideas, realised in the cosmical order, and towards a fuller intelligence of which human science is approximating. The assertion that matter is real would, when so understood, be an assertion that what we perceive in sense is *part* of an interpretable universe. It is actually interpreted to the extent that our scientific conceptions are in harmony with the divine Ideas exemplified in the natural order: Cf. *Siris*, § 335.

inert, unperceiving substance or substratum of some other qualities, as incomprehensible to us as colours are to a man born blind, because we have not a sense adapted to them. But, if we had a new sense, we should possibly no more doubt of their existence than a blind man made to see does of the existence of light and colours.—I answer, first, if what you mean by the word *Matter* be only the *unknown* support of *unknown* qualities, it is no matter whether there is such a thing or no, since it no way concerns us; and I do not see the advantage there is in disputing about we know not *what*, and we know not *why*.

78. But, secondly, if we had a new sense it could only furnish us with new ideas or sensations; and then we should have the same reason against *their* existing in an unperceiving substance that has been already offered with relation to figure, motion, colour, and the like. Qualities, as hath been shewn, are nothing else but *sensations* or *ideas*, which exist only in a *mind* perceiving them; and this is true not only of the ideas we are acquainted with at present, but likewise of all possible ideas whatsoever.

79. But, you will insist, what if I have no reason to believe the existence of Matter? what if I cannot assign any use to it, or explain anything by it, or even conceive what is meant by that word? yet still it is no contradiction to say that Matter exists, and that this Matter is in general a *substance*, or *occasion* of ideas; though indeed to go about to unfold the meaning or adhere to any particular explication of those words may be attended with great difficulties.—I *answer*, when words are used without a meaning, you may put them together as you please without danger of running into a contradiction. You may say, for example, that twice two is equal to seven, so long as you declare you do not take the words of that proposition in their usual acceptation, but for marks of you know not what. And, by the same reason,

you may say there is *an inert thoughtless substance without accidents* which is the occasion of our ideas. And we shall understand just as much by one proposition as the other.

80. In the *last* place, you will say, what if we give up the cause of material *Substance*, and stand to it that Matter is an unknown *Somewhat*—neither substance nor accident, spirit nor idea, inert, thoughtless, indivisible, immoveable, unextended, existing in no place? For, say you, whatever may be urged against *substance* or *occasion*, or any other positive or relative notion of Matter, hath no place at all, so long as this *negative* definition of Matter is adhered to. —I *answer*, you may, if so it shall seem good, use the word *matter* in the same sense as other men use *nothing*, and so make those terms convertible in your style. For, after all, this is what appears to me to be the result of that definition—the parts whereof when I consider with attention, either collectively or separate from each other, I do not find that there is any kind of effect or impression made on my mind different from what is excited by the term *nothing*.

81. You will reply, perhaps, that in the aforesaid definition is included what doth sufficiently distinguish it from nothing —the positive abstract idea of *quiddity*, *entity*, or *existence*. I own, indeed, that those who pretend to the faculty of framing abstract general ideas do talk as if they had such an idea, which is, say they, the most abstract and general notion of all; that is, to me, the most incomprehensible of all others. That there are a great variety of spirits of different orders and capacities, whose faculties both in number and extent are far exceeding those the Author of my being has bestowed on me, I see no reason to deny. And for me to pretend to determine, by my own few, stinted, narrow inlets of perception, what ideas the inexhaustible power of the Supreme Spirit may imprint upon them were certainly the utmost folly and presumption—since there may be, for aught

that I know, innumerable sorts of ideas or sensations, as different from one another, and from all that I have perceived, as colours are from sounds. But, how ready soever I may be to acknowledge the scantiness of my comprehension with regard to the endless variety of spirits and ideas that may possibly exist, yet for any one to pretend to a notion of Entity or Existence, *abstracted* from *spirit* and *idea*, from perceived and being perceived, is, I suspect, a downright repugnancy and trifling with words.

. . . .

IV

CONSEQUENCES OF THE PRINCIPLES

85. Having done with the Objections[1], which I endeavoured to propose in the clearest light, and gave them all the force and weight I could, we proceed in the next place to take a view of our tenets in their Consequences[2].

. . . .

---

[1] In the foregoing sections, we have arguments for and against Berkeley's new conception of Matter and the physical Cosmos. Instead of the unreflecting assumption, that things around us would be as we now perceive, although no one was perceiving them—he argues that they can be realised only in and through phenomena that are dependent for their realisation on being perceived—without any independent substance or power in the phenomena themselves. The meaninglessness of Matter, on any other view than this, might be called his *logical* argument for the necessary dependence of the material world upon Spirit. The need for resolving all the qualities of matter, into passive (although significant and therefore scientifically interpretable) phenomena, is his *psychological* argument. There is, in the third place, the *practical* argument, that existence for ever unrealised in a living experience, would after all make no difference to us in the conduct of our lives.

The chief objections to these Principles are the difficulty of reconciling this dependence of external things upon perception (*a*) with their continuous identity; (*b*) with the mathematical necessities and physical laws to which they must conform; (*c*) with our belief that other persons exist; (*d*) with the implied unsubstantiality and impotence of *persons* as well as of material *things*, if this new conception of matter is consistently carried out. Berkeley's *Commonplace Book* shows that this last difficulty at first influenced him enough to make his position then like Hume's total agnosticism.

[2] The remainder of this book of Philosophical Principles contains

86. From the Principles we have laid down it follows Human Knowledge may naturally be reduced to two heads—that of IDEAS and that of SPIRITS[1]. Of each of these I shall treat in order.

And *first* as to IDEAS or *unthinking things*. Our knowledge of these has been very much obscured and confounded, and we have been led into very dangerous errors, by supposing a two-fold existence of the objects of sense—the one *intelligible* or in the mind; the other *real* and without the mind, whereby unthinking things are thought to have a natural subsistence of their own, distinct from being perceived by spirits. This, which, if I mistake not, hath been shewn to be a most groundless and absurd notion, is the very root of Scepticism; for, so long as men thought that real things subsisted without the mind, and that their knowledge was only so far forth *real* as it was *conformable to real things*, it follows they could not be certain that they had any real knowledge at all. For, how can it be *known* that the things which are perceived are conformable to those which are not perceived, or exist without the mind[2]?

Berkeley's useful *application* of his new conception of the reality and function of the material world.—And first he shows its efficacy as against scepticism (§§ 86-96), and in freeing the mind from empty abstractions (§§ 97-100).

[1] 'Ideas and spirits.' In other words human knowledge is concerned with *natural phenomena* and with *self-conscious persons*. Berkeley's use of the word *idea* to signify the phenomena presented in nature to our senses; and his conclusion that the material world consists only of phenomena or sense appearances which co-exist and succeed one another in a uniform order, has led to his being called an *idealist*, which in this use of words means a *phenomenalist*. In his later writings, especially in *Siris*, his early 'idealism' becomes Platonic Idealism.

[2] This question expresses what has been regarded as the insuperable objection to a wholly *representative* perception of the material world.—How can we be assured of the *harmony* of the supposed representation with the real thing—*if the real thing is always unperceived?* We have no opportunity in that case to compare the two.

87. Colour, figure, motion, extension, and the like, considered only as so many *sensations* in the mind, are perfectly known, there being nothing in them which is not perceived. But, if they are looked on as notes or images, referred to *things* or *archetypes existing without the mind*, then are we involved all in scepticism. We see only the appearances, and not the real qualities of things[1]. What may be the extension, figure, or motion of anything really and absolutely, or in itself, it is impossible for us to know, but only the proportion or relation they bear to our senses. Things remaining the same, our ideas vary, and which of them, or even whether any of them at all, represent the true quality really existing in the thing, it is out of our reach to determine. So that, for aught we know, all we see, hear, and feel may be only phantom and vain chimera, and not at all agree with the real things existing *in rerum natura*. All this sceptical cant follows from our supposing a difference between *things* and *ideas*, and that the former had a subsistence without the mind or unperceived. It were easy to dilate on this subject, and shew how the arguments urged by sceptics in all ages depend on the supposition of external objects[2].

88. So long as we attribute a real existence to unthinking things, distinct from their being perceived, it is not only impossible for us to know with evidence the nature of any real unthinking being, but even that it exists. Hence it is that we see philosophers distrust their senses, and doubt of the existence of heaven and earth, of everything they see or feel, even of their own bodies. And, after all their labouring and struggle of thought, they are forced to own we cannot

---

[1] According to Berkeley the perceived appearances or natural phenomena, are the real things—named by him 'ideas' for the reason already given.

[2] The supposition, that is to say, that the real things are unperceived —because external to or behind the ideas which only represent them.

attain to any self-evident or demonstrative knowledge of the existence of sensible things[1]. But all this doubtfulness, which so bewilders and confounds the mind, and makes philosophy ridiculous in the eyes of the world, vanishes if we annex a meaning to our words, and not amuse ourselves with the terms 'absolute,' 'external,' 'exist,' &c.—signifying we know not what. For my part, I can as well doubt of my own being as of the being of those *things which I actually perceive by sense*[2]; it being a manifest contradiction that any sensible object should be immediately perceived by sight or touch, and at the same time have no existence in nature, since the very *existence* of an unthinking being consists in *being perceived*[3].

---

[1] Attempts have been made to *prove* that matter exists, all which, according to Berkeley's conception of what matter means, are unnecessary. Its living perception *is* its reality.

[2] As long, at least, as I, or some one else, is in the act of perceiving them. See Locke's *Essay*, b. IV. ch. 11. § 9.

[3] The difficulty is to suppose that we can have a knowledge of things that are permanent, if our knowledge of them is melted down into phenomena that are transitory. The difficulty raises a chief question in intellectual philosophy—to vindicate reality as given in experience. Berkeley argues that the favourite hypothesis of philosophers—that the real things are not themselves perceived, but have to be inferred—needlessly increases the difficulty. Let us, he says, recognise the real thing as *already presented* in perception; not as something dependent on a 'conformity,' impossible to ascertain, between the real thing and the representation in the mind of which alone, on this hypothesis, we are supposed to be percipient—and the difficulty is relieved. But is Berkeley's conception of things, as necessarily sense-dependent, consistent with their objective reality, as media of communication between persons?

On the connexion between scepticism and representative perception, see Hume's *Inquiry concerning Human Understanding*, sect. xii. pt. 1, which might be a text for discussing the 'immediate perception' of Reid and Hamilton, and for comparing it with the 'perception' and 'suggestion' of Berkeley. See also Hamilton's *Discussions*, 'Philosophy of Perception.'—For an account of various modifications of a representative perception which have been held by philosophers, see Reid's Second Essay on the Intellectual Powers, and Hamilton's appended Dissertations B and C in his edition of Reid. These Scotch psychologists

89. Nothing seems of more importance towards erecting a firm system of sound and real knowledge, which may be proof against the assaults of Scepticism, than to lay the beginning in a distinct explication of *what is meant by* THING, REALITY, EXISTENCE; for in vain shall we dispute concerning the *real existence* of things, or pretend to any knowledge thereof, so long as we have not fixed the meaning of those words[1]. THING or BEING is the most general name of all: it comprehends under it two kinds entirely distinct and heterogeneous, and which have nothing common but the name, viz. SPIRITS[2] and IDEAS. The former are active, indivisible substances: the latter are inert, fleeting, or dependent beings; which subsist not by themselves, but are supported by, or exist in, minds or spiritual substances.

[3] We comprehend our own existence by inward feeling or reflection, and that of other spirits by reason[4].—We may be said to have some knowledge or *notion* of our own minds, of spirits and active beings—whereof in a strict sense we have not ideas. In like manner, we know and have a *notion*

---

taught that an immediate revelation of Matter in certain of its qualities, is an ultimate fact,—the rejection of which logically involves total scepticism, because it involves distrust in the foundation of all belief; but they did not, like Berkeley, try to explain what is meant by the *reality* of Matter.

[1] This throws light on Berkeley's purpose, which was not to *prove* the reality of the material world, but—by showing what we are entitled to *mean* when we say that an external thing 'exists'—to make proof superfluous. He takes for granted that this reality may be analysed, and that analysis resolves it into *significant* because *ordered* sense-phenomena, which are virtually a Language.

[2] Spirits are not properly things.

[3] The remainder of this section was added in the Second Edition of the *Principles*, when he recognised the importance of the distinction which he then began to express by the contrasted terms *idea* and *notion* —a distinction which, in one form of expression or another, goes deep into his and every philosophy. His reason for recognising independent substance in Spirit, while he rejects it in Matter, is that ' we are *conscious* of personality and its permanence, but not so in the things around us.'

[4] i.e. by inference.

of relations between things or ideas—which relations are distinct from the ideas or things related, inasmuch as the latter may be perceived by us without our perceiving the former[1]. To me it seems that *ideas, spirits,* and *relations* are all, in their respective kinds, the object of human knowledge and subject of discourse, and that the term *idea* would be improperly extended to signify *everything we know or have any notion of*[2].

90. *Ideas imprinted on the senses* are *real things, or do really exist*: this we do not deny; but we deny they can subsist without the minds which perceive them; or that they are resemblances of any archetypes[3] existing without the mind;—since the very being of a sensation or idea consists in being perceived, and an idea can be like nothing but an idea. Again, the things perceived by sense may be termed *external*, with regard to their origin, in that they are not generated from within by the mind itself[4], but imprinted by a Spirit[5] distinct from that which perceives them.—Sensible objects may likewise be said to be 'without the mind' in another sense, namely when they exist in[6] some other mind; thus, when I shut my eyes, the things I saw may still exist, but it must be in another mind.

91. It were a mistake to think that what is here said derogates in the least from the reality of things. It is acknowledged, on the received principles, that extension, motion, and in a word all sensible qualities, have need of a support, as not being able to subsist by themselves. But

---

[1] This seems to say that we may know an absolutely isolated phenomenon.

[2] Note again how Berkeley calls the term *notion* into use in this special meaning.

[3] He means unperceived and unperceiving archetypes—not Platonic Ideas.

[4] Here Berkeley's view differs from Fichte's, so far as the latter seems to find in the individual Ego the origin of the material world, and thus lands in Panegoism.   [5] God.

[6] 'exist in,' i.e. are perceived by, some other mind.

the objects perceived by sense are allowed to be nothing but combinations of those qualities, and consequently cannot subsist by themselves. Thus far it is agreed on all hands. So that in denying the things perceived by sense an existence independent of a substance or support wherein they may exist, we detract nothing from the received opinion of their reality, and are guilty of no innovation in that respect. All the difference is that, according to us, the unthinking beings perceived by sense have no existence distinct from being perceived, and cannot therefore exist in any other substance than those unextended indivisible substances or *Spirits* which act and think and perceive them; whereas philosophers vulgarly hold the sensible qualities do exist in an inert, extended, unperceiving substance which they call *Matter*—to which they attribute a natural subsistence, exterior to all thinking beings, or distinct from being perceived by any mind whatsoever, even the Eternal Mind of the Creator, wherein they suppose only Ideas of the corporeal substances created by Him: if indeed they allow them to be at all created.

. . . .

97. Beside the external existence of the objects of perception, another great source of errors and difficulties with regard to *ideal* knowledge is the doctrine of 'abstract ideas,' such as it hath been set forth in the Introduction. The plainest things in the world, those we are most intimately acquainted with and perfectly know, *when they are considered in an abstract way*, appear strangely difficult and incomprehensible. Time, Place, and Motion, taken in particular or concrete, are what everybody knows; but, having passed through the hands of a metaphysician, they become too abstract and fine to be apprehended by men of ordinary sense. Bid your servant meet you at such a time in such a place, and he shall never stay to deliberate on the meaning of those words; in conceiving that particular time

and place, or the motion by which he is to get thither, he finds not the least difficulty. But if Time be taken exclusive of all those *particular* actions and ideas that diversify the day, merely for the continuation of existence, or Duration *in abstract*, then it will perhaps gravel even a philosopher to comprehend it[1].

98. For my own part, whenever I attempt to frame a simple idea of Time, abstracted from the succession of ideas in my mind, which flows uniformly and is participated by all beings, I am lost and embrangled[2] in inextricable difficulties[3]. I have no notion of it at all: only I hear others say it is infinitely divisible, and speak of it in such a manner as leads me to harbour odd thoughts of my existence;—since that doctrine lays one under an absolute necessity of thinking, either that he passes away innumerable ages without a thought, or else that he is annihilated every moment of his life, both which seem equally absurd. *Time* therefore being *nothing, abstracted from the succession of ideas in our minds*, it follows that the duration of any finite spirit must be estimated by the number of ideas or actions succeeding each other in that same spirit or mind. Hence, it is a plain consequence that the *soul always thinks*; and in truth whoever shall go about to

[1] 'Si non rogas intelligo.'

[2] 'Embrangled,' to 'brangle,' i. e. to twist or involve in perplexity.

[3] Locke's account of time (*Essay*, b. II. ch. 14. §§ 3, 5, 17) may be compared with this. Though change in the phenomena of which we are percipient, as a matter of fact, *develops in us* the idea of time, the ultimate mystery of that idea remains. In Berkeley's *Commonplace Book* we find such expressions as these, regarding Time, Duration, and Eternity:—'Time—train of ideas succeeding one another. Succession explained by before, between, after, and numbering. Duration infinitely divisible; time not so. The same τὸ νῦν now common to all intelligences. Time thought infinitely divisible on account of its measure. Time a sensation; therefore only in the mind. Eternity is only a train of innumerable ideas. Hence the immortality of the soul easily conceived, or rather the immortality of the person, that of the soul not being necessary for aught we can see.'

divide in his thoughts, or abstract, the *existence* of a spirit from its *cogitation*, will, I believe, find it no easy task[1].

. . . .

101. The two great provinces of speculative science conversant about *ideas received from Sense*, are Natural Philosophy and Mathematics; with regard to each of these I shall make some observations[2].

And first I shall say somewhat of Natural Philosophy. On this subject it is that the sceptics triumph. All that stock of arguments they produce to depreciate our faculties and make mankind appear ignorant and low, are drawn principally from this head, namely, that we are under an invincible blindness as to the *true* and *real* nature of things. This they exaggerate, and love to enlarge on. We are miserably bantered, say they, by our senses, and amused only with the outside and show of things. The real essence —the internal qualities and constitution—of every the meanest object, is hid from our view; something there is in every drop of water, every grain of sand, which it is beyond the power of human understanding to fathom or comprehend. But, it is evident from what has been shewn that all this complaint is groundless, and that we are influenced by false principles to that degree as to mistrust our senses, and think we know nothing of those things which we perfectly comprehend[3].

---

[1] Berkeley says in one of his letters: 'A succession of ideas I take to *constitute* time, and not to be only the *sensible measure* thereof, as Mr. Locke and others think. One of my earliest inquiries was about time, which led me into several paradoxes that I did not think fit or necessary to publish.' (See my *Life of Berkeley*, ch. v.)

With Berkeley 'the soul always thinks,' else it would lose its identity, for unconscious *Ego* is as impossible as unperceived matter. Hence since the *esse* of things is *percipi*, the *esse* of the Ego would be *percipere*.

[2] In Kant's 'Kritik' ('Aesthetic' and 'Analytic') we have his explanation and defence of mathematical and physical science, as against the sceptical dissolution of it into phenomena accidentally associated.

[3] For, under Berkeley's conception of the material world, there is

102. One great inducement to our pronouncing ourselves ignorant of the nature of things is the current opinion that everything includes *within itself* the cause of its properties; or that there is in each object an inward *essence* which is the source whence its discernible qualities flow, and whereon they depend[1]. Some have pretended to account for appearances by occult qualities: but of late they are mostly resolved into mechanical causes, to wit, the figure, motion, weight, and suchlike qualities[2], of insensible particles;—whereas, in truth, there is no other *agent* or *efficient cause* than *spirit*, it being evident that motion, as well as all other *ideas*, is perfectly inert. See sect. 25[3]. Hence, to endeavour to explain the production of colours or sounds, by figure, motion, magnitude and the like, must needs be labour in vain. And accordingly we see the attempts of that kind are not at all satisfactory. Which may be said in general of those instances wherein one idea or quality[4] is assigned for the cause of another. I need not say how many hypotheses and speculations are left out, and how much the study of nature is abridged by this doctrine[5].

. . . .

nothing to be comprehended in the material world except the phenomena or appearances of which it consists, and their relations of coexistence and succession, in virtue of which they constitute a system of sensible signs—a natural and divine language.

[1] This is the Aristotelian and Scholastic teaching, according to which the essential nature or formal cause of anything (οὐσία, τὸ τί ἦν εἶναι) explains its *secondary* qualities (ποιά), and is unfolded in its definition. The *form* or *essence* of a thing thus consists of what is essential to its existence *as that identical thing*, and is present in all its developments.

[2] The primary qualities, in respect of their differences of shape, size, motion, &c., were regarded by Locke and Descartes as the explanation of the differences in the secondary qualities of things.

[3] On the total powerlessness of matter.

[4] Phenomenon, i. e. sense-idea or appearance.

[5] Berkeley's conception of the material world is ultimately Spiritual in that it eliminates power from the things we see and touch, but retains it in Mind or Spirit. He sees in the order and interpretability of all

133. By what we have hitherto said, it is plain that very numerous and important errors have taken their rise from those false Principles which were impugned in the foregoing parts of this treatise ; and the opposites of those erroneous tenets at the same time appear to be most fruitful Principles, from whence do flow innumerable consequences highly advantageous to true philosophy, as well as to religion. Particularly MATTER, or the *absolute* existence of corporeal objects [1], hath been shewn to be that wherein the most avowed and pernicious enemies of all knowledge, whether human or divine, have ever placed their chief strength and confidence. And surely if by distinguishing the *real* existence of unthinking things from their *being perceived*, and allowing them a subsistence of their own out of the minds of spirits, no one thing is explained in nature, but on the contrary a great many inexplicable difficulties arise ; if the supposition of Matter is barely precarious, as not being grounded on so much as one single reason ; if its consequences cannot endure the light of examination and free inquiry, but screen themselves under the dark and general pretence of Infinites being incomprehensible ; if withal the removal of this Matter be not attended with the least evil consequence ; if it be not even missed in the world, but everything as well, nay much easier, conceived without it ; if, lastly, both Sceptics and Atheists are for ever silenced upon supposing only SPIRITS and IDEAS [2], and this scheme of things is perfectly agreeable

phenomena presented to the senses, the constant operation of the Universal or Divine Power.

[1] The denial of the existence of matter, as a substance and power independent of all conscious or percipient spirit, is not denial of the popular dogma that what is perceived in the senses is real. It only professes to be a deeper analysis of what the popular dogma means, making it reasonable.

[2] They are 'for ever silenced' if it may be concluded that Moral Reason is supreme in the universe, and Natural Order subordinate. But is that necessarily involved in the supposition that only *spirits*, and *phenomena dependent on a percipient* exist? Consider whether this

both to Reason and Religion—methinks we may expect it should be admitted and firmly embraced, though it were proposed only as an *hypothesis*, and the existence of Matter had been allowed possible, which yet I think we have evidently demonstrated that it is not.

. . . .

135. Having despatched what we intended to say concerning the knowledge of IDEAS[1], the method we proposed leads us in the next place to treat of SPIRITS—with regard to which, perhaps, human knowledge is not so deficient as is vulgarly imagined[2]. The great reason that is assigned for our being thought ignorant of the nature of Spirits is— our not having an *idea* of it. But, surely it ought not to be looked on as a defect in a human understanding that it does not perceive the *idea* of spirit[3], if it is manifestly impossible there should be any such idea. And this if I mistake not has been demonstrated in section 27; to which I shall here add—that a spirit has been shewn to be the only substance or support wherein unthinking beings or ideas can exist; but that this *substance* which *supports* or *perceives* ideas should itself be an idea, or like an idea, is evidently absurd.

136. It will perhaps be said that we want a *sense* (as some have imagined) proper to know *substances* withal; which, if we had, we might know our own soul as we do a triangle. To this I answer, that, in case we had a new sense bestowed

---

Principle is justified by reason, and whether it is the only one that effectually silences rejection of ethical supremacy or theistic optimism in the Universe.

[1] 'Ideas' = natural phenomena presented to the senses.

[2] In the preceding sections Berkeley has mentioned improvements in the physical sciences which should follow acceptance of his conception of Matter. He proceeds, in §§ 135-56, to trace its consequences, in its application to studies which are concerned with the origin and destiny of men, and the being and attributes of God.

[3] '*Idea* of spirit,' i.e. a picture of spirit in the sensuous imagination, or its appearance in sense as a natural phenomenon.

upon us, we could only receive thereby some new sensations or ideas of sense. But I believe nobody will say that what he means by the terms *soul* and *substance* is only some particular sort of idea or sensation[1]. We may therefore infer that, all things duly considered, it is not more reasonable to think our faculties defective, in that they do not furnish us with an *idea* of spirit or active thinking substance, than it would be if we should blame them for not being able to comprehend a *round square*.

137. From the opinion that spirits are to be known *after the manner of an idea or sensation*[2] have risen many absurd and heterodox tenets, and much scepticism about the nature of the soul. It is even probable that this opinion may have produced a doubt in some whether they had any soul at all distinct from their body; since upon inquiry they could not find they had an idea of it. That an *idea*, which is inactive, and the existence whereof consists in being perceived, should be the image or likeness of an agent subsisting by itself, seems to need no other refutation than barely attending to what is meant by those words. But perhaps you will say that though an idea cannot resemble a spirit in its thinking, acting, or subsisting by itself, yet it may in some other respects; and it is not necessary that an idea or image be in all respects like the original.

138. I answer, if it does not in those mentioned, it is impossible it should represent it in any other thing. Do but leave out the power of willing, thinking, and perceiving ideas, and there remains nothing else wherein the idea can be like a spirit. For, by the word *spirit* we mean only *that which thinks, wills, and perceives*: this, and this alone, constitutes the signification of that term. If therefore it

---

[1] Ideas, sensations, and phenomena are synonyms with Berkeley, as the student cannot be too often reminded.

[2] That is to say, 'the opinion' that we can have a *sensuous perception* of a spirit, as we have of a sensible thing.

is impossible that any degree of those powers should be represented in an idea, it is evident there can be no *idea* of a spirit.

139. But it will be objected that, if there is no *idea* signified by the terms 'soul,' 'spirit,' and 'substance,' they are wholly insignificant, or have no meaning in them[1]. I answer, those words do mean or signify a real thing—which is neither an idea nor like an idea, but that which perceives ideas, and wills, and reasons about them. What I am myself—that which I denote by the term *I*—is the same with what is meant by *soul* or *spiritual substance*. But if I should say that *I* was nothing, or that *I* was an idea, nothing could be more evidently absurd than either of these propositions. If it be said that this is only quarrelling at a word, and that, since the immediate significations of other names are by common consent called *ideas*, no reason can be assigned why that which is signified by the name *spirit* or *soul* may not partake in the same appellation, I answer—All the unthinking objects of the mind agree in that they are entirely passive, and their existence consists only in being perceived; whereas a soul or spirit is an active being, whose existence consists, not in being perceived, but in perceiving ideas and thinking[2]. It is therefore necessary—in order to prevent equivocation and confounding natures perfectly disagreeing and unlike, that we distinguish between SPIRIT and IDEA. See sect. 27.

---

[1] 'Rational psychology,' says Kant, 'has its origin in a mere misunderstanding. The unity of self-consciousness is confused with an intuition of the subject as an object; and the object thus supposed to be thus intuited is, moreover, substantiated. But this " subject " is really nothing more than a unity in thought, *in which no object is given*, and to which therefore the category of substance, which presupposes an object, cannot be applied. Therefore the subject cannot be known as a substance.' This of Kant seems to overlook the fact that the individual is present to himself in his own activities.

[2] If the existence of the *Ego* depends on *actual* perception, a person cannot become unconscious without ceasing to exist.

140. In a large sense indeed, we may be said to have an idea [or rather a notion [1]] of *spirit*; that is, we understand the meaning of the word, otherwise we could not affirm or deny anything of it [2]. Moreover, as we conceive the ideas that are in the minds of other spirits by means of our own, which we suppose to be resemblances of them; so we know *other spirits* by means of *our own soul*—which in that sense is *the image or idea of them*; it having a like respect to other spirits that blueness or heat by me perceived has to those ideas perceived by another [3].

---

[1] Added in Second Edition of the *Principles*. The term 'notion' introduced to signify what is unimaginable.

[2] By 'spiritual substance' Berkeley intends whatever is meant by the personal pronoun. This cannot, he urges, be an *idea*, or datum of sense. The *knower* cannot be *thus* known; yet, as I am presupposed in all my knowledge, I cannot be ignorant of *myself*. Hume afterwards applied Berkeley's own reasoning against *abstract matter* to this 'notion' of *Ego*, and argued that the knowing spirit, as well as the things of sense, is resolvable into passing conscious states, whose union in imagination gives rise to the illusion of personal identity. '*Treatise of Human Nature*, b. I. part iv. sect. 6.)—Berkeley's answer to this is given by anticipation in the *Dialogue between Hylas and Philonous*, where Philonous meets the objection, that 'there is no more *meaning* in *spiritual substance* than in *material substance*, so the one is to be exploded as well as the other.'

[3] That is to say, we become aware of the existence of other conscious beings, not by entering into their consciousness, but by inference, based partly on our own consciousness, and partly on the *signs* of similar conscious life in them, implied in our perceptions of their corporeal actions. We can conceive *conscious life numerically different from our own*, while *unperceived matter* is unimaginable negation.

Berkeley's account of the relation of human spirits to the Supreme Spirit, and to the System of Nature, is obscure. The question how far the human spirit is part of the Cosmos, its physical birth being an event or evolution, he does not touch;—nor yet our relation to the Universal Consciousness, of which, Pantheists say, we are *individual* phases—God being the *universal form* of which each of us is a finite and illusory manifestation.—Is not the root of individual personality found in the self-originated power by which a man is able to do evil, and to lose his power to act rightly, through self-caused paralysis of will?

141. The Natural Immortality of the Soul is a necessary consequence of the foregoing doctrine. But before we attempt to prove this, it is fit that we explain the meaning of that tenet. It must not be supposed that they who assert the natural immortality of the soul are of opinion that it is absolutely incapable of annihilation even by the infinite power of the Creator who first gave it being, but only that it is not liable to be broken or dissolved by the ordinary laws of nature or motion. They indeed who hold the soul of man to be only a thin vital flame, or system of animal spirits, make it perishing and corruptible as the body; since there is nothing more easily dissipated than such a being, which it is naturally impossible should survive the ruin of the tabernacle wherein it is enclosed. And this notion has been greedily embraced and cherished by the worst part of mankind, as the most effectual antidote against all impressions of virtue and religion. But it has been made evident that *bodies*, of what frame and texture soever, are barely passive ideas in the *mind*—which is more distant and heterogeneous from them than light is from darkness. We have shewn that the soul is indivisible, incorporeal, unextended, and it is consequently incorruptible. Nothing can be plainer than that the motions, changes, decays, and dissolutions which we hourly see befall natural bodies (and which is what we mean by the *course of nature*) cannot possibly affect an active, simple, uncompounded substance: such a being therefore is indissoluble by the force of nature; that is to say—the soul of man is *naturally* immortal [1].

[1] This is Berkeley's application of his conception of Matter to the question of the continued existence of self-conscious life in persons after the dissolution of the bodily organism in Death. From the necessary dependence of body on spirit, and the possible independence of the conscious spirit in man of its corporeal organism (which he assumes that he has already proved), he argues for the *natural* immortality of the human spirit. If this be so, there is no absurdity

142. After what has been said, it is, I suppose, plain that our souls are not to be known in the same manner as in supposing our continued personal consciousness after death — as *unbodied spirits*,—the dissolution of the body having no *natural* connexion with extinction of personal consciousness; though, *by a miracle*, God might at death cause our self-conscious lives to cease. 'I see no difficulty,' he says in one of his letters, 'in conceiving a change of state, such as is vulgarly called Death, as well without as with material *substance*. It is sufficient for that purpose that we allow *sensible bodies*, i.e. such as are perceived by sight and touch; the existence of which I am so far from questioning (as philosophers are used to do) that I establish it, I think, upon evident principles. Now, it seems very easy to conceive the *soul* to exist in a separate state (i.e. divested from those limits and laws of motion and perception with which she is embarrassed here), and to exercise herself on new ideas—without the intervention of those tangible things we call our bodies. It is even very possible to conceive how the soul may have ideas of colour without an eye, or of sounds without an ear.' (*Life of Berkeley*, ch. v.) Note how in this he distinguishes 'sensible bodies,' dependent for their existence on being perceived, from 'material substance,' supposed to exist independently of any percipient and sensation.

It was common among philosophers and theologians of the seventeenth century and afterwards to defend faith in a life after death by the metaphysical assumption of the indivisibility of mind, its independence of matter, and its merely contingent connexion with the body. Thus Bishop Butler takes for granted that 'all presumption of death's being the destruction of *living* beings must go upon the supposition that they are compounded and so discerptible'; adding that, since consciousness 'is a single and indivisible power, it should seem that the subject in which it resides must be so too.' And even if it should not be 'absolutely indiscerptible,' we have no way, he argues, of determining by experience 'what its bulk in space is; and till it can be shown that what I call *myself* is larger in bulk than the solid elementary particles of matter (atoms), which as there is no ground to think any *natural* power can dissolve, so there is no *natural* reason to think death to be *our* dissolution.' Referring to our connexion with our bodies, he says that 'upon the supposition that the living being each man calls *himself* is a single being ... *our organised bodies are no more ourselves, or part of ourselves, than any other matter around us*.' 'It is as easy to conceive,' he continues, 'that we may exist out of bodies as in them; that we might have animated bodies of any other organs, and senses wholly different from those now given us; and that we may hereafter animate these same, or new bodies, variously modified and organised, as to conceive how we can animate such bodies as our present; and the dissolution of all these several organised bodies, supposing ourselves

senseless, inactive objects, or by way of *idea*. Spirits and *ideas* are things so wholly different, that when we say 'they exist,' 'they are known,' or the like, these words must not be thought to signify anything common to both natures. There is nothing alike or common in them; and to expect that by any multiplication or enlargement of our faculties we may be enabled to know a spirit as we do a triangle, seems as absurd as if we should hope to see a sound. This is inculcated because I imagine it may be of moment towards clearing several important questions, and preventing some very dangerous errors concerning the Nature of the Soul. [¹We may not, I think, strictly be said to have

to have successively animated them, would have no more conceivable tendency to destroy the living beings, ourselves, or deprive us of living faculties, than the dissolution of any foreign matter' (*Analogy*, pt. I. ch. 1).

This train of thought is more foreign to the present generation, when science insists that self-conscious life in constant correlation with a corporeal frame is a fact proved by sufficient induction; whatever may be the abstract metaphysical possibility of conceiving the conscious being to exist independently of body. The only personal life we have any experience of, it is argued, is one that is found in organic union with the corporeal structure, in correlation with which it develops. Speculations like those of Berkeley and Butler would be condemned as dreams.

Faith in continued self-conscious life after death seems to have its rationale in ethical considerations rather than in physical or in metaphysical arguments. Does not a theistically constituted universe, with its moral implications, suggest that physical death is not the extinction of the moral agent after a short life in this mixed world, with its irregular distribution of happiness and opportunity? Moral experience of the organised unity I call *myself* seems to justify the previsive inference that the physical change called death is not the end of *me*. In one view the rising of the sun to-morrow, and the conscious life after death of any person who has not yet died, as future, are both 'beyond experience.' In another definition of experience, neither is 'beyond' it: the one may be involved in the rational constitution of natural, and the other in the constitution of moral experience.

¹ What follows to the end of this section was introduced in the second edition of the *Principles*, as well as other passages in which *notion* is distinguished from *idea* or sense-presented phenomenon.

an *idea* of an active being, or of an action, although we may be said to have a *notion* of them. I have some knowledge or notion of my mind, and its acts about ideas—inasmuch as I know or understand what is meant by these words. What I know, that I have some notion of.—I will not say that the terms *idea* and *notion* may not be used convertibly, if the world will have it so; but yet it conduceth to clearness and propriety that we distinguish things very different by different names. It is also to be remarked that, all *relations* including *an act of the mind*, we cannot so properly be said to have an idea, but rather a notion of the relations and habitudes between things [1]. But if, in the modern way, the word *idea* is extended to *spirits*, and *relations* and *acts*, this is, after all, an affair of verbal concern [2].]

. . . .

145. From what has been said, it is plain that we cannot know the existence of *other spirits* [3] otherwise than by their operations, or the ideas by them excited in us. I perceive several motions, changes, and combinations of ideas, that inform me there are certain particular agents, like myself, which accompany them and concur in their production. Hence, the knowledge I have of other spirits is not imme-

---

[1] There is perhaps a faint anticipation of Kantism in this employment of the term *notion* to signify conscious mind, and the relations which its intellectual acts involve. But critical analysis, like Kant's, of the relations presupposed in real experience is foreign to Berkeley.

[2] Berkeley hardly proves that we cannot have an intellectual 'notion' of substance as manifested in its sensible phenomena. What he says goes to show that we find in *self* that to which there is nothing analogous in the phenomena of which we are percipient in our five senses—that our continuous individual personality is an irreducible fact, *sui generis*, and untranslatable into a natural phenomenon that can be presented to the senses.

[3] '*Other spirits*,' e.g. other men. We only see their bodies and bodily motions: their self-conscious life or proper personality is necessarily invisible.

diate, as is the knowledge of my ideas; but depending on the intervention of ideas, by me referred to agents or spirits distinct from myself, as effects or concomitant signs[1].

146. But, though there be some things which convince us *human* agents are concerned in producing them, yet it is evident to every one that those things which are called the Works of Nature—that is, the far greater part of the ideas or sensations perceived by us—are not produced by, or dependent on, the wills of *men*. There is therefore some other Spirit that causes them; since it is repugnant[2] that they should subsist by themselves. See sect. 29. But, if we attentively consider the constant regularity, order, and concatenation of natural things; the surprising magnificence, beauty and perfection of the larger, and the exquisite contrivance of the smaller parts of the creation, together with the exact harmony and correspondence of the whole; but above all the never-enough-admired laws of pain and plea-

---

[1] This is one of the most fruitful sections in the *Principles*. How can one individual mind communicate with another individual mind through a *mind-dependent* body, such as Berkeley supposes human bodies, and the whole material world, to be? It has been alleged that, under Berkeley's conception of the material world, I have no reason to believe in the existence of other men;—that, at most, I can discern only my own existence and God. I find that *I* can will, and I suppose that what our wills fail to do is God's doing; so *my* volitions and *His* determine all changes.—Berkeley, however, might argue that, under his view of nature, the supremacy of Divine Will is a security that we are not deceived when changes in phenomena presented to our senses *suggest* the intentions and meanings of persons like ourselves as their cause. (Is this, we may ask, mere 'suggestion' or is it 'inference of reason'? See *Vindication of Theory of Vision*, §§ 11, 12, 42.) The difficulty still is to understand *how* the appearances which I perceive when I use my senses—if they are wholly subjective or self-contained, and numerically different from those of which any other mind is conscious—can be *media of communication with another mind*. In § 147 he says vaguely that God 'maintains that intercourse between spirits whereby they are able to perceive the existence of each other.'

[2] 'Repugnant,' for it would paralyse its indispensable presupposition of efficient causation.

sure, and the instincts or natural inclinations, appetites, and passions of animals—I say if we consider all these things, and at the same time attend to the meaning and import of the attributes One, Eternal, Infinitely Wise, Good, and Perfect, we shall clearly perceive that they belong to the aforesaid Spirit, 'who works all in all,' and 'by whom all things consist.'

147. Hence, it is evident that God is known as certainly and immediately as any other mind or spirit whatsoever distinct from ourselves. We may even assert that the existence of God is far more evidently perceived than the existence of men; because the effects of Nature are infinitely more numerous and considerable than those ascribed to human agents. There is not any one mark that denotes a man, or effect produced by him, which does not more strongly evince the being of that Spirit who is the Author of Nature. For, it is evident that in affecting other persons the will of man has no other object than barely the motion of the limbs of his body; but that such a motion should be attended by, or excite any idea in the mind of another, depends wholly on the will of the Creator. He alone it is who, 'upholding all things by the word of His power,' maintains that intercourse between spirits whereby they are able to perceive the existence of each other. And yet this pure and clear light which enlightens every one is itself invisible [1].

148. It seems to be a general pretence of the unthinking herd that they cannot *see* God. Could we but see Him, say they, as we see a man, we should believe that He is, and believing obey His commands. But alas, we need only open our eyes to see the Sovereign Lord of all things, with a more full and clear view than we do any one of our fellow-creatures. Not that I imagine we see God (as some

---

[1] The reasoning in this and the two next sections is expanded in the Dialogue on *Divine Visual Language*.

will have it) by a direct and immediate view; or see corporeal things, not by themselves, but by seeing that which represents them in the essence of God, which doctrine is, I must confess, to me incomprehensible[1]. But I shall explain my meaning:—A human *spirit* or *person* is not perceived by sense, as not being an idea; when therefore we see the colour, size, figure, and motions of a man, we perceive only certain sensations or ideas excited in our own minds; and these being exhibited to our view in sundry distinct collections, serve to mark out unto us the existence of finite and created spirits like ourselves. Hence it is plain *we do not see a man*—if by *man* is meant that which lives, moves, perceives, and thinks as we do—but only such a certain collection of ideas[2] as directs us to think there is a distinct principle of thought and motion, like to ourselves, accompanying and represented by it. *And after the same manner we see God*; all the difference is that, whereas some one finite and narrow assemblage of ideas denotes a particular human mind, whithersoever we direct our view, we do at all times and in all places perceive manifest tokens of the Divinity—everything we see, hear, feel, or anywise perceive by Sense, being a *sign* or *effect* of the power of God; as is our perception of those very motions which are produced by men[3].

---

[1] He refers to Malebranche, whose doctrine—that we perceive the material world 'in God'—was an attempt to reconcile the Cartesian duality of self-conscious and unextended substance, on the one hand, extended and unconscious substance, on the other. Berkeley does not, like Malebranche, say that we perceive things by perceiving God, and that we perceive them in Him (whatever that may mean); but only that phenomena are presented in our perceptions according to what we call 'natural order,' which is really the immediate issue and sensible expression of the mind of God. The phenomena present in our senses, which are wholly passive, cannot, he argues, be like the Divine Spirit, who is wholly active. See Berkeley's *Works*, vol. I. p. 308.

[2] 'Ideas,' i.e. natural appearances presented to our senses.

[3] The *present* existence of God and the *present* existence of *other*

149. It is therefore plain that nothing can be more evident to any one that is capable of the least reflection than the existence of God, or a Spirit who is intimately present to our minds—producing in them all that variety of *ideas* or *sensations* which continually affect us; on whom we have an absolute and entire dependence, in short 'in whom we live, and move, and have our being.' That the discovery of this great truth, which lies so near and obvious to the mind, should be attained to by the reason of so very few, is a sad instance of the stupidity and inattention of men, who, though they are surrounded with such clear manifestations of the Deity, are yet so little affected by them that they seem, as it were, blinded with excess of light.

150. But you will say, Hath Nature no share in the production of natural things, and must they be all ascribed to the immediate and sole operation of God? I answer, if by *Nature* is meant only the visible series of effects or sensations imprinted on our minds, according to certain fixed and general laws, then it is plain that Nature, taken in this sense, cannot produce anything at all[1]. But, if by *Nature* is meant some being distinct from God, as well as from the laws of nature, and things perceived by sense, I must confess that word is to me an empty sound without any intelligible meaning annexed to it. Nature, in this acceptation, is a vain chimera, introduced by those heathens who had not just notions of the omnipresence and infinite perfection of God[2]. But, it is more unaccountable that it should be

human spirits are both reached, it seems, through sense signs, according to Berkeley, and at first only in the way of 'suggestion.' The *Dialogue on Visual Language* is an expansion of this section. Neither here nor there does he refer to the moral presupposition of God given in conscience, and its 'supremacy,' which is practically perfect ethical supremacy in the universe.

[1] In a word 'natural causes' are not, properly speaking, causes at all; they only instrumentally transmit the originating efficacy of spirit, and signify its meaning.

[2] Thus in the Greek conception of Nature (φύσις) as something inter-

received among Christians, professing belief in the Holy Scriptures, which constantly ascribe those effects to the *immediate* hand of God that heathen philosophers are wont to impute to Nature. 'The Lord He causeth the vapours to ascend; He maketh lightnings with rain; He bringeth forth the wind out of His treasures.' Jerem. x. 13. 'He turneth the shadow of death into the morning, and maketh the day dark with night.' Amos v. 8. 'He visiteth the earth, and maketh it soft with showers: He blesseth the springing thereof, and crowneth the year with His goodness; so that the pastures are clothed with flocks, and the valleys are covered over with corn.' See Psal. lxv. But, notwithstanding that this is the constant language of Scripture, yet we have I know not what aversion from believing that God concerns Himself so nearly in our affairs. Fain would we suppose Him at a great distance off, and substitute some *blind unthinking* deputy in His stead, though (if we may believe Saint Paul) 'He be not far from every one of us.'

151. It will, I doubt not, be objected that the slow, gradual, and roundabout methods observed in the production of natural things do not seem to have for their cause the *immediate* hand of an Almighty Agent. Besides, monsters, untimely births, fruits blasted in the blossom, rains falling in desert places, miseries incident to human life, and the like, are so many arguments that the whole frame of nature is not immediately actuated and superintended by a Spirit of infinite wisdom and goodness[1]. But

---

mediate between Necessity and Chance—the efficient cause of the Cosmos, of which God is the final cause. So too in the impersonal 'force' of modern scientific assumption. Are conservation and transformation of force more than names for that *law* of change in the universe under which every perishing phenomenon has its equivalent in a new one, in the orderly metamorphosis which the passing phenomena of sense are continually undergoing?

[1] So J. S. Mill, in his *Autobiography* and posthumous *Essays*, in

the answer to this objection is in a good measure plain from sect. 62; it being visible that the aforesaid Methods of Nature are absolutely necessary, in order to working by the most simple and general rules, and after a steady and consistent manner; which argues both the wisdom and goodness of God. Such is the artificial contrivance of this mighty Machine of Nature that, whilst its motions and various phenomena strike on our senses, the hand which actuates the whole is itself unperceivable to men of flesh and blood. 'Verily' (saith the prophet) 'thou art a God that hidest thyself[1].' Isaiah xlv. 15. But, though the Lord conceal Himself from the eyes of the sensual and lazy, who will not be at the least expense of thought, yet to an unbiassed and attentive mind nothing can be more plainly legible than the intimate presence of an All-wise Spirit, who fashions, regulates, and sustains the whole system of beings. It is clear, from what we have elsewhere observed, that the operating according to general and stated laws is so necessary for our guidance in the affairs of Life, and letting us into the secret of Nature, that without it all reach and compass of thought, all human sagacity and design, could serve to no manner of purpose; it were even impossible there should be any such faculties or powers in the mind. See sect. 31. Which one consideration abundantly outbalances whatever particular inconveniences may thence arise[2].

152. But we should further consider that the very blem-

---

which he conjectures a Manichæist solution of the difficulties of our moral experience, instead of referring them to the free agency of men or other finite persons.

[1] So Pascal in the *Pensées*, on God as a God 'that hideth himself.'

[2] We should be virtually irrational if we lived in a physical Chaos instead of the Cosmos; for sense-phenomena would then have no meaning on which our cognitive power might be exercised. The rationally-constituted Cosmos is the correlate of our faculty of intelligence, and material phenomena give concrete meaning to abstract thought.

ishes and defects of Nature are not without their use, in that they make an agreeable sort of variety, and augment the beauty of the rest of the creation, as shades in a picture serve to set off the brighter and more enlightened parts. We would likewise do well to examine whether our taxing the waste of seeds and embryos, and accidental destruction of plants and animals, before they come to full maturity, as an imprudence in the Author of Nature, be not the effect of prejudice contracted by our familiarity with impotent and saving mortals. In man indeed a thrifty management of those things which he cannot procure without much pains and industry may be esteemed wisdom. But, we must not imagine that the inexplicably fine machine of an animal or vegetable costs the great Creator any more pains or trouble in its production than a pebble does; nothing being more evident than that an Omnipotent Spirit can indifferently produce everything by a mere *fiat* or act of his will[1]. Hence, it is plain that the splendid profusion of natural things should not be interpreted weakness or prodigality in the agent who produces them, but rather be looked on as an argument of the riches of his power.

153. As for the mixture of pain or uneasiness which is in the world, pursuant to the general Laws of Nature, and the actions of finite, imperfect spirits, this, in the state we are in at present, is indispensably necessary to our well-being. *But our prospects are too narrow.* We take, for instance, the idea of some one particular pain into our thoughts, and account *it* evil; whereas, if we enlarge our view, so as to comprehend the various ends, connexions, and dependencies of things, on what occasions and in what proportions we are affected with pain and pleasure, the nature of human freedom, and the design with which we are put into the

---

[1] By a power that is independent of nature. We suppose nature and natural laws to be constantly sustained by Supreme Active Reason, not evolved in blind necessity.

world; we shall be forced to acknowledge that those particular things which, considered in themselves, appear to be evil, have the nature of good, when considered as linked with the whole system of beings[1].

[1] So afterwards Butler. '*Our whole nature* leads us to ascribe moral perfection to God, and to deny all imperfection of Him. And *this* must for ever be a practical proof of His moral character. From thence we conclude that virtue must be the happiness and vice the misery of every creature; and that regularity, order, and right cannot but prevail finally, in a universe under His government. *But we are in no sort judges what are the necessary means of accomplishing this end.*' (*Analogy*, Introduction.) See also his Sermon on the 'Ignorance of Man.'—In the *Theodicée* of Leibniz, published in the same year as the *Principles* of Berkeley, these difficulties are discussed.

They gave rise to Manichæism, the doctrine of Manes, a Persian philosopher of the third century, who appears to have held Eternal Duality in the Universal Power to be an explanation of the mingled good and evil that is in the universe. The existence of free agents,—who, as free, must be free to act wickedly,—might seem to be a modified Manichæism; especially if accompanied by the supposition that the universe into which finite agents can introduce sin is incapable of ultimate freedom from evil, and that it is thus a failure, which it is doubtful whether the Manichæans themselves meant to say. Is the creation of finite creators of acts which *may* be evil as well as good, Divine creation of evil? A sense of the importance of responsible (because free) agents in the universe has, through Christianity, grown in the mediæval and modern world; as compared with an indifference towards individual personality in the œconomy of things on the part of Greek and other ancient philosophers.

Our limited knowledge of the origin and destiny of the universe is at the root of objections at the present day to the recognition of Active Moral Reason as its ultimate explanation. Hume proceeds partly on this, when he treats the universe as a 'singular effect,' the phenomena of which can be interpreted only so far as this life of sense is concerned (and even that in merely probable interpretations), but which at last dissolves in 'a riddle, an ænigma, an inexplicable mystery.' Does not true philosophical analysis show that our knowledge of the universe cannot be even so much as this without being more than this? Is not final assurance of Omnipotent Goodness the fundamental postulate of human experience, virtually presupposed in the scientific postulate of constant order in nature?

A DIALOGUE CONCERNING THE PRINCIPLES

Philonous. Good morrow, *Hylas*: I did not expect to find you abroad so early.

Hylas. It is indeed something unusual; but my thoughts were so taken up with a subject I was discoursing of last night, that finding I could not sleep, I resolved to rise and take a turn in the garden.

Phil. It happened well, to let you see what innocent and agreeable pleasures you lose every morning. Can there be a pleasanter time of the day, or a more delightful season of the year? That purple sky, those wild but sweet notes of birds, the fragrant bloom upon the trees and flowers, the gentle influence of the rising sun, these and a thousand nameless beauties of nature inspire the soul with secret transports; its faculties too being at this time fresh and lively, are fit for these meditations, which the solitude of a garden and tranquillity of the morning naturally dispose us to. But I am afraid I interrupt your thoughts: for you seemed very intent on something.

Hyl. It is true, I was, and shall be obliged to you if you will permit me to go on in the same vein; not that I would by any means deprive myself of your company, for my thoughts always flow more easily in conversation with a friend, than when I am alone: but my request is, that you would suffer me to impart my reflections to you.

Phil. With all my heart, it is what I should have requested myself if you had not prevented me.

Hyl. I was considering the odd fate of those men who have in all ages, through an affectation of being distinguished from the vulgar, or some unaccountable turn of thought, pretended either to believe nothing at all, or to believe the most extravagant things in the world. This however might be borne, if their paradoxes and scepticism did not draw after them some consequences of general disadvantage to mankind. But the mischief lieth here; that when men of less leisure see them who are supposed to have spent their whole time in the pursuits of knowledge professing an entire ignorance of all things, or advancing such notions as are repugnant to plain and commonly received principles, they will be tempted to entertain suspicions concerning the most important truths, which they had hitherto held sacred and unquestionable.

Phil. I entirely agree with you, as to the ill tendency of the affected doubts of some philosophers, and fantastical conceits of others. I am even so far gone of late in this way of thinking, that I have quitted several of the sublime notions I had got in their schools for vulgar opinions. And I give it you on my word, since this revolt from metaphysical notions, to the plain dictates of nature and common sense, I find my understanding strangely enlightened, so that I can now easily comprehend a great many things which before were all mystery and riddle.

Hyl. I am glad to find there was nothing in the accounts I heard of you.

Phil. Pray, what were those?

Hyl. You were represented in last night's conversation, as one who maintained the most extravagant opinion that ever entered into the mind of man, to wit, that there is no such thing as *material substance* in the world.

Phil. That there is no such thing as what Philosophers

call *material substance*, I am seriously persuaded: but, if I were made to see anything absurd or sceptical in this, I should then have the same reason to renounce this that I imagine I have now to reject the contrary opinion.

Hyl. What! can anything be more fantastical, more repugnant to common sense, or a more manifest piece of Scepticism, than to believe there is no such thing as *matter?*

Phil. Softly, good *Hylas.* What if it should prove, that you, who hold there is, are, by virtue of that opinion, a greater sceptic, and maintain more paradoxes and repugnances to common sense, than I who believe no such thing?

Hyl. You may as soon persuade me, the part is greater than the whole, as that, in order to avoid absurdity and Scepticism, I should ever be obliged to give up my opinion in this point.

Phil. Well then, are you content to admit that opinion for true, which, upon examination, shall appear most agreeable to common sense, and remote from Scepticism?

Hyl. With all my heart. Since you are for raising disputes about the plainest things in nature, I am content for once to hear what you have to say.

Phil. Pray, *Hylas*, what do you mean by a *sceptic?*

Hyl. I mean what all men mean—one that doubts of everything.

Phil. He then who entertains no doubt concerning some particular point, with regard to that point cannot be thought a sceptic.

Hyl. I agree with you.

Phil. Whether doth doubting consist in embracing the affirmative or negative side of a question?

Hyl. In neither; for whoever understands English, cannot but know that *doubting* signifies a suspense between both.

Phil. He then that denieth any point, can no more be said to doubt of it, than he who affirmeth it with the same degree of assurance.

Hyl. True.

Phil. And, consequently, for such his denial is no more to be esteemed a sceptic than the other.

Hyl. I acknowledge it.

Phil. How cometh it to pass then, *Hylas*, that you pronounce me a *sceptic*, because I deny what you affirm, to wit, the existence of Matter? Since, for aught you can tell, I am as peremptory in my denial, as you in your affirmation.

Hyl. Hold, *Philonous*, I have been a little out in my definition; but every false step a man makes in discourse is not to be insisted on. I said indeed that a *sceptic* was one who doubted of everything; but I should have added, or who denies the reality and truth of things.

Phil. What things? Do you mean the principles and theorems of sciences? But these you know are universal intellectual notions, and consequently independent of Matter; the denial therefore of this doth not imply the denying them.

Hyl. I grant it. But are there no other things? What think you of distrusting the senses, of denying the real existence of sensible things, or pretending to know nothing of them. Is not this sufficient to denominate a man a *sceptic?*

Phil. Shall we therefore examine which of us it is that denies the reality of sensible things, or professes the greatest ignorance of them; since, if I take you rightly, he is to be esteemed the greatest *sceptic?*

Hyl. That is what I desire.

Phil. What mean you by Sensible Things?

Hyl. Those things which are perceived by the senses. Can you imagine that I mean anything else?

Phil. Pardon me, *Hylas*, if I am desirous clearly to apprehend your notions, since this may much shorten our inquiry. Suffer me then to ask you this farther question. Are those things only perceived by the senses which are perceived immediately? Or, may those things properly be said to be *sensible* which are perceived mediately, or not without the intervention of others?

Hyl. I do not sufficiently understand you.

Phil. In reading a book, what I immediately perceive are the letters, but mediately, or by means of these, are suggested to my mind the notions of God, virtue, truth, &c. Now, that the letters are truly sensible things, or perceived by sense, there is no doubt: but I would know whether you take the things suggested by them to be so too.

Hyl. No, certainly; it were absurd to think *God* or *virtue* sensible things, though they may be signified and suggested to the mind by sensible marks, with which they have an arbitrary connexion.

Phil. It seems then, that by *sensible things* you mean those only which can be perceived *immediately* by sense?

Hyl. Right.

Phil. Doth it not follow from this, that though I see one part of the sky red, and another blue, and that my reason doth thence evidently conclude there must be some cause of that diversity of colours, yet that cause cannot be said to be a sensible thing, or perceived by the sense of seeing?

Hyl. It doth.

Phil. In like manner, though I hear variety of sounds, yet I cannot be said to hear the causes of those sounds?

Hyl. You cannot.

Phil. And when by my touch I perceive a thing to be hot and heavy, I cannot say, with any truth or propriety, that I feel the cause of its heat or weight?

Hyl. To prevent any more questions of this kind, I tell you once for all, that by *sensible things* I mean those only which are perceived by sense, and that in truth the senses perceive nothing which they do not perceive immediately: for they make no inferences. The deducing therefore of causes or occasions from effects and appearances, which alone are perceived by sense, entirely relates to reason.

Phil. This point then is agreed between us—that *sensible things are those only which are immediately perceived by sense.* You will farther inform me, whether we immediately perceive by sight anything beside light, and colours, and figures; or by hearing, anything but sounds; by the palate, anything beside tastes; by the smell, beside odours; or by the touch, more than tangible qualities.

Hyl. We do not.

Phil. It seems, therefore, that if you take away all sensible qualities, there remains nothing sensible?

Hyl. I grant it.

Phil. Sensible things therefore are nothing else but so many sensible qualities, or combinations of sensible qualities?

Hyl. Nothing else.

Phil. Heat then is a sensible thing?

Hyl. Certainly.

Phil. Doth the reality of sensible things consist in being perceived? or, is it something distinct from their being perceived, and that bears no relation to the mind?

Hyl. To *exist* is one thing, and to be *perceived* is another.

Phil. I speak with regard to sensible things only: and of these I ask, whether by their real existence you mean a subsistence exterior to the mind, and distinct from their being perceived?

Hyl. I mean a real absolute being, distinct from, and without any relation to their being perceived.

Phil. Heat therefore, if it be allowed a real being, must exist without the mind?

Hyl. It must.

Phil. Tell me, *Hylas*, is this real existence equally compatible to all degrees of heat, which we perceive; or is there any reason why we should attribute it to some, and deny it to others, and if there be, pray let me know that reason.

Hyl. Whatever degree of heat we perceive by sense, we may be sure the same exists in the object that occasions it.

Phil. What! the greatest as well as the least?

Hyl. I tell you, the reason is plainly the same in respect of both: they are both perceived by sense; nay, the greater degree of heat is more sensibly perceived; and consequently, if there is any difference, we are more certain of its real existence than we can be of the reality of a lesser degree.

Phil. But is not the most vehement and intense degree of heat a very great pain?

Hyl. No one can deny it.

Phil. And is any unperceiving thing capable of pain or pleasure?

Hyl. No certainly.

Phil. Is your material substance a senseless being, or a being endowed with sense and perception?

Hyl. It is senseless without doubt.

Phil. It cannot therefore be the subject of pain?

Hyl. By no means.

Phil. Nor consequently of the greatest heat perceived by sense, since you acknowledge this to be no small pain?

Hyl. I grant it.

Phil. What shall we say then of your external object; is it a material substance, or no?

Hyl. It is a material substance with the sensible qualities inhering in it.

Phil. How then can a great heat exist in it, since you own it cannot in a material substance? I desire you would clear this point.

Hyl. Hold, *Philonous*, I fear I was out in yielding intense heat to be a pain. It should seem rather, that pain is something distinct from heat, and the consequence or effect of it.

Phil. Upon putting your hand near the fire, do you perceive one simple uniform sensation, or two distinct sensations?

Hyl. But one simple sensation.

Phil. Is not the heat immediately perceived?

Hyl. It is.

Phil. And the pain?

Hyl. True.

Phil. Seeing therefore they are both immediately perceived at the same time, and the fire affects you only with one simple, or uncompounded idea, it follows that this same simple idea is both the intense heat immediately perceived, and the pain; and, consequently, that the intense heat immediately perceived, is nothing distinct from a particular sort of pain.

Hyl. It seems so.

Phil. Again, try in your thoughts, *Hylas*, if you can conceive a vehement sensation to be without pain or pleasure.

Hyl. I cannot.

Phil. Or can you frame to yourself an idea of sensible pain or pleasure, in general, abstracted from every particular idea of heat, cold, tastes, smells? &c.

Hyl. I do not find that I can.

Phil. Doth it not therefore follow, that sensible pain is nothing distinct from those sensations or ideas—in an intense degree?

Hyl. It is undeniable; and, to speak the truth, I begin to suspect a very great heat cannot exist but in a mind perceiving it.

Phil. What! are you then in that *sceptical* state of suspense, between affirming and denying?

Hyl. I think I may be positive in the point. A very violent and painful heat cannot exist without the mind.

Phil. It hath not therefore, according to you, any real being?

Hyl. I own it.

Phil. Is it therefore certain, that there is no body in nature really hot?

Hyl. I have not denied there is any real heat in bodies. I only say, there is no such thing as an intense real heat.

Phil. But did you not say before that all degrees of heat were equally real; or, if there was any difference, that the greater were more undoubtedly real than the lesser?

Hyl. True: but it was because I did not then consider the ground there is for distinguishing between them, which I now plainly see. And it is this:—because intense heat is nothing else but a particular kind of painful sensation; and pain cannot exist but in a perceiving being; it follows that no intense heat can really exist in an unperceiving corporeal substance. But this is no reason why we should deny heat in an inferior degree to exist in such a substance.

Phil. But how shall we be able to discern those degrees of heat which exist only in the mind from those which exist without it?

Hyl. That is no difficult matter. You know the least pain cannot exist unperceived; whatever, therefore, degree of heat is a pain exists only in the mind. But, as for all other degrees of heat, nothing obliges us to think the same of them.

Phil. I think you granted before that no unperceiving being was capable of pleasure, any more than of pain.

Hyl. I did.

Phil. And is not warmth, or a more gentle degree of heat than what causes uneasiness, a pleasure?

Hyl. What then?

Phil. Consequently, it cannot exist without the mind in an unperceiving substance, or body.

Hyl. So it seems.

Phil. Since, therefore, as well those degrees of heat that are not painful, as those that are, can exist only in a thinking substance; may we not conclude that external bodies are absolutely incapable of any degree of heat whatsoever?

Hyl. On second thoughts, I do not think it so evident that warmth is a pleasure as that a great degree of heat is a pain.

Phil. I do not pretend that warmth is as great a pleasure as heat is a pain. But, if you grant it to be even a small pleasure, it serves to make good my conclusion.

Hyl. I could rather call it an *indolence*. It seems to be nothing more than a privation of both pain and pleasure. And that such a quality or state as this may agree to an unthinking substance, I hope you will not deny.

Phil. If you are resolved to maintain that warmth, or a gentle degree of heat, is no pleasure, I know not how to convince you otherwise, than by appealing to your own sense. But what think you of cold?

Hyl. The same that I do of heat. An intense degree of cold is a pain; for to feel a very great cold, is to perceive a great uneasiness: it cannot therefore exist without the mind; but a lesser degree of cold may, as well as a lesser degree of heat.

Phil. Those bodies, therefore, upon whose application to our own, we perceive a moderate degree of heat, must be concluded to have a moderate degree of heat or warmth in them; and those, upon whose application we feel a like degree of cold, must be thought to have cold in them.

Hyl. They must.

Phil. Can any doctrine be true that necessarily leads a man into an absurdity?

Hyl. Without doubt it cannot.

Phil. Is it not an absurdity to think that the same thing should be at the same time both cold and warm?

Hyl. It is.

Phil. Suppose now one of your hands hot, and the other cold, and that they are both at once put into the same vessel of water, in an intermediate state; will not the water seem cold to one hand, and warm to the other?

Hyl. It will.

Phil. Ought we not therefore, by your principles, to conclude it is really both cold and warm at the same time, that is, according to your own concession, to believe an absurdity?

Hyl. I confess it seems so.

Phil. Consequently, the principles themselves are false, since you have granted that no true principle leads to an absurdity.

Hyl. But, after all, can anything be more absurd than to say, *there is no heat in the fire?*

Phil. To make the point still clearer; tell me whether, in two cases exactly alike, we ought not to make the same judgment?

Hyl. We ought.

Phil. When a pin pricks your finger, doth it not rend and divide the fibres of your flesh?

Hyl. It doth.

Phil. And when a coal burns your finger, doth it any more?

Hyl. It doth not.

Phil. Since, therefore, you neither judge the sensation itself occasioned by the pin, nor anything like it to be in the pin; you should not, conformably to what you have now granted, judge the sensation occasioned by the fire, or anything like it, to be in the fire.

Hyl. Well, since it must be so, I am content to yield this point, and acknowledge that heat and cold are only sensations existing in our minds. But there still remain qualities enough to secure the reality of external things.

Phil. But what will you say, *Hylas*, if it shall appear that the case is the same with regard to all other sensible qualities, and that they can no more be supposed to exist without the mind, than heat and cold?

Hyl. Then indeed you will have done something to the purpose; but that is what I despair of seeing proved.

Phil. Let us examine them in order. What think you of *tastes*—do they exist without the mind, or no?

Hyl. Can any man in his senses doubt whether sugar is sweet, or wormwood bitter?

Phil. Inform me, *Hylas*. Is a sweet taste a particular kind of pleasure or pleasant sensation, or is it not?

Hyl. It is.

Phil. And is not bitterness some kind of uneasiness or pain?

Hyl. I grant it.

Phil. If therefore sugar and wormwood are unthinking corporeal substances existing without the mind, how can sweetness and bitterness, that is, pleasure and pain, agree to them?

Hyl. Hold, *Philonous*, I now see what it was deluded me all this time. You asked whether heat and cold, sweetness and bitterness, were not particular sorts of pleasure and pain; to which I answered simply, that they were. Whereas I should have thus distinguished:—those qualities, as perceived by us, are pleasures or pains; but not as existing in the external objects. We must not therefore conclude absolutely, that there is no heat in the fire, or sweetness in the sugar, but only that heat or sweetness, as perceived by us, are not in the fire or sugar. What say you to this?

Phil. I say it is nothing to the purpose. Our discourse proceeded altogether concerning sensible things, which you defined to be, *the things we immediately perceive by our senses.* Whatever other qualities, therefore, you speak of, as distinct from these, I know nothing of them, neither do they at all belong to the point in dispute. You may, indeed, pretend to have discovered certain qualities which you do not perceive, and assert those insensible qualities exist in fire and sugar. But what use can be made of this to your present purpose, I am at a loss to conceive. Tell me then once more, do you acknowledge that heat and cold, sweetness and bitterness (meaning those qualities which are perceived by the senses), do not exist without the mind?

Hyl. I see it is to no purpose to hold out, so I give up the cause as to those mentioned qualities. Though I profess it sounds oddly, to say that sugar is not sweet.

Phil. But, for your farther satisfaction, take this along with you: that which at other times seems sweet, shall, to a distempered palate, appear bitter. And, nothing can be plainer than that divers persons perceive different tastes in the same food; since that which one man delights in, another abhors. And how could this be, if the taste was something really inherent in the food?

Hyl. I acknowledge I know not how.

Phil. In the next place, *odours* are to be considered. And, with regard to these, I would fain know whether what hath been said of tastes doth not exactly agree to them? Are they not so many pleasing or displeasing sensations?

Hyl. They are.

Phil. Can you then conceive it possible that they should exist in an unperceiving thing?

Hyl. I cannot.

Phil. Or, can you imagine that filth and ordure affect those brute animals that feed on them out of choice, with the same smells which we perceive in them?

Hyl. By no means.

Phil. May we not therefore conclude of smells, as of the

other forementioned qualities, that they cannot exist in any but a perceiving substance or mind?

Hyl. I think so.

Phil. Then as to *sounds*, what must we think of them: are they accidents really inherent in external bodies, or not?

Hyl. That they inhere not in the sonorous bodies is plain from hence; because a bell struck in the exhausted receiver of an air-pump sends forth no sound. The air, therefore, must be thought the subject of sound.

Phil. What reason is there for that, *Hylas*?

Hyl. Because, when any motion is raised in the air, we perceive a sound greater or lesser, according to the air's motion; but without some motion in the air, we never hear any sound at all.

Phil. And granting that we never hear a sound but when some motion is produced in the air, yet I do not see how you can infer from thence, that the sound itself is in the air.

Hyl. It is this very motion in the external air that produces in the mind the sensation of *sound*. For, striking on the drum of the ear, it causeth a vibration, which by the auditory nerves being communicated to the brain, the soul is thereupon affected with the sensation called *sound*.

Phil. What! is sound then a sensation?

Hyl. I tell you, as perceived by us, it is a particular sensation in the mind.

Phil. And can any sensation exist without the mind?

Hyl. No, certainly.

Phil. How then can sound, being a sensation, exist in the air, if by the *air* you mean a senseless substance existing without the mind?

Hyl. You must distinguish, *Philonous*, between sound as it is perceived by us, and as it is in itself; or (which is the same thing) between the sound we immediately perceive, and that which exists without us. The former, indeed, is a particular kind of sensation, but the latter is merely a vibrative or undulatory motion in the air.

Phil. I thought I had already obviated that distinction, by the answer I gave when you were applying it in a like case before. But, to say no more of that, are you sure then that sound is really nothing but motion?

Hyl. I am.

Phil. Whatever therefore agrees to real sound, may with truth be attributed to motion?

Hyl. It may.

Phil. It is then good sense to speak of *motion* as of a thing that is *loud, sweet, acute, or grave.*

Hyl. I see you are resolved not to understand me. Is it not evident those accidents or modes belong only to sensible sound, or *sound* in the common acceptation of the word, but not to *sound* in the real and philosophic sense; which, as I just now told you, is nothing but a certain motion of the air?

Phil. It seems then there are two sorts of sound—the one vulgar, or that which is heard, the other philosophical and real?

Hyl. Even so.

Phil. And the latter consists in motion?

Hyl. I told you so before.

Phil. Tell me, *Hylas*, to which of the senses, think you, the idea of motion belongs? to the hearing?

Hyl. No, certainly; but to the sight and touch.

Phil. It should follow then, that, according to you, real sounds may possibly be *seen* or *felt*, but never *heard*.

Hyl. Look you, *Philonous*, you may, if you please, make a jest of my opinion, but that will not alter the truth of things. I own, indeed, the inferences you draw me into, sound something oddly; but common language, you know, is framed by, and for the use of the vulgar: we must not therefore wonder, if expressions adapted to exact philosophic notions seem uncouth and out of the way.

Phil. Is it come to that? I assure you, I imagine myself to have gained no small point, since you make so light of departing from common phrases and opinions; it being a main part of our inquiry, to examine whose notions are widest of the common road, and most repugnant to the general sense of the world. But, can you think it no more than a philosophical paradox, to say that *real sounds are never heard*, and that the idea of them is obtained by some other sense? And is there nothing in this contrary to nature and the truth of things?

Hyl. To deal ingenuously, I do not like it. And, after the concessions already made, I had as well grant that sounds too have no real being without the mind.

Phil. And I hope you will make no difficulty to acknowledge the same of *colours*.

Hyl. Pardon me: the case of colours is very different. Can anything be plainer than that we see them on the objects?

Phil. The objects you speak of are, I suppose, corporeal Substances existing without the mind?

Hyl. They are.

Phil. And have true and real colours inhering in them?

Hyl. Each visible object hath that colour which we see in it.

Phil. How! is there anything visible but what we perceive by sight?

Hyl. There is not.

Phil. And, do we perceive anything by sense which we do not perceive immediately?

Hyl. How often must I be obliged to repeat the same thing? I tell you, we do not.

Phil. Have patience, good *Hylas*; and tell me once more, whether there is anything immediately perceived by the senses, except sensible qualities. I know you asserted there was not; but I would now be informed, whether you still persist in the same opinion.

Hyl. I do.

Phil. Pray, is your corporeal substance either a sensible quality, or made up of sensible qualities?

Hyl. What a question that is! who ever thought it was?

Phil. My reason for asking was, because in saying, *each visible object hath that colour which we see in it,* you make visible objects to be corporeal substances; which implies either that corporeal substances are sensible qualities, or else that there is something beside sensible qualities perceived by sight: but, as this point was formerly agreed between us, and is still maintained by you, it is a clear consequence, that your corporeal substance is nothing distinct from sensible qualities.

Hyl. You may draw as many absurd consequences as you please, and endeavour to perplex the plainest things: but you shall never persuade me out of my senses. I clearly understand my own meaning.

Phil. I wish you would make me understand it too. But, since you are unwilling to have your notion of corporeal substance examined, I shall urge that point no farther. Only be pleased to let me know, whether the same colours which we see exist in external bodies, or some other.

Hyl. The very same.

Phil. What! are then the beautiful red and purple we see on yonder clouds really in them? Or do you imagine they have in themselves any other form than that of a dark mist or vapour?

Hyl. I must own, *Philonous,* those colours are not really in the clouds as they seem to be at this distance. They are only apparent colours.

Phil. Apparent call you them? how shall we distinguish these apparent colours from real?

Hyl. Very easily. Those are to be thought apparent which, appearing only at a distance, vanish upon a nearer approach.

Phil. And those, I suppose, are to be thought real which are discovered by the most near and exact survey.

Hyl. Right.

Phil. Is the nearest and exactest survey made by the help of a microscope, or by the naked eye?

Hyl. By a microscope, doubtless.

Phil. But a microscope often discovers colours in an object different from those perceived by the unassisted sight. And, in case we had microscopes magnifying to any assigned degree, it is certain that no object whatsoever, viewed through them, would appear in the same colour which it exhibits to the naked eye.

Hyl. And what will you conclude from all this? You cannot argue that there are really and naturally no colours on objects : because by artificial managements they may be altered, or made to vanish.

Phil. I think it may evidently be concluded from your own concessions, that all the colours we see with our naked eyes are only apparent as those on the clouds, since they vanish upon a more close and accurate inspection which is afforded us by a microscope. Then, as to what you say by way of prevention : I ask you whether the real and natural state of an object is better discovered by a very sharp and piercing sight, or by one which is less sharp?

Hyl. By the former without doubt.

Phil. Is it not plain from *Dioptrics* that microscopes make the sight more penetrating, and represent objects as they would appear to the eye in case it were naturally endowed with a most exquisite sharpness?

Hyl. It is.

Phil. Consequently the microscopical representation is to be thought that which best sets forth the real nature of the thing, or what it is in itself. The colours, therefore, by it perceived are more genuine and real than those perceived otherwise.

Hyl. I confess there is something in what you say.

Phil. Besides, it is not only possible but manifest, that there actually are animals whose eyes are by nature framed to perceive those things which by reason of their minuteness escape our sight. What think you of those inconceivably small animals perceived by glasses? must we suppose they are all stark blind? Or, in case they see, can it be imagined their sight hath not the same use in preserving their bodies from injuries, which appears in that of all other animals? And if it hath, is it not evident they must see particles less than their own bodies, which will present them with a far different view in each object from that which strikes our senses? Even our own eyes do not always represent objects to us after the same manner. In the *jaundice* every one knows that all things seem yellow. Is it not therefore highly probable those animals in whose eyes we discern a very different texture from that of ours, and whose bodies abound with different humours, do not see the same colours in every object that we do? From all which, should it not seem to follow that all colours are equally apparent, and that none of those which we perceive are really inherent in any outward object?

Hyl. It should.

Phil. The point will be past all doubt, if you consider that, in case colours were real properties or affections inherent in external bodies, they could admit of no alteration without some change wrought in the very bodies themselves: but, is it not evident from what hath been said that, upon the use of microscopes, upon a change happening in the humours of the eye, or a variation of distance, without any manner of real alteration in the thing itself, the colours of any object are either changed, or totally disappear? Nay, all other circumstances remaining the same, change but the situation of some objects, and they shall present different colours to the eye. The same thing happens upon viewing an object in various degrees of light. And what is more known than that the same bodies appear differently coloured by candle-light from what they do in the open day? Add to these the experiment of a prism which, separating the heterogeneous rays of light, alters the colour of any object, and will cause the whitest to appear of a deep blue or red to the naked eye. And now tell me whether you are still of opinion that every body hath its true real colour inhering in it; and, if you think it hath, I would fain know farther from you, what certain distance and position of the object, what peculiar texture and formation of the eye, what degree or kind of light is necessary for ascertaining that true colour, and distinguishing it from apparent ones.

Hyl. I own myself entirely satisfied, that they are all equally apparent, and that there is no such thing as colour really inhering in external bodies, but that it is altogether in the light. And what confirms me in this opinion is that in proportion to the light colours are still more or less vivid; and if there be no light, then are there no colours perceived. Besides, allowing there are colours on external objects, yet, how is it possible for us to perceive them? For no external body affects the mind, unless it acts first on our organs of sense. But the only action of bodies is motion: and motion cannot be communicated otherwise than by impulse. A distant object therefore cannot act on the eye, nor consequently make itself or its properties perceivable to the soul. Whence it plainly follows that it is immediately some contiguous substance, which, operating on the eye, occasions a perception of colours: and such is light.

Phil. How! is light then a substance?

Hyl. I tell you, *Philonous*, external light is nothing but a thin fluid substance, whose minute particles being agitated with a brisk motion, and in various manners reflected from the different surfaces of outward objects to the eyes, communicate different motions to the optic nerves; which, being propagated to the brain, cause therein various impressions; and these are attended with the sensations of red, blue, yellow, &c.

Phil. It seems then the light doth no more than shake the optic nerves.

Hyl. Nothing else.

Phil. And, consequent to each particular motion of the nerves, the mind is affected with a sensation, which is some particular colour.

Hyl. Right.

Phil. And these sensations have no existence without the mind.

Hyl. They have not.

Phil. How then do you affirm that colours are in the light; since by *light* you understand a corporeal substance external to the mind?

Hyl. Light and colours, as immediately perceived by us, I grant cannot exist without the mind. But, in themselves they are only the motions and configurations of certain insensible particles of matter.

Phil. Colours then, in the vulgar sense, or taken for the immediate objects of sight, cannot agree to any but a perceiving substance.

Hyl. That is what I say.

Phil. Well then, since you give up the point as to those sensible qualities which are alone thought colours by all mankind beside, you may hold what you please with regard to those invisible ones of the philosophers. It is not my business to dispute about them; only I would advise you to bethink yourself, whether, considering the inquiry we are upon, it be prudent for you to affirm—*the* red and blue which we see are not real colours, but certain unknown motions and figures, which no man ever did or can see, are truly so. Are not these shocking notions, and are not they subject to as many ridiculous inferences, as those you were obliged to renounce before in the case of sounds?

Hyl. I frankly own, *Philonous*, that it is in vain to stand out any longer. Colours, sounds, tastes, in a word all those termed *secondary qualities*, have certainly no existence without the mind. But, by this acknowledgment I must not be supposed to derogate anything from the reality of Matter or external objects; seeing it is no more than several philosophers maintain, who nevertheless are the farthest imaginable from denying Matter. For the clearer understanding of this, you must know sensible qualities are by philosophers divided into *primary* and *secondary*. The former are Extension, Figure, Solidity, Gravity, Motion, and Rest. And these they hold exist really in bodies. The latter are those above enumerated; or, briefly, all sensible qualities beside the Primary, which they assert are only so many sensations or ideas existing nowhere but in the mind. But all this, I doubt not, you are apprised of. For my part, I have been a long time sensible there was such an opinion current among philosophers, but was never thoroughly convinced of its truth until now.

Phil. You are still then of opinion that *extension* and *figures* are inherent in external unthinking substances?

Hyl. I am.

Phil. But what if the same arguments which are brought against Secondary Qualities will hold good against these also?

Hyl. Why then I shall be obliged to think, they too exist only in the mind.

Phil. Is it your opinion the very figure and extension

which you perceive by sense exist in the outward object or material substance?

Hyl. It is.

Phil. Have all other animals as good grounds to think the same of the figure and extension which they see and feel?

Hyl. Without doubt, if they have any thought at all.

Phil. Answer me, *Hylas*. Think you the senses were bestowed upon all animals for their preservation and well-being in life? or were they given to men alone for this end?

Hyl. I make no question but they have the same use in all other animals.

Phil. If so, is it not necessary they should be enabled by them to perceive their own limbs, and those bodies which are capable of harming them?

Hyl. Certainly.

Phil. A mite therefore must be supposed to see his own foot, and things equal or even less than it, as bodies of some considerable dimension; though at the same time they appear to you scarce discernible, or at best as so many visible points?

Hyl. I cannot deny it.

Phil. And to creatures less than the mite they will seem yet larger?

Hyl. They will.

Phil. Insomuch that what you can hardly discern will to another extremely minute animal appear as some huge mountain?

Hyl. All this I grant.

Phil. Can one and the same thing be at the same time in itself of different dimensions?

Hyl. That were absurd to imagine.

Phil. But, from what you have laid down it follows that both the extension by you perceived, and that perceived by the mite itself, as likewise all those perceived by lesser animals, are each of them the true extension of the mite's foot; that is to say, by your own principles, you are led into an absurdity.

Hyl. There seems to be some difficulty in the point.

Phil. Again, have you not acknowledged that no real inherent property of any object can be changed without some change in the thing itself?

Hyl. I have.

Phil. But, as we approach to or recede from an object, the visible extension varies, being at one distance ten or a hundred times greater than at another. Doth it not therefore follow from hence likewise that it is not really inherent in the object?

Hyl. I own I am at a loss what to think.

Phil. Your judgment will soon be determined, if you will venture to think as freely concerning this quality as you have done concerning the rest. Was it not admitted as a good argument, that neither heat nor cold was in the water, because it seemed warm to one hand and cold to the other?

Hyl. It was.

Phil. Is it not the very same reasoning to conclude, there is no extension or figure in an object, because to one eye it shall seem little, smooth, and round, when at the same time it appears to the other, great, uneven, and angular?

Hyl. The very same. But does this latter fact ever happen?

Phil. You may at any time make the experiment, by looking with one eye bare, and with the other through a microscope.

Hyl. I know not how to maintain it, and yet I am loath to give up *extension*, I see so many odd consequences following upon such a concession.

Phil. Odd, say you? After the concessions already made, I hope you will stick at nothing for its oddness.

But, on the other hand, should it not seem very odd, if the general reasoning which includes all other sensible qualities did not also include extension? If it be allowed that no idea nor anything like an idea can exist in an unperceiving substance, then surely it follows that no figure or mode of extension, which we can either perceive or imagine, or have any idea of, can be really inherent in Matter; not to mention the peculiar difficulty there must be in conceiving a material substance, prior to and distinct from extension, to be the *substratum* of extension. Be the sensible quality what it will—figure, or sound, or colour; it seems alike impossible it should subsist in that which doth not perceive it.

Hyl. I give up the point for the present, reserving still a right to retract my opinion, in case I shall hereafter discover any false step in my progress to it.

Phil. That is a right you cannot be denied. Figures and extension being despatched, we proceed next to *motion*. Can a real motion in any external body be at the same time both very swift and very slow?

Hyl. It cannot.

Phil. Is not the motion of a body swift in a reciprocal proportion to the time it takes up in describing any given space? Thus a body that describes a mile in an hour moves three times faster than it would in case it described only a mile in three hours.

Hyl. I agree with you.

Phil. And is not time measured by the succession of ideas in our minds?

Hyl. It is.

Phil. And is it not possible ideas should succeed one another twice as fast in your mind as they do in mine, or in that of some spirit of another kind?

Hyl. I own it.

Phil. Consequently, the same body may to another seem

to perform its motion over any space in half the time that it doth to you. And the same reasoning will hold as to any other proportion: that is to say, according to your principles (since the motions perceived are both really in the object) it is possible one and the same body shall be really moved the same way at once, both very swift and very slow. How is this consistent either with common sense, or with what you just now granted?

Hyl. I have nothing to say to it.

Phil. Then as for *solidity*; either you do not mean any sensible quality by that word, and so it is beside our inquiry: or if you do, it must be either hardness or resistance. But both the one and the other are plainly relative to our senses: it being evident that what seems hard to one animal may appear soft to another, who hath greater force and firmness of limbs. Nor is it less plain that the resistance I feel is not in the body.

Hyl. I own the very sensation of resistance, which is all you immediately perceive, is not in the *body*; but the cause of that sensation is.

Phil. But the causes of our sensations are not things immediately perceived, and therefore not sensible. This point I thought had been already determined.

Hyl. I own it was; but you will pardon me if I seem a little embarrassed: I know not how to quit my old notions.

Phil. To help you out, do but consider that if *extension* be once acknowledged to have no existence without the mind, the same must necessarily be granted of motion, solidity, and gravity—since they all evidently suppose extension. It is therefore superfluous to inquire particularly concerning each of them. In denying extension, you have denied them all to have any real existence.

Hyl. I wonder, *Philonous*, if what you say be true, why those philosophers who deny the Secondary Qualities any real existence, should yet attribute it to the Primary. If there is no difference between them, how can this be accounted for?

Phil. It is not my business to account for every opinion of the philosophers. But, among other reasons which may be assigned for this, it seems probable that pleasure and pain being rather annexed to the former than the latter may be one. Heat and cold, tastes and smells, have something more vividly pleasing or disagreeable than the ideas of extension, figure, and motion affect us with. And, it being too visibly absurd to hold that pain or pleasure can be in an unperceiving Substance, men are more easily weaned from believing the external existence of the Secondary than the Primary Qualities. You will be satisfied there is something in this, if you recollect the difference you made between an intense and more moderate degree of heat; allowing the one a real existence, while you denied it to the other. But, after all, there is no rational ground for that distinction; for, surely an indifferent sensation is as truly *a sensation* as one more pleasing or painful; and consequently should not any more than they be supposed to exist in an unthinking subject.

Hyl. It is just come into my head, *Philonous*, that I have somewhere heard of a distinction between absolute and sensible extension. Now, though it be acknowledged that *great* and *small*, consisting merely in the relation which other extended beings have to the parts of our own bodies, do not really inhere in the Substances themselves; yet nothing obliges us to hold the same with regard to *absolute extension*, which is something abstracted from *great* and *small*, from this or that particular magnitude or figure. So likewise as to motion; *swift* and *slow* are altogether relative to the succession of ideas in our own minds. But, it doth not follow, because those modifications of motion exist not without the mind, that therefore absolute motion abstracted from them doth not.

Phil. Pray what is it that distinguishes one motion, or one part of extension, from another? Is it not something sensible, as some degree of swiftness or slowness, some certain magnitude or figure peculiar to each?

Hyl. I think so.

Phil. These qualities, therefore, stripped of all sensible properties, are without all specific and numerical differences, as the schools call them.

Hyl. They are.

Phil. That is to say, they are extension in general, and motion in general.

Hyl. Let it be so.

Phil. But it is a universally received maxim that *Everything which exists is particular.* How then can motion in general, or extension in general, exist in any corporeal Substance?

Hyl. I will take time to solve your difficulty.

Phil. But I think the point may be speedily decided. Without doubt you can tell whether you are able to frame this or that idea. Now I am content to put our dispute on this issue. If you can frame in your thoughts a distinct abstract idea of motion or extension; divested of all those sensible modes, as swift and slow, great and small, round and square, and the like, which are acknowledged to exist only in the mind, I will then yield the point you contend for. But, if you cannot, it will be unreasonable on your side to insist any longer upon what you have no notion of.

Hyl. To confess ingenuously, I cannot.

Phil. Can you even separate the ideas of extension and motion from the ideas of all those qualities which they who make the distinction term *secondary*?

Hyl. What! is it not an easy matter to consider extension and motion by themselves, abstracted from all other sensible qualities? Pray how do the mathematicians treat of them?

Phil. I acknowledge, *Hylas*, it is not difficult to form general propositions and reasonings about those qualities, without mentioning any other; and, in this sense, to consider or treat of them abstractedly. But, how doth it follow that, because I can pronounce the word *motion* by itself, I can form the idea of it in my mind exclusive of body? Or, because theorems may be made of extension and figures, without any mention of great or small, or any other sensible mode or quality, that therefore it is possible such an abstract idea of extension, without any particular size or figure, or sensible quality, should be distinctly formed, and apprehended by the mind? Mathematicians treat of quantity, without regarding what other sensible qualities it is attended with, as being altogether indifferent to their demonstrations. But, when laying aside the words, they contemplate the bare ideas, I believe you will find, they are not the pure abstracted ideas of extension.

Hyl. But what say you to *pure intellect?* May not abstracted ideas be framed by that faculty?

Phil. Since I cannot frame abstract ideas at all, it is plain I cannot frame them by the help of pure intellect; whatsoever faculty you understand by those words. Besides, not to inquire into the nature of pure intellect and its spiritual objects, as *virtue, reason, God*, or the like, thus much seems manifest—that sensible things are only to be perceived by sense, or represented by the imagination. Figures, therefore, and extension, being originally perceived by sense, do not belong to pure intellect: but, for your farther satisfaction, try if you can frame the idea of any figure, abstracted from all particularities of size, or even from other sensible qualities.

Hyl. Let me think a little —— I do not find that I can.

Phil. And can you think it possible that should really exist in nature which implies a repugnancy in its conception?

Hyl. By no means.

Phil. Since therefore it is impossible even for the mind to disunite the ideas of extension and motion from all other sensible qualities, doth it not follow, that where the one exist there necessarily the other exist likewise?

Hyl. It should seem so.

Phil. Consequently, the very same arguments which you admitted as conclusive against the Secondary Qualities are, without any farther application of force, against the Primary too. Besides, if you will trust your senses, is it not plain all sensible qualities coexist, or to them appear as being in the same place? Do they ever represent a motion, or figure, as being divested of all other visible and tangible qualities?

Hyl. You need say no more on this head. I am free to own, if there be no secret error or oversight in our proceedings hitherto, that all sensible qualities are alike to be denied existence without the mind. But, my fear is that I have been too liberal in my former concessions, or overlooked some fallacy or other. In short, I did not take time to think.

Phil. For that matter, *Hylas*, you may take what time you please in reviewing the progress of our inquiry. You are at liberty to recover any slips you might have made, or offer whatever you have omitted which makes for your first opinion.

Hyl. One great oversight I take to be this—that I did not sufficiently distinguish the *object* from the *sensation*. Now, though this latter may not exist without the mind, yet it will not thence follow that the former cannot.

Phil. What object do you mean? The object of the senses?

Hyl. The same.

Phil. It is then immediately perceived?

Hyl. Right.

Phil. Make me to understand the difference between what is immediately perceived, and a sensation.

Hyl. The sensation I take to be an act of the mind perceiving: besides which, there is something perceived; and this I call the *object*. For example, there is red and yellow on that tulip. But then the act of perceiving those colours is in me only, and not in the tulip.

Phil. What tulip do you speak of? Is it that which you see?

Hyl. The same.

Phil. And what do you see beside colour, figure, and extension?

Hyl. Nothing.

Phil. What you would say then is that the red and yellow are coexistent with the extension; is it not?

Hyl. That is not all; I would say they have a real existence without the mind, in some unthinking substance.

Phil. That the colours are really in the tulip which I see is manifest. Neither can it be denied that this tulip may exist independent of your mind or mine; but, that any immediate object of the senses—that is, any idea, or combination of ideas—should exist in an unthinking substance, or exterior to all minds, is in itself an evident contradiction. Nor can I imagine how this follows from what you said just now, to wit, that the red and yellow were on the tulip *you saw*, since you do not pretend to *see* that unthinking substance.

Hyl. You have an artful way, *Philonous*, of diverting our inquiry from the subject.

Phil. I see you have no mind to be pressed that way. To return then to your distinction between *sensation* and *object*; if I take you right, you distinguish in every perception two things, the one an action of the mind, the other not.

Hyl. True.

Phil. And this action cannot exist in, or belong to, any unthinking thing; but, whatever beside is implied in a perception may?

Hyl. That is my meaning.

Phil. So that if there was a perception without any act of the mind, it were possible such a perception should exist in an unthinking substance?

Hyl. I grant it. But it is impossible there should be such a perception.

Phil. When is the mind said to be active?

Hyl. When it produces, puts an end to, or changes, anything.

Phil. Can the mind produce, discontinue, or change anything, but by an act of the will?

Hyl. It cannot.

Phil. The mind therefore is to be accounted *active* in its perceptions so far forth as *volition* is included in them?

Hyl. It is.

Phil. In plucking this flower I am active; because **I** do it by the motion of my hand, which was consequent upon my volition; so likewise in applying it to my nose. But is either of these smelling?

Hyl. No.

Phil. I act too in drawing the air through my nose; because my breathing so rather than otherwise is the effect of my volition. But neither can this be called *smelling*: for, if it were, I should smell every time I breathed in that manner?

Hyl. True.

Phil. Smelling then is somewhat consequent to all this?

Hyl. It is.

Phil. But I do not find my will concerned any farther. Whatever more there is—as that I perceive such a particular smell, or any smell at all—this is independent of my will, and therein I am altogether passive. Do you find it otherwise with you, *Hylas*?

Hyl. No, the very same.

Phil. Then, as to seeing, is it not in your power to open your eyes, or keep them shut; to turn them this or that way?

Hyl. Without doubt.

Phil. But, doth it in like manner depend on your will that in looking on this flower you perceive *white* rather than any other colour? Or, directing your open eyes towards yonder part of the heaven, can you avoid seeing the sun? Or is light or darkness the effect of your volition?

Hyl. No certainly.

Phil. You are then in these respects altogether passive?

Hyl. I am.

Phil. Tell me now, whether *seeing* consists in perceiving light and colours, or in opening and turning the eyes?

Hyl. Without doubt, in the former.

Phil. Since therefore you are in the very perception of light and colours altogether passive, what is become of that action you were speaking of as an ingredient in every sensation? And, doth it not follow from your own concessions, that the perception of light and colours, including no action in it, may exist in an unperceiving substance? And is not this a plain contradiction?

Hyl. I know not what to think of it.

Phil. Besides, since you distinguish the *active* and *passive* in every perception, you must do it in that of pain. But how is it possible that pain, be it as little active as you please, should exist in an unperceiving substance? In short, do but consider the point, and then confess ingenuously, whether light and colours, tastes, sounds, &c., are not all equally passions or sensations in the soul. You may indeed call them *external objects*, and give them in words what subsistence you please. But, examine your own thoughts, and then tell me whether it be not as I say?

Hyl. I acknowledge, *Philonous*, that, upon a fair observation of what passes in my mind, I can discover nothing else but that I am a thinking being, affected with variety of sensations; neither is it possible to conceive how a sensation should exist in an unperceiving substance.—But then, on the other hand, when I look on sensible things in a different view, considering them as so many modes and qualities, I find it necessary to suppose a material *substratum*, without which they cannot be conceived to exist.

Phil. Material *substratum* call you it? Pray, by which of your senses came you acquainted with that being?

Hyl. It is not itself sensible; its modes and qualities only being perceived by the senses.

Phil. I presume then it was by reflection and reason you obtained the idea of it?

Hyl. I do not pretend to any proper positive idea of it. However, I conclude it exists, because qualities cannot be conceived to exist without a support.

Phil. It seems then you have only a relative notion of it, or that you conceive it not otherwise than by conceiving the relation it bears to sensible qualities?

Hyl. Right.

Phil. Be pleased therefore to let me know wherein that relation consists.

Hyl. Is it not sufficiently expressed in the term *substratum*, or *substance*?

Phil. If so, the word *substratum* should import that it is spread under the sensible qualities or accidents?

Hyl. True.

Phil. And consequently under extension?

Hyl. I own it.

Phil. It is therefore somewhat in its own nature entirely distinct from extension?

Hyl. I tell you, extension is only a mode, and Matter is something that supports modes. And is it not evident the thing supported is different from the thing supporting?

Phil. So that something distinct from, and exclusive of, extension is supposed to be the *substratum* of extension?

Hyl. Just so.

Phil. Answer me, *Hylas*. Can a thing be spread without extension? or is not the idea of extension necessarily included in *spreading*?

Hyl. It is.

Phil. Whatsoever therefore you suppose spread under anything must have in itself an extension distinct from the extension of that thing under which it is spread?

Hyl. It must.

Phil. Consequently, every corporeal substance being the *substratum* of extension must have in itself another extension, by which it is qualified to be a *substratum*: and so on to infinity? And I ask whether this be not absurd in itself, and repugnant to what you granted just now, to wit, that the *substratum* was something distinct from and exclusive of extension?

Hyl. Aye but, *Philonous*, you take me wrong. I do not mean that Matter is *spread* in a gross literal sense under extension. The word *substratum* is used only to express in general the same thing with *substance*.

Phil. Well then, let us examine the relation implied in the term *substance*. Is it not that it stands under accidents?

Hyl. The very same.

Phil. But, that one thing may stand under or support another, must it not be extended?

Hyl. It must.

Phil. Is not therefore this supposition liable to the same absurdity with the former?

Hyl. You still take things in a strict literal sense; that is not fair, *Philonous*.

Phil. I am not for imposing any sense on your words: you are at liberty to explain them as you please. Only, I beseech you, make me understand something by them. You tell me Matter supports or stands under accidents. How! is it as your legs support your body?

Hyl. No; that is the literal sense.

Phil. Pray let me know any sense, literal or not literal, that you understand it in. . . . How long must I wait for an answer, *Hylas*?

Hyl. I declare I know not what to say. I once thought I understood well enough what was meant by Matter's supporting accidents. But now, the more I think on it the less can I comprehend it; in short I find that I know nothing of it.

Phil. It seems then you have no idea at all, neither relative nor positive, of Matter; you know neither what it is in itself, nor what relation it bears to accidents?

Hyl. I acknowledge it.

Phil. And yet you asserted that you could not conceive how qualities or accidents should really exist, without conceiving at the same time a material support of them?

Hyl. I did.

Phil. That is to say, when you conceive the real existence of qualities, you do withal conceive something which you cannot conceive?

Hyl. I was wrong I own. But still I fear there is some fallacy or other. Pray what think you of this? It is just come into my head that the ground of all our mistake lies in your treating of each quality by itself. Now, I grant that each quality cannot singly subsist without the mind. Colour cannot without extension, neither can figure without some other sensible quality. But, as the several qualities united or blended together form entire sensible things, nothing hinders why such things may not be supposed to exist without the mind.

Phil. Either, *Hylas*, you are jesting, or have a very bad memory. Though indeed we went through all the qualities by name one after another; yet my arguments, or rather your concessions, nowhere tended to prove that the Secondary Qualities did not subsist each alone by itself; but, that they were not at all without the mind. Indeed, in treating of figure and motion we concluded they could not exist without the mind, because it was impossible even in thought to separate them from all secondary qualities, so as to conceive them existing by themselves. But then this was not the only argument made use of upon that occasion. But (to pass by all that hath been hitherto said, and reckon it for nothing, if you will have it so) I am content to put the whole upon this issue. If you can conceive it possible for any mixture or combination of qualities, or any sensible object whatever, to exist without the mind, then I will grant it actually to be so.

Hyl. If it comes to that the point will soon be decided. What more easy than to conceive a tree or house existing by itself, independent of, and unperceived by, any mind whatsoever? I do at this present time conceive them existing after that manner.

Phil. How say you, *Hylas*, can you see a thing which is at the same time unseen?

Hyl. No, that were a contradiction.

Phil. Is it not as great a contradiction to talk of *conceiving* a thing which is *unconceived*?

Hyl. It is.

Phil. The tree or house therefore which you think of is conceived by you?

Hyl. How should it be otherwise?

Phil. And what is conceived is surely in the mind?

Hyl. Without question, that which is conceived is in the mind.

Phil. How then came you to say, you conceived a

house or tree existing independent and out of all minds whatsoever?

Hyl. That was I own an oversight; but stay, let me consider what led me into it.—It is a pleasant mistake enough. As I was thinking of a tree in a solitary place where no one was present to see it, methought that was to conceive a tree as existing unperceived or unthought of—not considering that I myself conceived it all the while. But now I plainly see that all I can do is to frame ideas in my own mind. I may indeed conceive in my own thoughts the idea of a tree, or a house, or a mountain, but that is all. And this is far from proving that I can conceive them *existing out of the minds of all Spirits.*

Phil. You acknowledge then that you cannot possibly conceive how any one corporeal sensible thing should exist otherwise than in a mind?

Hyl. I do.

Phil. And yet you will earnestly contend for the truth of that which you cannot so much as conceive?

Hyl. I profess I know not what to think; but still there are some scruples remain with me. Is it not certain I *see* things at a distance? Do we not perceive the stars and moon, for example, to be a great way off? Is not this, I say, manifest to the senses?

Phil. Do you not in a dream too perceive those or the like objects?

Hyl. I do.

Phil. And have they not then the same appearance of being distant?

Hyl. They have.

Phil. But you do not thence conclude the apparitions in a dream to be without the mind?

Hyl. By no means.

Phil. You ought not therefore to conclude that sensible

objects are without the mind, from their appearance or manner wherein they are perceived.

Hyl. I acknowledge it. But doth not my sense deceive me in those cases?

Phil. By no means. The idea or thing which you immediately perceive, neither sense nor reason informs you that it actually exists without the mind. By sense you only know that you are affected with such certain sensations of light and colour, &c. And these you will not say are without the mind.

Hyl. True: but, beside all that, do you not think the sight suggests something of *outness* or *distance*?

Phil. Upon approaching a distant object, do the visible size and figure change perpetually, or do they appear the same at all distances?

Hyl. They are in a continual change.

Phil. Sight therefore doth not suggest or any way inform you that the visible object you immediately perceive exists at a distance, or will be perceived when you advance farther onward; there being a continued series of visible objects succeeding each other during the whole time of your approach.

Hyl. It doth not; but still I know, upon seeing an object, what object I shall perceive after having passed over a certain distance: no matter whether it be exactly the same or no: there is still something of distance suggested in the case.

Phil. Good *Hylas*, do but reflect a little on the point, and then tell me whether there be any more in it than this: —From the ideas you actually perceive by sight, you have by experience learned to collect what other ideas you will (according to the standing order of nature) be affected with, after such a certain succession of time and motion.

Hyl. Upon the whole, I take it to be nothing else.

Phil. Now, is it not plain that if we suppose a man born

blind was on a sudden made to see, he could at first have no experience of what may be suggested by sight?

Hyl. It is.

Phil. He would not then, according to you, have any notion of distance annexed to the things he saw; but would take them for a new set of sensations existing only in his mind?

Hyl. It is undeniable.

Phil. But, to make it still more plain: is not *distance* a line turned endwise to the eye?

Hyl. It is.

Phil. And can a line so situated be perceived by sight?

Hyl. It cannot.

Phil. Doth it not therefore follow that distance is not properly and immediately perceived by sight?

Hyl. It should seem so.

Phil. Again, is it your opinion that colours are at a distance?

Hyl. It must be acknowledged they are only in the mind.

Phil. But do not colours appear to the eye as coexisting in the same place with extension and figures?

Hyl. They do.

Phil. How can you then conclude from sight that figures exist without, when you acknowledge colours do not; the sensible appearance being the very same with regard to both?

Hyl. I know not what to answer.

Phil. But, allowing that distance was truly and immediately perceived by the mind, yet it would not thence follow it existed out of the mind. For, whatever is immediately perceived is an idea: and can any *idea* exist out of the mind?

Hyl. To suppose that were absurd: but, inform me, *Philonous,* can we perceive or know nothing beside our ideas?

Phil. As for the rational deducing of causes from effects, that is beside our inquiry. And, by the senses you can best tell whether you perceive anything which is not immediately perceived. And I ask you, whether the things immediately perceived are other than your own sensations or ideas? You have indeed more than once, in the course of this conversation, declared yourself on those points; but you seem, by this last question, to have departed from what you then thought.

Hyl. To speak the truth, *Philonous*, I think there are two kinds of objects:—the one perceived immediately, which are likewise called *ideas*; the other are real things or external objects, perceived by the mediation of ideas, which are their images and representations. Now, I own ideas do not exist without the mind; but the latter sort of objects do. I am sorry I did not think of this distinction sooner; it would probably have cut short your discourse.

Phil. Are those external objects perceived by sense, or by some other faculty?

Hyl. They are perceived by sense.

Phil. How! is there anything perceived by sense which is not immediately perceived?

Hyl. Yes, *Philonous*, in some sort there is. For example, when I look on a picture or statue of Julius Cæsar, I may be said after a manner to perceive him (though not immediately) by my senses.

Phil. It seems then you will have our ideas, which alone are immediately perceived, to be pictures of external things: and that these also are perceived by sense, inasmuch as they have a conformity or resemblance to our ideas?

Hyl. That is my meaning.

Phil. And, in the same way that Julius Cæsar, in himself invisible, is nevertheless perceived by sight; real things, in themselves imperceptible, are perceived by sense.

Hyl. In the very same.

Phil. Tell me, *Hylas*, when you behold the picture of

Julius Cæsar, do you see with your eyes any more than some colours and figures, with a certain symmetry and composition of the whole?

Hyl. Nothing else.

Phil. And would not a man who had never known anything of Julius Cæsar see as much?

Hyl. He would.

Phil. Consequently he hath his sight, and the use of it, in as perfect a degree as you?

Hyl. I agree with you.

Phil. Whence comes it then that your thoughts are directed to the Roman emperor, and his are not? This cannot proceed from the sensations or ideas of sense by you then perceived; since you acknowledge you have no advantage over him in that respect. It should seem therefore to proceed from reason and memory: should it not?

Hyl. It should.

Phil. Consequently, it will not follow from that instance that anything is perceived by sense which is not immediately perceived. Though I grant we may, in one acceptation, be said to perceive sensible things mediately by sense—that is, when, from a frequently perceived connexion, the immediate perception of ideas by one sense suggests to the mind others, perhaps belonging to another sense, which are wont to be connected with them. For instance, when I hear a coach drive along the streets, immediately I perceive only the sound; but, from the experience I have had that such a sound is connected with a coach, I am said to hear the coach. It is nevertheless evident that, in truth and strictness, nothing can be *heard* but *sound*; and the coach is not then properly perceived by sense, but suggested from experience. So likewise when we are said to see a red-hot bar of iron; the solidity and heat of the iron are not the objects of sight, but suggested to the imagination by the colour and figure which are properly perceived by that sense. In short, those things alone are actually and strictly perceived by any sense, which would have been perceived in case that same sense had then been first conferred on us. As for other things, it is plain they are only suggested to the mind by experience, grounded on former perceptions. But, to return to your comparison of Cæsar's picture, it is plain, if you keep to that, you must hold the real things or archetypes of our ideas are not perceived by sense, but by some internal faculty of the soul, as reason or memory. I would therefore fain know what arguments you can draw from reason for the existence of what you call *real things* or *material objects*. Or, whether you remember to have seen them formerly as they are in themselves; or, if you have heard or read of any one that did.

Hyl. I see, *Philonous*, you are disposed to raillery; but that will never convince me.

Phil. My aim is only to learn from you the way to come at the knowledge of *material beings*. Whatever we perceive is perceived immediately or mediately: by sense; or by reason and reflection. But, as you have excluded sense, pray shew me what reason you have to believe their existence; or what *medium* you can possibly make use of to prove it, either to mine or your own understanding.

Hyl. To deal ingenuously, *Philonous*, now I consider the point, I do not find I can give you any good reason for it. But, thus much seems pretty plain, that it is at least possible such things may really exist. And, as long as there is no absurdity in supposing them, I am resolved to believe as I did, till you bring good reasons to the contrary.

Phil. What! is it come to this, that you only believe the existence of material objects, and that your belief is founded barely on the possibility of its being true? Then you will have me bring reasons against it: though another would think it reasonable the proof should lie on him who holds the affirmative. And, after all, this very point which you are now resolved to maintain, without any reason, is in effect what you have more than once during this discourse seen good reason to give up. But, to pass over all this; if I understand you rightly, you say our ideas do not exist without the mind; but that they are copies, images, or representations, of certain originals that do?

Hyl. You take me right.

Phil. They are then like external things?

Hyl. They are.

Phil. Have those things a stable and permanent nature, independent of our senses; or are they in a perpetual change, upon our producing any motions in our bodies—suspending, exerting, or altering, our faculties or organs of sense?

Hyl. Real things, it is plain, have a fixed and real nature, which remains the same notwithstanding any change in our senses, or in the posture and motion of our bodies: which indeed may affect the ideas in our minds, but it were absurd to think they had the same effect on things existing without the mind.

Phil. How then is it possible that things perpetually fleeting and variable as our ideas should be copies or images of anything fixed and constant? Or, in other words, since all sensible qualities, as size, figure, colour, &c., that is, our ideas, are continually changing upon every alteration in the distance, medium, or instruments of sensation: how can any determinate material objects be properly represented or painted forth by several distinct things, each of which is so different from and unlike the rest? Or, if you say it resembles some one only of our ideas, how shall we be able to distinguish the true copy from all the false ones?

Hyl. I profess, *Philonous*, I am at a loss. I know not what to say to this.

Phil. But neither is this all. Which are material objects in themselves—perceptible or imperceptible?

Hyl. Properly and immediately nothing can be perceived but ideas. All material things, therefore, are in themselves insensible, and to be perceived only by our ideas.

Phil. Ideas then are sensible, and their archetypes or originals insensible?

Hyl. Right.

Phil. But how can that which is sensible be like that which is insensible? Can a real thing, in itself *invisible*, be like a *colour*; or a real thing, which is not *audible*, be like a *sound*? In a word, can anything be like a sensation or idea, but another sensation or idea?

Hyl. I must own, I think not.

Phil. Is it possible there should be any doubt on the point? Do you not perfectly know your own ideas?

Hyl. I know them perfectly; since what I do not perceive or know can be no part of my idea.

Phil. Consider, therefore, and examine them, and then tell me if there be anything in them which can exist without the mind? or if you can conceive anything like them existing without the mind?

Hyl. Upon inquiry, I find it is impossible for me to conceive or understand how anything but an idea can be like an idea. And it is most evident that *no idea can exist without the mind*.

Phil. You are therefore, by your principles, forced to deny the reality of sensible things; since you made it to consist in an absolute existence exterior to the mind. That is to say, you are a downright sceptic. So I have gained my point, which was to shew your principles led to Scepticism.

. . . .

Hyl. You say your own soul supplies you with some sort of an idea or image of God. But, at the same time, you acknowledge you have, properly speaking, no *idea* of your own soul. You even affirm that spirits are a sort of beings altogether different from ideas. Consequently that no idea can be like a spirit. We have therefore no idea of any spirit. You admit nevertheless that there is spiritual Substance, although you have no idea of it; while you deny there can be such a thing as material Substance, because you have no notion or idea of it. Is this fair dealing? To act consistently, you must either admit Matter or reject Spirit. What say you to this?

Phil. I say, in the first place, that I do not deny the existence of material substance, merely because I have no notion of it, but because the notion of it is inconsistent; or, in other words, because it is repugnant that there should be a notion of it. Many things, for ought I know, may exist, whereof neither I nor any other man hath or can have any idea or notion whatsoever. But then those things must be possible; that is, nothing inconsistent must be included in their definition. I say, secondly, that, although we believe things to exist which we do not perceive, yet we may not believe that any particular thing exists, without some reason for such belief: but I have no reason for believing the existence of Matter. I have no immediate intuition thereof: neither can I immediately from my sensations, ideas, notions, actions, or passions, infer an unthinking, unperceiving, inactive Substance—either by probable deduction, or necessary consequence. Whereas the being of my Self, that is, my own soul, mind, or thinking principle, I evidently know by reflection. You will forgive me if I repeat the same things in answer to the same objections. In the very notion or definition of *material Substance*, there is included a manifest repugnance and inconsistency. But this cannot be said of the notion of Spirit. That ideas should exist in what doth not perceive, or be produced by what doth not act, is repugnant.

But, it is no repugnancy to say that a perceiving thing should be the subject of ideas, or an active thing the cause of them. It is granted we have neither an immediate evidence nor a demonstrative knowledge of the existence of other finite spirits; but it will not thence follow that such spirits are on a foot with material substances: if to suppose the one be inconsistent, and it be not inconsistent to suppose the other; if the one can be inferred by no argument, and there is a probability for the other; if we see signs and effects indicating distinct finite agents like ourselves, and see no sign or symptom whatever that leads to a rational belief of material Substance. I say, lastly, that I have a notion of Spirit, though I have not, strictly speaking, an idea of it. I do not perceive it as an idea, or by means of an idea, but know it by reflection.

Hyl. Notwithstanding all you have said, to me it seems that, according to your own way of thinking, and in consequence of your own principles, it should follow that *you* are only a system of floating ideas, without any substance to support them. Words are not to be used without a meaning. And as there is no more meaning in *spiritual Substance* than in *material Substance*, the one is to be exploded as well as the other.

Phil. How often must I repeat, that I know or am conscious of my own being; and that *I myself* am not my ideas, but somewhat else—a thinking, active principle that perceives, knows, wills, and operates about ideas. I know that I, one and the same self, perceive both colours and sounds: that a colour cannot perceive a sound, nor a sound a colour: that I am therefore one individual principle, distinct from colour and sound; and, for the same reason, from all other sensible things and inert ideas. But, I am not in like manner conscious either of the existence or essence of Matter. On the contrary, I know that nothing inconsistent can exist, and that the existence of Matter implies an inconsistency. Farther, I know what I mean when I affirm that there is a spiritual substance or support of ideas; that is, that a spirit knows and perceives ideas. But, I do not know what is meant when it is said that an unperceiving substance hath inherent in it and supports either ideas or the archetypes of ideas. There is therefore upon the whole no parity of case between Spirit and Matter.

. . . .

Hyl. I must needs own, *Philonous,* nothing seems to have kept me from agreeing with you more than somehow *mistaking the question.* In denying Matter, at first glimpse I am tempted to imagine you deny the things we see and feel: but, upon reflection, find there is no ground for it. What think you, therefore, of retaining the name *Matter,* and applying it to *sensible things?* This may be done without any change in your sentiments: and, believe me, it would be a means of reconciling them to some persons who may be more shocked at an innovation in words than in opinion.

Phil. With all my heart: retain the word *Matter,* and apply it to the objects of sense, if you please; provided you do not attribute to them any subsistence distinct from their being perceived. I shall never quarrel with you for an expression. *Matter,* or *material substance,* are terms introduced by philosophers; and, as used by them, imply a sort of independency, or a subsistence distinct from being perceived by a mind: but are never used by common people; or, if ever, it is to signify the immediate objects of sense. One would think, therefore, so long as the names of all particular things, with the terms *sensible, substance, body, stuff,* and the like, are retained, the word *Matter* should be never missed in common talk. And in philosophical discourses it seems the best way to leave it quite out: since there is not, perhaps, any one thing that hath more favoured and strengthened the depraved bent of the mind towards Atheism than the use of that general confused term.

Hyl. Well but, *Philonous*, since I am content to give up the notion of an unthinking substance exterior to the mind, I think you ought not to deny me the privilege of using the word *Matter* as I please, and annexing it to a collection of sensible qualities subsisting only in the mind. I freely own there is no other substance, in a strict sense, than *Spirit*. But I have been so long accustomed to the term *Matter* that I know not how to part with it. To say, there is no *Matter* in the world, is still shocking to me. Whereas one may say, There is no *Matter*, if by that term be meant an unthinking substance existing without the mind: but if by *Matter* is meant some sensible thing, whose existence consists in being perceived, then there is *Matter*. This distinction gives it quite another turn; and men will come into your notions with small difficulty, when they are proposed in that manner. For, after all, the controversy about *Matter*, in the strict acceptation of it, lies altogether between you and the philosophers: whose Principles, I acknowledge, are not near so natural, or so agreeable to the common sense of mankind, and Holy Scripture, as yours. There is nothing we either desire or shun but as it makes, or is apprehended to make, some part of our happiness or misery. But what hath happiness or misery, joy or grief, pleasure or pain, to do with Absolute Existence; or with unknown Entities, abstracted from all relation to us? It is evident, things regard us only as they are pleasing or displeasing: and they can please or displease only so far forth as they are perceived. Farther, therefore, we are not concerned; and thus far you leave things as you found them. Yet still there is something new in this doctrine. It is plain, I do not now think with the philosophers, nor yet altogether with the vulgar. I would know how the case stands in that respect; precisely, what you have added to, or altered in my former notions.

Phil. I do not pretend to be a setter-up of new notions. My endeavours tend only to unite and place in a clearer light that truth which was before shared between the vulgar and the philosophers:—the former being of opinion, that *those things they immediately perceive are the real things;* and the latter, that *the things immediately perceived are ideas which exist only in the mind.* Which two notions, put together, do, in effect, constitute the substance of what I advance.

Hyl. I have been a long time distrusting my senses; methought I saw things by a dim light, and through false glasses. Now the glasses are removed, and a new light breaks in upon my understanding. I am clearly convinced that I see things in their native forms, and am no longer in pain about their *unknown natures* or *absolute existence.* This is the state I find myself in at present: though, indeed, the course that brought me to it I do not yet thoroughly comprehend. You set out upon the same principles that Academics, Cartesians, and the like sects usually do; and for a long time it looked as if you were advancing their Philosophical Scepticism; but, in the end, your conclusions are directly opposite to theirs.

Phil. You see, Hylas, the water of yonder fountain, how it is forced upwards, in a round column, to a certain height; at which it breaks, and falls back into the basin from whence it rose; its ascent as well as descent proceeding from the same uniform law or principle of *gravitation.* Just so, the same Principles which, at first view, lead to Scepticism, pursued to a certain point, bring men back to Common Sense.

SECOND PART

THE VISIBLE WORLD

A DIVINE LANGUAGE

SELECTIONS FROM

BERKELEY'S 'NEW THEORY OF VISION,' 'ALCIPHRON,
OR THE MINUTE PHILOSOPHER,' AND THE
'THEORY OF VISION VINDICATED'

Mens agitat molem.—VIRGIL.
Homo Naturae minister et interpres.—BACON.

PREFATORY NOTE

THE *Essay towards a New Theory of Vision* was published in 1709, a year before the *Principles*. It is the first in chronological order of those writings of Berkeley, illustrated in the Second Part of the *Selections*, which,—ostensibly concerned with the Visible World, the psychology of the Senses and sense-suggestion,—treat by implication of the philosophy of Science, and ultimately of our knowledge of God. Twenty-three years after the publication of the juvenile *Theory of Vision*, theological inferences involved in that theory were deduced in *Alciphron, or the Minute Philosopher*, in a Dialogue on the Visible World interpreted as the language of God. And in the following year this thought was pursued in the *Theory of Visual Language Further Vindicated and Explained*. The selections which follow are taken from these three works, harmonised by the foregoing Philosophical Principles.

According to Berkeley's Principles, the supposition that Matter exists independently of a percipient mind is unintelligible: it involves the absurdity of experience existing without any one living to make experience real.

Yet all bodies exist 'without mind,' if what is meant by 'without' is, that they are extended or exist 'in space.' And that they thus exist in space, or consist of *partes extra partes*, cannot be doubted. Do we not *see* them so existing in seeing that they are extended; and also in seeing that each extra-organic body is *placed* relatively to other extra-organic bodies, and to the living body of the percipient? What, Berkeley asks, is the deepest and truest meaning of 'outness' or 'externality'; and is the *outwardness* of bodies originally seen? This question leads us into the heart of the psychology of external perception.

The *New Theory of Vision* is so far Berkeley's answer. But in it he holds in reserve the bolder doctrine of his book of *Principles*, namely, that the material world cannot in *any* of its qualities exist out of living perception: he is satisfied with the more limited conclusion, that *coloured extension* is dependent on a percipient who can see. The claim to independent externality on behalf of what is perceived by *touch* is meanwhile postponed. He argues that, because outwardness is unintelligible apart from the experience we have when we touch things and move our bodies, therefore it cannot be perceived originally by *sight*. This argument should be examined critically by the student, as a central part of the psychology of the Senses and the rise of mere sense-perception into physical science.

Berkeley's account of the Visible World advances from the things of sense in their relation to our organism, through their natural laws as interpreted in the physical sciences, to our faith in Divine or Universal Mind, as the philosophical explanation of all changes of the sensible world, and therefore as the ultimate *rationale* of sense-perception. So our power of seeing things in 'ambient space' is virtually a power of seeing interpretable signs of the constant agency of God.

The *Essay on Vision* was the first elaborate attempt to show that our ordinary visual perceptions of extended things are not our *original* perceptions of Sight; that they are *expectations* which are so connected with what we see, that sight becomes foresight. According to Adam Smith this theory is 'one of the finest examples of philosophical analysis that is to be found either in our own or in any other language.' 'Whatever I say upon the subject,' he adds, 'if not directly borrowed from Berkeley, has been suggested by what he has said.' Berkeley refers the early growth of our knowledge of space, in its three dimensions of length, breadth, and thickness, to ideas of contact, muscular resistance, and locomotive effort that are suggested by visual sensations, with which they have been connected in our experience. The former in process of time by habit come to do duty for the latter; so that we can be admonished by this language seeing of what sensations of touch will affect us, at such and such distances of time, in consequence of such and such actions.

Berkeley started with the assumption that Colour is the proper and direct object of sight. Without denying that the colour we see is superficially extended, he analysed coloured extension, in order to show that this extension is different in kind from the extension presented to us in touch, in which he holds that real 'outness' consists. He argues that when one sees a thing 'at a distance,' he is really foreseeing coming sensations, of which what he sees are the signs. *Seeing becomes predicting.* If people never experienced locomotive sensations, they could not understand what the word Space means; for it means *room to move in*,—an idea we could not have had without experience of movement. The so-called 'sight' of outwardness is therefore power of interpreting visual phenomena. This power, he further argues, is (*a*) not instinctive; (*b*) nor so connected with what we originally see that it can be realised *a priori*: it is (*c*) gradually suggested, in the same way as words suggest their meanings in human languages.

This is the answer given by Berkeley to the question, How it comes to pass that we *learn* to perceive, by what we see, what is not seen; and what indeed neither resembles, nor causes, nor is caused by, nor has any necessary connexion with what is seen? This answer implies that what we see is connected with its tactual meaning by natural law; not merely by the tendency to associate ideas that have by accident often been together in our experience. The ultimate reason of Law in Nature, or the philosophy of natural Science (almost unconsciously on the part of Berkeley) is thus proposed for reflection. Natural law is resolved into *divinely* established connexion among the phenomena of which nature is composed: this connexion is said to be 'arbitrary,' because God might have made the law different. This *arbitrariness* is what Berkeley intends in his metaphor of external nature as 'Visual Language.' But the 'arbitrariness' must not be confounded with caprice; for it means the perfectly rational will of the Divine Agent. An important difference between the words of men, and the words daily addressed to us by God in the providential language of the senses is, that the connexion between human words and their meanings is due to human convention, whereas the connexion between *what we see* and *the experience which in consequence we expect* is grounded on faith in the reasonable Will of God. As he puts it, 'visible ideas are the language whereby the Governing Spirit, on whom we depend, informs us what tangible ideas He is about to imprint upon us, in case we excite this or that motion in our own bodies.' When applied to the phenomena presented in the five senses, and not merely in sight, this implies that Order in Nature is the expression of Divine Rational Will—that the Natural Government of things is subordinate in the Divine System of the Universe to the Moral Government of persons—and that our knowledge of the natural laws of the material world cannot be *a priori*, but must be gathered by experiment.

Berkeley's psychological analysis of seeing implies that if

a person born blind were suddenly endowed with sight, he could *at first* have no knowledge of visual outness; that the visible world must all seem to be 'in his mind,' prior to further experience. This is a conclusion which might be tested by experiments on individuals as well as by mental analysis. Appropriate tests would be—(*a*) cases of born-blind persons who have been made to see; (*b*) the imagination of space possessed by the born-blind; (*c*) experiments on persons able to see, but who had no sense of movement (if such persons could be found); (*d*) facts of sight in human infants; (*e*) in the lower animals. Berkeley contributes no original observations gathered on any of these fields.

His discussions on Visual Signs and their interpretation may be used by the student as aids to the study of the human mind in its ascent from the Five Senses and their original perceptions, by sensuous Imagination through suggestion; inductive discovery of laws in Nature, with the ground in reason of scientific inferences; all culminating in recognition of the relation between natural order and the Supreme Active Reason that operates beyond and within Nature.

In the 'Dialogue on Visual Language' which follows the selections from the 'New Theory,' the subject is unfolded in its theological relations. The significant phenomena presented in sight are taken as striking illustrations of the omnipresent agency of God, and as affording the same sort of assurance of the presence of God as we have of the presence of our fellow men when they stand before us and speak to us.

I have appended to the Second Part some extracts from Berkeley's 'Vindication' of this conception of Vision as Divine Language — the last philosophical publication of his middle life, which appeared in 1733, in which, with added explanations, the subject is presented in some fresh lights.

The rationale of Theism that is offered in Berkeley's visual psychology lies in his treatment of Natural Order as virtually the language of omnipresent Deity. He leaves too much in the background the still deeper conception of Omnipotent Goodness in the omnipresent Power, and the ethico-theological presupposition that is implied in our confidence in natural law and in the original constitution of man.

I

A NEW THEORY OF VISION

1. My *design* is (*a*) to shew the manner wherein we perceive by Sight the Distance, Magnitude, and Situation of objects; also (*b*) to consider the difference there is betwixt the ideas of Sight and Touch, and whether there be any idea common to both senses [1].

2. It is, I think, agreed by all that Distance, of itself and immediately, cannot be seen. For, distance being a line directed endwise to the eye, it projects only one point in the fund of the eye, which point remains invariably the same, whether the distance be longer or shorter [2].

---

[1] The design is, to compare the phenomena immediately presented in Sight with those immediately presented in Touch, and to show how we learn gradually in *seeing* to apprehend *invisible* phenomena of the natural world. It is an analysis of the genesis of our adult perception of visible things. It is founded upon deductions from the laws and tendencies of the human mind, as these operate in the adult, but are latent in infancy. From this we are naturally led to consider the office of all the Senses, and the expansion of sense-perception in the formation of science, in connexion with this analysis of Sight, 'the most perfect and delightful' of them.

[2] Sect. 2–51 explain how we seem to 'see' Distance, or an interval between two points, one of which is invisible. Sect. 2 takes for granted, but without distinct proof or adequate definition of terms, that distance is necessarily invisible *directly*, and that it can be seen only through the medium of visual signs by which it is suggested. Now the 'distance'

3. I find it also acknowledged that the estimate we make of the distance of objects *considerably remote* is rather an act of judgment [1] grounded on experience than of sense. For example, when I perceive a great number of intermediate objects, such as houses, fields, rivers, and the like, which I have experienced to take up a considerable space, I thence form a judgment or conclusion, that the object I see beyond them is at a great distance. Again, when an object appears faint and small which at a near distance I have experienced to make a vigorous and large appearance, I instantly conclude it to be far off.—And this, it is evident, is the result of experience; without which, from the faintness and littleness, I should not have inferred anything concerning the distance of objects [2].

intended seems to be space in its third dimension, i.e. depth, or outness from the eye in the line of sight; not superficial extension. In relation to the distance which cannot be seen—viz. depth, or distance which is in the line of sight—the percipient is supposed to be *at the end* of a straight line, the interval between the two extremes of which must be invisible, because only one of them can be present. When we see superficial distance, on the other hand, we are *at the side*, and not at the end of the line—at a point where the distance forms a larger or smaller angle with the eye; so that this sort of distance is called *lateral, transverse,* or *angular.* Any distance that is strictly in the line of sight, in order to become visible, must, by a change in the point of view of the percipient, be as it were transformed into lateral distance, i.e. from a relation in the third dimension of space into plane superficial extension. But it has then ceased to be the sort of distance that is invisible.

Some of Berkeley's critics have referred to sect. 2 as if it fully stated his famous 'theory of vision,' and also his 'argument in support of it.' It is merely a statement of one of the alleged facts on which the theory rests.

[1] See the account of what Locke calls *judgment* (i.e. faith in probability), in his *Essay*, b. IV. ch. 14, 15, 16. Like Berkeley here, Locke opposes it, as 'grounded on experience' with its contingencies, to *knowledge proper,* which is due to intuition or to demonstration.

[2] What does Berkeley, here and in what follows, intend by '*necessary* connexion'? Is it only a factitious, *a posteriori* necessity; generated, as Hume would say, by custom objectively manifested in nature, and consequent habit generated in the individual and the race? Or is it a

4. But, when an object is placed at so near a distance as that the interval between the eyes bears any sensible proportion to it, the opinion of speculative men is, that the two optic axes (the fancy that we see only with one eye at once being exploded), concurring at the object, do there make an angle, by means of which, according as it is greater or lesser, the object is perceived to be nearer or farther off.

5. Betwixt which and the foregoing manner of estimating distance there is this remarkable difference ;—that, whereas there was no apparent *necessary*[1] connexion between small distance and a large and strong appearance, or between great distance and a little and faint appearance, there appears a very necessary connexion between an obtuse angle and near distance, and an acute angle and farther distance. It does not in the least depend upon experience, but may be evidently known by any one before he had experienced it, that the nearer the concurrence of the optic axes the greater the angle, and the remoter their concurrence is the lesser will be the angle comprehended by them[2].

necessity due to the eternal constitution of things? That it is meant to be more than the former seems implied in the subsequent analysis of our faith in the actual laws of nature into 'suggestion' determined by custom. Necessity he illustrates by pure mathematics; although the outcome of this *Essay* tends to refer mathematical necessity itself to the will of God.

[1] What artists call aerial and linear perspectives are here taken as acknowledged signs of 'considerably remote' distances. But the main question is, *the manner in which* we learn to see *near* distances in the line of sight outwards. In Berkeley's day even, it was 'agreed by all' that 'the remoter distances' outwards are 'suggested' by 'arbitrary signs'; near distances were supposed to be demonstrated from (not merely suggested by) necessary relations of lines and angles. This last supposition Berkeley proceeds to refute in the following sections.

[2] Here again, what *sort* of 'necessity' does he intend in the connexion (§§ 5, 7) between angles and distances, and between divergency of rays and degrees of distance? The varieties in the possible meaning of the ambiguous term 'necessity' (which may be either logical,

6. There is another way, mentioned by optic writers, whereby they will have us judge of those distances in respect of which the breadth of the pupil hath any sensible bigness. And that is the greater or lesser divergency of the rays, which, issuing from the visible point, do fall on the pupil—that point being judged nearest which is seen by most diverging rays, and that remoter which is seen by less diverging rays; and so on, the apparent distance still increasing, as the divergency of the rays decreases, till at length it becomes infinite when the rays that fall on the pupil are to sense parallel. And after this manner it is said we perceive distance when we look only with one eye.

7. In this case also it is plain we are not beholden to experience: it being a certain, necessary truth that, the nearer the direct rays falling on the eye approach to a parallelism, the farther off is the point of their intersection, or the visible point from whence they flow.

8. Now though the accounts here given of perceiving *near* distance by sight are received for true, and accordingly made use of in determining the apparent places of objects, they do nevertheless seem to me very unsatisfactory, and that for these following reasons:—

9. *First*, It is evident that, when the mind perceives any idea, not immediately and of itself, it must be by the means of some other idea. Thus, for instance, the passions which are in the mind of another are of themselves to me invisible. I may nevertheless perceive them by sight, though not immediately, yet by means of the colours they produce in

---

mathematical, metaphysical, physical, or moral necessity) should be here distinguished by the student. Is there ground for *ultimately* distinguishing the necessity in virtue of which *this* is the cause of *that* from the necessity for *a* cause of *every* change; also for distinguishing mathematical from metaphysical necessity; and both from the logical obligation to avoid a contradiction in terms?

the countenance. We often see shame or fear in the looks of a man, by perceiving the changes of his countenance to red or pale.

10. Moreover, it is evident that no idea[1] which is not itself perceived can be to me the means of perceiving any other idea[2]. If I do not perceive the redness or paleness of a man's face themselves, it is impossible I should perceive by them the passions which are in his mind.

11. Now, from sect. 2, it is plain that distance is in its own nature imperceptible[3]; and yet it is perceived by sight. It remains, therefore, that it be brought into view by means of some other idea, that is itself immediately perceived in the act of vision.

12. But those lines and angles by means whereof some men pretend to explain the perception of distance, are themselves not at all perceived, nor are they in truth ever thought of by those unskilful in optics. I appeal to any one's experience, whether, upon sight of an object, he computes its distance by the bigness of the angle made by the meeting of the two optic axes? or whether he ever thinks of the greater or lesser divergency of the rays which arrive from any point to his pupil? nay, whether it be not perfectly impossible for him to perceive by sense the various angles wherewith the rays, according to their greater or lesser divergence, do fall on the eye? Every one is himself the best judge of what he perceives, and what not. In vain

---

[1] 'idea,' here as elsewhere = phenomenon presented in sense.

[2] Here 'perceived' means apprehending *immediate* data of sense: 'perceiving' sometimes means being aware through what he calls 'suggestion') of what is signified by sense-given data. So in the following sections what is 'imperceptible,' because not actually felt in sense, is yet 'perceived,' i.e. 'judged' through suggestion. The former is immediate, and the latter acquired perception.

[3] That is to say, distance outwards or in the line of sight, is not immediately presentable in sense—cannot be an idea or phenomenon so presented. Accordingly it must be perceived through some sign.

shall any man tell me, that I perceive certain lines and angles which introduce into my mind the various ideas of distance, so long as I myself am conscious of no such thing.

13. Since therefore those angles and lines are not themselves perceived by sight, it follows, from sect. 10, that the mind does not by them judge of the distance of objects.

14. *Secondly*, The truth of this assertion will be yet farther evident to any one that considers those lines and angles have no real existence in nature, being only an hypothesis framed by the mathematicians, and by them introduced into optics that they might treat of that science in a geometrical way.

15. The *third* and last reason I shall give for rejecting that doctrine is, that though we should grant the real existence of those optic angles, &c., and that it was possible for the mind to perceive them, yet these principles would not be found sufficient to explain the phenomena of distance, as shall be shewn hereafter.

16. Now, it being already shewn that distance is *suggested*[1]

---

[1] Note in § 16 the first use in the *Essay* of the term SUGGESTION— already referred to as expressive of the way in which our acquired power of *interpreting what we see*, and thus *going beyond bare visual sense of colour*, is explained by Berkeley. He explains acquired visual perception by resolving it into what he calls suggestion.—An important question is, What does he mean by Suggestion? Is it more than blind Habit? Does it involve reason? (See *Vindication*, sect. 42.) The answer to this question goes (so far) to settle Berkeley's starting-point, as either empirical like Hume's, or as anticipating Reid, if not even Kant, in this constructive principle of his early philosophy. — Reid, in his *Inquiry*, often uses the word 'suggestion' when treating of the five senses, and the relations of their data to one another, making it mean conviction of which no further explanation can be given than what he calls the Common Sense. 'I know no word,' he says, 'more proper than *suggestion* to express a power of the mind which seems entirely to have escaped the notice of philosophers, and to which we owe many of our simple notions which are neither impressions nor ideas, as well as many original principles of belief. . . . There is a sort of suggestion which is not natural or original: it is the result of experience and habit. . . .

to the mind, by the mediation of some other idea which is itself perceived in the act of seeing, it remains that we inquire *what* ideas or sensations there be that attend vision unto which we may suppose the ideas of distance are connected, and by which they are introduced into the mind[1].

But I think it appears that there are also *natural suggestions*, e. g. that sensation suggests the notion of present existence, and the belief that what we perceive or feel does now exist; that memory suggests the notion of past existence, and the belief that what we remember did exist in time past; and that our sensations and thoughts suggest the notion of a mind, and the belief of its existence, and of its relation to our thoughts. By a like natural principle it is that a beginning of existence, or any change in nature, suggests to us the notion of a cause, and compels our belief of its existence. And in like manner, certain sensations of touch, by the constitution of our nature, suggest to us extension, solidity, and motion, which are nowise like sensations, although they have been hitherto confounded with them' (*Inquiry*, ch. II. sect. 7). 'This class of intimations,' says Stewart, with reference to this passage, 'result from *the original frame of the human mind*, and were quite overlooked by Berkeley.'—The question which Berkeley would solve by 'suggestion' is really the great one afterwards proposed by Hume, in his *Inquiry concerning Human Understanding*, section IV, and which the remainder of that work is an attempt to answer:—' What is the nature of that evidence which assures us of any matter of fact that lies *beyond* the present testimony of our senses or the records of our memory?' This is just to ask what the ultimate constructive principle of our sciences of nature is, in virtue of which present phenomena of sense issue first in *acquired perceptions*, and then in *physical science*. That, Hume says, is Custom. With Berkeley sense-perception is evolved by 'suggestion,' to which the origin of our judgments of Extension is referred. Berkeley's explanation may be compared with Kant's, by whom phenomena of sense were supposed to be translated into perceptions, under 'forms' that belong to intellect and not to sense, but which are true, because they are forms under which phenomena *must* be experienced by *us* if they are experienced at all. Compare Berkeley's 'suggestion' also with the transformed sensations of Condillac, and with the 'principle of common sense' of Reid.

The truth seems to be that Berkeley's 'suggestion' means *habit*, but habit that may be *unconsciously* rational. One result of what he says is to show the efficacy of early habits.

[1] §§ 16-27 give three sorts of 'arbitrary signs' of 'near distances'—recognition of their *arbitrariness* being what Berkeley considers the

And, *first*, it is certain by experience, that when we look at a near object with both eyes, according as it approaches or recedes from us, we alter the disposition of our eyes, by lessening or widening the interval between the pupils. This disposition or turn of the eyes is attended with a sensation [1], which seems to me to be that which in this case brings the idea of greater or lesser distance into the mind.

17. Not that there is any natural or necessary connexion between the sensation we perceive by the turn of the eyes and greater or lesser distance. But—because the mind has, by constant experience, found the different sensations corresponding to the different dispositions of the eyes to be attended each with a different degree of distance in the object—there has grown an habitual or customary connexion [2] between those two sorts of ideas; so that the mind no sooner perceives the sensation arising from the different turn it gives the eyes, in order to bring the pupils nearer or farther asunder, but it withal perceives the different idea of distance which was wont to be connected with that sensation. Just as, upon hearing a certain sound, the idea is immediately suggested to the understanding which custom had united with it.

18. Nor do I see how I can easily be mistaken in this matter. I know evidently that distance is not perceived of

---

important outcome of his whole investigation into vision, as it empties natural law and physical science of *a priori* necessity, reducing them to effects of Divine will which form an interpretable language.

[1] This *muscular* 'sensation' connected with this adjustment of the eye is of course not itself *seen*: it is *felt*. It may be called *visual*, but it is not *visible*. Thus the visual signs through which we learn to see things in their places are some of them (like this one) invisible while others are seen.

[2] The 'customary connexion,' elsewhere called arbitrary, is not therefore capricious. The 'suggestions' to which it gives rise may involve unconscious reason; and 'arbitrary' may be understood to mean *reasonable will*, as opposed to *blind necessity*—and this divine arbitrariness would be the constant motive power of the universe.

itself—that, by consequence, it must be perceived by means of some other idea, which is immediately perceived, and varies with the different degrees of distance. I know also that the sensation arising from the turn of the eyes is of itself immediately perceived, and various degrees thereof are connected with different distances, which never fail to accompany them into my mind, when I view an object distinctly with both eyes whose distance is so small that in respect of it the interval between the eyes has any considerable magnitude.

19. I know it is a received opinion that, by altering the disposition of the eyes, the mind perceives whether the angle of the optic axes, or the lateral angles comprehended between the interval of the eyes or the optic axes, are made greater or lesser; and that, accordingly, by a kind of natural geometry, it judges the point of their intersection to be nearer or farther off. But that this is not true I am convinced by my own experience, since I am not conscious that I make any such use of the perception I have by the turn of my eyes. And for me to make those judgments, and draw those conclusions from it, without knowing that I do so, seems altogether incomprehensible.

20. From all which it follows, that the judgment we make of the distance of an object viewed with both eyes is entirely the result of experience[1]. If we had not constantly found certain sensations, arising from the various dispositions of the eyes, attended with certain degrees of distance, we should never make those sudden judgments from them concerning the distance of objects; no more than we would pretend to judge of a man's thought by his pronouncing words we had never heard before.

---

[1] 'Experience,' i.e. phenomena presented to the senses, at first automatically organised into experience by 'suggestion'—which he held sufficient to explain the 'judgment,' or presumption of probability, that is latent in acquired perception.

21. *Secondly*, an object placed at a certain distance from the eye, to which the breadth of the pupil bears a considerable proportion, being made to approach, is seen more confusedly. And the nearer it is brought the more confused appearance it makes. And, this being found constantly to be so, there arises in the mind an habitual connexion between the several degrees of confusion and distance; the greater confusion still implying the lesser distance, and the lesser confusion the greater distance of the object [1].

22. This confused appearance of the object doth therefore seem to be the medium whereby the mind judges of distance, in those cases wherein the most approved writers of optics will have it judge by the different divergency with which the rays flowing from the radiating point fall on the pupil. No man, I believe, will pretend to see or feel those imaginary angles that the rays are supposed to form according to their various inclinations on his eye. But he cannot choose seeing whether the object appear more or less confused. It is therefore a manifest consequence from what has been demonstrated that, instead of the greater or lesser divergency of the rays, the mind makes use of the greater or lesser confusedness of the appearance, thereby to determine the apparent place of an object.

23. Nor doth it avail to say there is not any necessary connexion between confused vision and distance great or small. For I ask any man what necessary connexion he sees between the redness of a blush and shame? And yet no sooner shall he behold that colour to arise in the face of another but it brings into his mind the idea of that passion which hath been observed to accompany it.

---

[1] This explanation of our acquired power of seeing *near* distances, tends towards an acknowledgment of what is now called Inseparable Association. See Mill's *Examination of Hamilton*, ch. XIV. But can scientific experience be resolved into blind association? It may explain, in a physical way, connexions in an individual mind; surely not the perception of objective reality.

24. What seems to have misled the writers of optics in this matter is, that they imagine men judge of distance as they do of a conclusion in mathematics; betwixt which and the premises it is indeed absolutely requisite there be an apparent necessary connexion [1]. But it is far otherwise in the sudden judgments men make of distance. We are not to think that brutes and children, or even grown reasonable men, whenever they perceive an object to approach or depart from them, do it by virtue of geometry and demonstration.

25. That one idea may suggest another to the mind, it will suffice that they have been observed to go together, without any demonstration of the necessity of their coexistence, or without as much as knowing what it is that makes them so to coexist. Of this there are innumerable instances, of which no one can be ignorant [2].

26. Thus, greater confusion having been constantly attended with nearer distance, no sooner is the former idea perceived but it suggests the latter to our thoughts. And, if it had been the ordinary course of nature that the farther off an object were placed the more confused it should appear, it is certain the very same perception that now makes us think an object approaches would then have

---

[1] In this Berkeley thus early seems to recognise intellectual necessity in mathematical demonstration.

[2] Here and throughout Berkeley presupposes a natural tendency in each person to connect in his thoughts, ever after, those phenomena of sense which have been connected in his previous experience—a tendency the strength of which may be so confirmed through repetition, that *his* mind at last *becomes unable* to separate them. This is the *associative* tendency, since made so much of by some psychologists, which thus, with Berkeley as with Aristotle, is mixed up with the psychology of the senses. Because it is dependent on the variable experience of each person, it has been called a *subjective* law or tendency, in contrast to relations which issue from irreversible necessities that are of the essence of reason, and therefore common to all intelligence. The difference between the blind tendency to associate and the necessary relations of reason is obscured in association psychology.

made us to imagine it went farther off—that perception, abstracting from custom and experience, being equally fitted to produce the idea of great distance, or small distance, or no distance at all.

27. *Thirdly*, an object being placed at the distance above specified, and brought nearer to the eye, we may nevertheless prevent, at least for some time, the appearance's growing more confused, by straining the eye. In which case that sensation supplies the place of confused vision, in aiding the mind to judge of the distance of the object; it being esteemed so much the nearer by how much the effort or straining of the eye in order to distinct vision is greater.

28. I have here set down those *sensations* or *ideas* that seem to be the constant and general occasions of introducing into the mind the different ideas of near distance. It is true, in most cases, that divers other circumstances contribute to frame our idea of distance, viz. the particular number, size, kind, &c. of the things seen[1]. Concerning which, as well as all other the forementioned occasions which suggest distance, I shall only observe, they have none of them, in their own nature, any relation or connexion with it: nor is it possible they should ever signify the various degrees thereof, otherwise than as by experience they have been found to be connected with them[2].

. . . .

---

[1] *Visible* signs mix with those that are *merely visual*. The latter appear to be *felt in the eye*, but are not themselves *seen*.

[2] The visual 'signs' given in the preceding sections are all either (*a*) visible or (*b*) *invisible*. Under neither head is Berkeley's list exhaustive, nor even accurate as far as it goes. Recent German and British physiologists have discovered others: Müller, Helmholtz, and Lotze have mentioned visual signs not recognised by Berkeley. The student should here generalise the chief visual signs of the distances of objects, including the muscular sensations which accompany focal adjustment of the crystalline lens; the muscular sensations due to convergence of the axes of both eyes; the smallness and indistinctness

41. From what hath been premised, it is a manifest consequence, that a man born blind, being made to see, would at first have no idea of Distance by sight: the sun and stars, the remotest objects as well as the nearer, would all seem to be in his eye, or rather in his mind[1]. The objects intromitted by sight would seem to him (as in truth they are) no other than a new set of thoughts or sensations, each whereof is as near to him as the perceptions of pain or pleasure, or the most inward passions of his soul. For, our judging objects perceived by sight to be at any distance, or without the mind, is (vid. sect. 28) entirely the effect of experience, which one in those circumstances could not yet have attained to.

42. It is indeed otherwise upon the common supposition —that men judge of distance by the angle of the optic axes, just as one in the dark, or a blind man by the angle comprehended by two sticks, one whereof he held in each hand. For, if this were true, it would follow that one blind from his birth, being made to see, should stand in need of no new experience, in order to perceive distance by sight. But that this is false has, I think, been sufficiently demonstrated[2].

of the visible image; the number of intervening objects; as well as the phenomena of binocular vision. But these and other matters of biological psychology were for Berkeley questions of detail, irrelevant to the general principle of *divinely arbitrary sense-symbolism* which was mainly in his view. The distinction between the *sensory* and *motor nerves*, important in connexion with the correlative difference between passive and active sense-consciousness, was unknown to him; also much else now known as to the nervous system and its relations by physiological psychologists.

In §§ 29-40, here omitted, Berkeley proceeds to verify his invisible and visible signs, by showing that one class of them can explain a curious optical phenomenon that had baffled Barrow and others.

[1] 'In his eye' and 'in his mind'—i.e. existing *dependently* on the organ, or on the sentient mind.

[2] He does not, as one might expect, ask for *experimental* verification of his conclusions in cases of born-blind persons made to see.

43. ¹And perhaps, upon a strict inquiry, we shall not find that even those who from their birth have grown up in a continued habit of seeing are irrecoverably prejudiced on the other side, to wit, in thinking what they see to be at a distance from them. For, at this time it seems agreed on all hands, by those who have had any thoughts of that matter, *that colours, which are the proper and immediate object of sight*², *are not without the mind*³. But then, it will be said, by *sight* we have *also* the ideas of *extension*, and *figure*, and *motion*; all which may well be thought without and at some distance from the mind, though colour should not. In answer to this, I appeal to any man's experience, whether the visible extension of any object do not appear as near to him as the colour of that object; nay, whether they do not both seem to be in the very same place. Is not the extension we see coloured, and is it

---

¹ Berkeley now advances from (*a*) the argument that our power to see distance *outwards* is due to *suggestion*, and proceeds (*b*) to draw similar conclusions from the fact that *phenomena of colour* are the *only* phenomena which we immediately see. Having shown, by the preceding reasons, that distances outwards, whether near or remote, are not *actually seen*, but are *suggested by divinely arbitrary signs*, he now proceeds to deny the externality of colour—'externality' meaning its being extended in space, in independence of a percipient.

One may here ask, why *touch* is popularly regarded as the test of externality, as when *visibility without tangibility* is supposed to imply that what is seen is illusory unless it can be touched? Berkeley, though he argued for the ideal or mind-dependent nature of what is seen, sooner than for the ideal or mind-dependent nature of what can be touched, does not make the distinction between the illusory and the real turn *ultimately* upon the tangibility of the real. (See *Principles*, sect. 28-33.) But see Mansel's *Metaphysics*, p. 346; also Brown's *Lectures*, xxiv.

² With psychologists generally, since Aristotle (*De Anima*, b. II. ch. 7), he assumes that colour, and whatever colour implies, is the only *original* datum of sight, all else popularly included in 'seeing' being gradually learned through suggestion.

³ 'Not without the mind,' i.e. not independent of sentient intelligence—not able to *exist* without being felt or perceived; therefore incapable of being 'at a distance' from embodied mind.

possible for us, so much as in thought, to separate and abstract colour from extension? Now, where the extension is, there surely is the figure, and there the motion too. I speak of those which are perceived by sight[1].

44. But, for a fuller explication of this point, and to shew that the immediate objects of sight are not so much as the ideas or resemblances of things placed at a distance, it is requisite that we look nearer into the matter, and carefully observe what is meant in common discourse when one says, that which he sees is at a distance from him. Suppose, for example, that looking at the moon I should say it were fifty or sixty semidiameters of the earth distant from me. Let us see what moon this is spoken of. It is plain it cannot be the visible moon, or anything like the visible moon, or that which I see—which is only a round luminous plain, of about thirty visible points in diameter. For, in case I am carried from the place where I stand directly towards the moon, it is manifest the object varies still as I

---

[1] Berkeley started, in § 2, with the *assumption* that *distance in the line of sight is in its nature invisible*; on this foundation he proceeded in the proof, given in §§ 3-28, that all distances outward are perceptions of sight only so far as they are 'suggestions' gradually acquired through experience of the meaning of visual and visible signs.— He enters in this section on a second line of proof. He argues that *what we see cannot be independent of perception*. This is founded on a second assumption, also sustained by concurrent authority—that *colour* is the only immediate or original object of sight. Locke had said that we can see distances between bodies, and between parts of the same body. But does colour involve distance? What Berkeley wants to show is, that 'distance' and 'extension' are ambiguous words —the distances and extensions we see being different in *kind* from those we touch. The common philosophical opinion had been, that light or colour is what we see—including whatever extension is necessarily involved in seeing colour; for it was supposed that colour, as originally seen, was in some sort extended, involving an immediate perception of extension. The question still unconsidered was the nature of *visible* extension. Is it of two dimensions or of three? Is the coloured extension we see identical with, or even similar to, the extension we touch? Berkeley argues that it is not. See §§ 121-46.

go on; and, by the time that I am advanced fifty or sixty semidiameters of the earth, I shall be so far from being near a small, round, luminous flat that I shall perceive nothing like it—this object having long since disappeared, and, if I would recover it, it must be by going back to the earth from whence I set out. Again, suppose I perceive by sight the faint and obscure idea of something, which I doubt whether it be a man, or a tree, or a tower, but judge it to be at the distance of about a mile. It is plain I cannot mean that what I see is a mile off, or that it is the image or likeness of anything which is a mile off; since that every step I take towards it the appearance alters, and from being obscure, small, and faint, grows clear, large, and vigorous. And when I come to the mile's end, that which I saw first is quite lost, neither do I find anything in the likeness of it [1].

45. In these and the like instances, the truth of the matter, I find, stands thus:—Having of a long time experienced

---

[1] The sceptical objections of the Eleatics and others to the trustworthiness of our senses, referred to by Descartes in his *Meditations*, and by Malebranche in the first book of his *Recherche*, may have suggested the illustrations in this section. The sceptical difficulty rises out of the assumption that the extended colour we see, when the tangible object is near, is the *same* extended colour that we see, when the tangible object is more remote. Berkeley insists that what is *seen* in these cases is different, but that *what is signified or suggested by what is seen* may still be the same. He does not here pursue the deeper question of what is ultimately meant by *sameness* in sensible things—foreign to an Essay on Sight. This he had to meet in defending his conception of Matter, as necessarily dependent on percipient mind.

Compare, and analyse critically, Hume's illustration of his position —that 'nothing can be present to the mind but an image or perception,' and that the senses are only 'inlets through which these images are conveyed, without being able to produce any immediate intercourse between the mind and the [outward] object. *The table which we see* seems to diminish as we remove further from it: but *the real table* which exists independent of us suffers no alteration' (*Essay on* 'Sceptical Philosophy,' Part 1).

certain ideas perceivable by *touch*[1]—as distance, tangible figure, and solidity—to have been connected with certain ideas of sight, I do, upon perceiving these ideas of sight, forthwith conclude what tangible ideas are, by the wonted ordinary course of nature, like to follow. Looking at an object, I perceive a certain visible figure and colour, with some degree of faintness and other circumstances, which, from what I have formally observed, determine me to think that if I advance forward so many paces, miles, &c., I shall be affected with such and such ideas of touch. So that, in truth and strictness of speech, I neither see distance itself, nor anything that I take to be at a distance. I say, neither distance nor things placed at a distance are themselves, or their ideas, truly perceived by sight. This I am persuaded of, as to what concerns myself. And I believe whoever will look narrowly into his own thoughts, and examine what he means by saying he sees this or that thing at a distance, will agree with me, that what he sees only *suggests* to his understanding that, after having passed a certain distance, *to be measured by the motion of his body, which is perceivable by touch*, he shall come to perceive such and such tangible ideas, which have been usually connected with such and such visible ideas[2]. But, that one might be deceived by

[1] This is the first introduction of the phenomena of 'touch'—a term which with Berkeley includes not merely (*a*) the *sense of simple contact*, but also (*b*) the *sense of muscular resistance*, and (*c*) the *sentient activity connected with the movements of our bodies, or any of their organs*. From this point he begins to unfold his antithesis of the visible and the tangible worlds—*coloured* and *resistant* extension. To explain by 'suggestion' the union of these opposite elements in our *acquired* perceptions of sight is the aim of this theory of Visual Symbolism, or tactual meanings in visual signs.

[2] The important office of our sensuous consciousness of bodily movement and muscular resistance, in the development of self-consciousness and knowledge of extra-organic things, might be illustrated in connexion with this fact. It is in our active collision with the material world that we begin to distinguish between 'I can' and 'I cannot'; and the conceptions and convictions of personality, personal identity, and personal responsibility are thus gradually drawn forth.

these suggestions of sense, and that there is no necessary connexion between visible and tangible ideas suggested by them, we need go no farther than the next looking-glass or picture to be convinced[1].—Note that, when I speak of tangible ideas, I take the word *idea* for any the immediate object of sense or understanding—in which large signification it is commonly used by the moderns[2].

46. From what we have shewn, it is a manifest consequence that the ideas of Space, Outness, and things placed at a distance are not, strictly speaking, the object of sight: they are not otherwise perceived by the eye than by the ear. Sitting in my study I hear a coach drive along the street; I look through the casement and see it; I walk out and enter into it. Thus, common speech would incline one to think I heard, saw, and touched the same thing, to wit, the coach. It is nevertheless certain the ideas intromitted by each sense are widely different, and distinct from each other; but, having been observed constantly to go together, they are spoken of as one and the same thing. By the variation of the noise, I perceive the different distances of the coach, and know that it approaches before I look out. Thus, by the ear I perceive distance just after the same manner as I do by the eye[3].

---

[1] Consider and examine critically the meaning and relevancy of this illustration.

[2] 'moderns'—Locke and Descartes for instance. With Locke (*Essay*, Introduction, § 8), 'ideas' mean whatever we are conscious of— 'whatsoever is the object of the understanding when a man thinks;' and what we are conscious, i.e. immediately percipient of, in sense-perception, includes primary qualities of things, and also sensations which the primary qualities are supposed to occasion, namely, secondary qualities. By Descartes, 'idea' was sometimes applied to the mental perception and sometimes to the organic motion or physical impression with which the perception was believed to be connected by Divine appointment.

[3] In short the 'perception' in both cases is a 'suggested' expectation. Acquired sight is foresight.

47. I do not nevertheless say I hear distance, in like manner as I say that I see it—the ideas perceived by hearing not being so apt to be confounded with the ideas of touch as those of sight are. So likewise a man is easily convinced that bodies and external things are not properly the object of hearing, but only sounds—by the mediation whereof the idea of this or that body, or distance, is suggested to his thoughts[1]. But then one is with more difficulty brought to discern the difference there is betwixt the ideas of sight and touch: though it be certain, a man no more sees and feels the same thing, than he hears and feels the same thing.

48. One reason of which seems to be this. It is thought a great absurdity to imagine that one and the same thing should have any more than one extension and one figure. But, the extension and figure of a body being let into the mind two ways, and that indifferently, either by sight or touch, it seems to follow that we see the same extension and the same figure which we feel.

49. But, if we take a close and accurate view of the matter, it must be acknowledged that *we never see and feel one and the same object.* That which is seen is one thing, and that which is felt is another. If the visible figure and extension be not the same with the tangible figure and extension, we are not to infer that one and the same thing has divers extensions. The true consequence is that the objects of sight and touch are two distinct things. It may perhaps require some thought rightly to conceive this distinction.

---

[1] The original data peculiar to the sense of Hearing should be here analysed by the student, and compared with those of Sight and of Touch, as systems of audible and visual signs. The chief natural languages of sense, as well as all verbal or articulate languages, consist either of audible signs or of visual signs. Visible signs it should be remembered are seen, whereas visual signs may be felt in the organ of sight without being seen—e. g. motions in the eye, &c.

And the difficulty seems not a little increased, because the combination of visible ideas hath constantly the same name as the combination of tangible ideas wherewith it is connected—which doth of necessity arise from the use and end of language.

50. In order, therefore, to treat accurately and unconfusedly of vision, we must bear in mind that there are two sorts of objects apprehended by the eye—the one primarily and immediately, the other secondarily and by intervention of the former. Those of the first sort neither are nor appear to be without the mind, or at any distance off. They may, indeed, grow greater or smaller, more confused, or more clear, or more faint. But they do not, cannot approach or recede from us. Whenever we say an object is at a distance, whenever we say it draws near, or goes farther off, we must always mean it of the latter sort, which properly belong to the touch, and are not so truly *perceived* as *suggested* by the eye, in like manner as thoughts by the ear[1].

51. No sooner do we hear the words of a familiar language pronounced in our ears but the ideas corresponding thereto present themselves to our minds: in the very same instant the sound and its meaning enter the understanding; so closely are they united that it is not in our power to keep out the one except we exclude the other also. We even act in all respects as if we heard the very thoughts themselves. So likewise the secondary objects, or those which are only suggested by sight, do often more strongly affect us, and are more regarded, than the proper objects of that sense; a'ong with which they enter into the mind, and with which they have a far more strict connexion than ideas have with words. Hence it is we find it so difficult to discriminate between

---

[1] Whether what is perceived in touching is as dependent on a percipient mind as what is perceived in seeing, Berkeley does not discuss in this juvenile *Essay*. That is the wider question considered in his *Principles of Human Knowledge*.

the immediate and mediate[1] objects of sight, and are so prone to attribute to the former what belongs only to the latter. They are, as it were, most closely twisted, blended, and incorporated together. And the prejudice is confirmed and riveted in our thoughts by a long tract of time, by the use of language, and want of reflection. However, I doubt not but any one that shall attentively consider what we have already said, and shall say upon this subject before we have done (especially if he pursue it in his own thoughts), may be able to deliver himself from that prejudice. Sure I am, it is worth some attention to whoever would understand the true nature of vision[2].

52. I have now done with distance, and proceed to shew how it is that we perceive by sight the Magnitude of objects[3]. —It is the opinion of some that we do it by angles, or by angles in conjunction with distance. But, neither angles nor distance being perceivable by sight, and the things we see[4] being in truth at no distance from us, it follows that, as we have shewn lines and angles not to be the medium the mind makes use of in apprehending the apparent place, so neither are they the medium whereby it apprehends the apparent magnitude of objects.

53. It is well known that the same extension at a near

---

[1] 'mediate' or suggested.

[2] The attempt to define the original data of any of the senses *taken singly* illustrates this difficulty; but it is more obtrusive in sight and in touch, because perception of extension, and discernment of its relations (the chief difficulty in the analysis), seem to occur in visual and tactual perceptions exclusively. In his *Commonplace Book* (p. 494) Berkeley well remarks that 'extension is *blended* with tangible or visible ideas, and afterwards by the mind prescinded [abstracted] therefrom.'

[3] Sect. 52-87 treat of the necessary invisibility of the real Magnitudes of things—the tactual distances between their parts. Cf. *Vindication*, sect. 54-61.

[4] 'see,' i. e. see immediately, as distinguished from visual suggestion or acquired seeing.

distance shall subtend a greater angle, and at a farther distance a lesser angle. And by this principle (we are told) the mind estimates the magnitude of an object, comparing the angle under which it is seen with its distance, and thence inferring the magnitude thereof. What inclines men to this mistake (beside the humour of making one see by geometry) is, that the same perceptions or ideas which suggest distance do also suggest magnitude. But, if we examine it, we shall find they suggest the latter as immediately as the former. I say, they do not first suggest distance and then leave it to the judgment to use that as a medium whereby to collect the magnitude; but they have as close and immediate a connexion with the magnitude as with the distance; and suggest magnitude as independently of distance, as they do distance independently of magnitude. All which will be evident to whoever considers what has been already said and what follows.

54. It has been shewn there are two sorts of objects apprehended by sight, each whereof has its distinct magnitude or extension—the one, properly tangible, i. e. to be perceived and measured by touch, and not immediately falling under the sense of seeing; the other, properly and immediately visible, by mediation of which the former is brought in view. Each of these magnitudes are greater or lesser, according as they contain in them more or fewer points, they being made up of points or minimums. For, whatever may be said of extension in abstract, it is certain sensible extension is not infinitely divisible. There is a *minimum tangibile*, and a *minimum visibile*, beyond which sense cannot perceive[1]. This every one's experience will inform him.

---

[1] There is a *minimum visibile* at which *we* cease to be percipient of colour, and also a *minimum tangibile* at which all sense of resistance and contact disappears. This point is, for us, the necessary limit (in imagination) of (visible or tangible) reality.

Though Berkeley regards extension as, in itself, necessarily dependent

55. The magnitude of the object which exists without the mind, and is at a distance, continues always invariably the same: but, the visible object still changing as you approach to or recede from the tangible object, it hath no fixed and determinate greatness. Whenever therefore we speak of the magnitude of any thing, for instance a tree or a house, we must mean the tangible magnitude; otherwise there can be nothing steady and free from ambiguity spoken of it[1]. Now, though the tangible and visible magnitude do in truth belong to two distinct objects, I shall nevertheless (especially since those objects are called by the same name, and are observed to coexist), to avoid tediousness and singularity of speech, sometimes speak of them as belonging to one and the same thing[2].

56. Now, in order to discover by what means the magnitude of tangible objects is perceived by sight, I need only reflect on what passes in my own mind, and observe what those things be which (as signs) introduce the ideas of greater or lesser into my thoughts when I look on any object[3]. And these I find to be, *first*, the magnitude or

---

on a percipient mind, he does not mean that mind, in perceiving extension, itself becomes extended. With him, extension—existing only as a greater or smaller number of coloured or resistant *minima*, all dependent on sentient mind, nevertheless does not exist *as an attribute of mind*. (Cf. *Principles*, sect. 49.) Mind, he might say, *can* be conscious without being percipient of what is extended; on the other hand, what is extended *cannot* exist without a living mind to realise it.

[1] But is not this 'unsteadiness' or 'flux' found in what we touch as well as in what we see—though less obtrusively? A felt thing is felt to be larger or smaller according to the state of the organism of the percipient at the time of the perception. Every perception is relative to the state of the bodily organ.

[2] Ordinary language identifies what careful analysis of the original data of the senses seems to Berkeley to distinguish. Does ordinary language involve a truer analysis of extension than Berkeley entertains, and if not, why not?

[3] The 'signs' which 'suggest,' and so enable us to 'judge' of, the real magnitudes of things, are analysed in the following sections. They

extension of the visible object, which, being immediately perceived by sight, is connected with that other which is tangible and placed at a distance : *secondly*, the confusion or distinctness : and *thirdly*, the vigorousness or faintness of the aforesaid visible appearance. *Cæteris paribus*, by how much the greater or lesser the visible object is, by so much the greater or lesser do I conclude the tangible object to be. But, be the idea immediately perceived by sight never so large, yet, if it be withal confused, I judge the magnitude of the thing to be but small. If it be distinct and clear, I judge it greater. And, if it be faint, I apprehend it to be yet greater. What is here meant by confusion and faintness has been explained in sect. 35.

57. Moreover, the judgments we make of greatness do, in like manner as those of distance, depend on the disposition of the eye ; also on the figure, number, and situation of intermediate objects, and other circumstances that have been observed to attend great or small tangible magnitudes. Thus, for instance, the very same quantity of visible extension which in the figure of a tower doth suggest the idea of great magnitude shall in the figure of a man suggest the idea of much smaller magnitude. That this is owing to the experience we have had of the usual bigness of a tower and a man, no one, I suppose, need be told.

58. It is also evident that confusion or faintness have no more a *necessary* connexion with little or great magnitude than they have with little or great distance. As they suggest the latter, so they suggest the former to our minds. And, by consequence, if it were not for experience, we should no more judge[1] a faint or confused appearance to be connected

---

are concluded to be (*a*) the proportion of the field of sight which the object occupies, (*b*) the clearness or indistinctness of its outlines, (*c*) the lightness or faintness of its colours, (*d*) the number of intervening visible objects, and (*e*) the amount of muscular strain or sensation in directing both eyes to the object.

[1] 'Judge,' i. e. assume to be *proved* by sufficient experience—again in

with great or little magnitude than we should that it was connected with great or little distance.

59. Nor will it be found that great or small visible magnitude hath any *necessary* relation to great or small tangible magnitude—so that the one may certainly and infallibly be inferred from the other.—But, before we come to the proof of this, it is fit we consider the difference there is betwixt the extension and figure which is the proper object of touch, and that other which is termed visible; and how the former is principally, though not immediately, taken notice of when we look at any object. This has been before mentioned, but we shall here inquire into the cause thereof. We regard the objects that environ us in proportion as they are adapted to benefit or injure our own bodies, and thereby produce in our minds the sensations of pleasure or pain. Now, bodies operating on our organs by an immediate application, and the hurt and advantage arising therefrom depending altogether on the tangible, and not at all on the visible, qualities of any object—this is a plain reason why those should be regarded by us much more than these. And for this end the visive sense seems to have been bestowed on animals, to wit, that, by the perception of *visible* ideas[1] (which in themselves are not capable of affecting or anywise altering the frame of their bodies), they may be able to foresee (from the experience they have had what tangible ideas are connected with such and such visible ideas) the damage or benefit which is like to ensue upon the application of their own bodies to this or that body

Locke's meaning of 'judgment'; in contrast with what is either intuitively or demonstratively 'known.' Even with Berkeley rational judgments turn out to be unconsciously presupposed in the sub-conscious and mechanical 'suggestions' of experience; but he does not unfold them critically as Kant would do.

[1] 'perception of visible ideas,' i.e. of the visible symbols. He proceeds to explain why we associate *reality* with touch rather than with sight.

which is at a distance. Which foresight, how necessary it is for the preservation of an animal, every one's experience can inform him[1]. Hence it is that, when we look at an object, the tangible figure and extension thereof are principally attended to; whilst there is small heed taken of the visible figure and magnitude, which, though more immediately perceived, do less sensibly affect us, and are not fitted to produce any alteration in our bodies.

60. That the matter of fact is true will be evident to any one who considers that a man placed at ten foot distance is thought as great as if he were placed at a distance only of five foot; which is true, not with relation to the visible, but tangible greatness of the object: the visible magnitude being far greater at one station than it is at the other.

61. Inches, feet, &c. are settled, stated lengths, whereby we measure objects and estimate their magnitude. We say, for example, an object appears to be six inches, or six foot long. Now, that this cannot be meant of visible inches, &c. is evident, because a visible inch is itself no constant determinate magnitude, and cannot therefore serve to mark out and determine the magnitude of any other thing. Take an inch marked upon a ruler; view it successively, at the distance of half a foot, a foot, a foot and a half, &c. from the eye: at each of which, and at all the intermediate distances, the inch shall have a different visible extension, i. e. there shall be more or fewer points discerned in it. Now, I ask which of all these various extensions is that stated determinate one that is agreed on for a common measure of other magnitudes? No reason can be assigned why we should

---

[1] Most of what is commonly called 'vision' is really *prevision*, and proceeds on sub-conscious assumption of the omnipresence of law or order in nature. In all developed visual perception we go beyond mere sense; still more in all the inferences of physical science, and on the same assumption of constant natural order. But in science this assumption is more conscious of its rational ground, and is not the issue of habit only, as at the lower stage of mere sense-suggestion.

pitch on one more than another. And, except there be some invariable determinate extension fixed on to be marked by the word inch, it is plain it can be used to little purpose; and to say a thing contains this or that number of inches shall imply no more than that it is extended, without bringing any particular idea of that extension into the mind. Farther, an inch and a foot, from different distances, shall both exhibit the same visible magnitude, and yet at the same time you shall say that one seems several times greater than the other. From all which it is manifest, that the judgments we make of the magnitude of objects by sight are altogether in reference to their tangible extension. Whenever we say an object is great or small, of this or that determinate measure, I say, it must be meant of the tangible and not the visible extension, which, though immediately perceived, is nevertheless little taken notice of [1].

62. Now, that there is no necessary connexion between these two distinct extensions is evident from hence—because our eyes might have been framed in such a manner as to be able to see nothing but what were less than the *minimum tangibile*. In which case it is not impossible we might have perceived all the immediate objects of sight the very same that we do now; but unto those visible appearances there would not be connected those different tangible magnitudes that are now. Which shews the judgments we make of the magnitude of things placed at a distance, from the various greatness of the immediate objects of sight, do not arise from any essential or necessary, but only a customary [2] tie which has been observed betwixt them.

[1] But if extension is only an empirical datum of sense, and if tangible as well as coloured extension fluctuates relatively to the state of the sense-organism, we need an objective criterion of the former as well as of the latter. What is it?

[2] So Hume afterwards, who tried to reduce faith in 'necessary' connexion to the physical issue of habit, induced by the custom of previous experience. 'All inferences from experience,' he maintains, are *effects*

63. Moreover, it is not only certain that any idea of sight might not have been connected with this or that idea of touch we now observe to accompany it, but also that the greater visible magnitudes might have been connected with and introduced into our minds lesser tangible magnitudes, and the lesser visible magnitudes greater tangible magnitudes. Nay, that it actually is so, we have daily experience that object which makes a strong and large appearance not seeming near so great as another the visible magnitude whereof is much less, but more faint, and the appearance upper, or which is the same thing, painted lower on the retina, which faintness and situation suggest both greater magnitude and greater distance.

64. From which, and from sect. 57 and 58, it is manifest that, as we do not perceive the magnitude of objects immediately by sight, so neither do we perceive them by the mediation of anything which has a necessary connexion with them. Those ideas that now suggest unto us the various magnitudes of external objects before we touch them might possibly have suggested no such thing ; or they might have signified them in a direct contrary manner, so that the very same ideas on the perception whereof we judge an object to be small might as well have served to make us conclude it great : those ideas being in their own nature equally fitted to bring into our minds the idea of small or great, or no size at all, of outward objects, just as the words of any language are in their own nature indifferent to signify this or that thing, or nothing at all.

65. As we see distance so we see magnitude. And we see both in the same way that we see shame or anger in the looks of a man. Those passions are themselves invisible ; they are nevertheless let in by the eye along with

---

of custom, not *conclusions of reasoning*. Custom is the guide of life.' (*Inquiry*, V. p. 1.) With Bishop Butler, 'probability is the guide of life.' (*Analogy*, Introd.) So too Locke.

colours and alterations of countenance which are the immediate object of vision, and which signify them for no other reason than barely because they have been observed to accompany them. Without which experience we should no more have taken blushing for a sign of shame than of gladness.

66. We are nevertheless exceedingly prone to imagine those things which are perceived only by the mediation of others to be themselves the immediate objects of sight, or at least to have in their own nature a fitness to be suggested by them before ever they had been experienced to coexist with them. From which prejudice every one perhaps will not find it easy to emancipate himself, by any the clearest convictions of reason. And there are some grounds to think that, if there was one only invariable and universal language in the world, and that men were born with the faculty of speaking it, it would be the opinion of some, that the ideas in other men's minds were properly perceived by the ear, or had at least a necessary and inseparable tie with the sounds that were affixed to them. All which seems to arise from want of a due application of our discerning faculty, thereby to discriminate between the ideas that are in our understandings, and consider them apart from each other; which would preserve us from confounding those that are different, and make us see what ideas do, and what do not, include or imply this or that other idea [1].

. . . .

[1] Mark the stress put in these sections on the *divine arbitrariness* of the connexion between those visual signs which suggest tangible magnitudes, and that which they signify—a fundamental principle throughout the *Essay*: for, as according to the analogy of articulate language, any term might *a priori* have been made the sign of any meaning, so any sort of sense-phenomenon might have been connected by divine Will with any other sort, under divinely maintained 'natural' law. Compare this with Hume, when he says that 'if we reason *a priori* anything may

77. For the further clearing up of this point, it is to be observed, that what we immediately and properly see are only lights and colours in sundry situations and shades, and degrees of faintness and clearness, confusion and distinctness. All which visible objects are only in the mind [1]; nor do they suggest aught external [2], whether distance or magnitude, otherwise than by habitual connexion, as words do things. We are also to remark, that beside the straining of the eyes, and beside the vivid and faint, the distinct and confused appearances (which, bearing some proportion to lines and angles, have been substituted instead of them in the foregoing part of this Treatise), there are other means which suggest both distance and magnitude—particularly the situation of visible points or objects, as upper or lower; the former suggesting a farther distance and greater magnitude, the latter a nearer distance and lesser magnitude—all which is an effect only of custom and experience, there being really nothing intermediate in the line of distance between the uppermost and the lowermost, which are both equidistant, or rather at no distance from the eye; as there is also nothing in upper or lower which by necessary connexion should suggest greater or lesser magnitude. Now, as these customary experimental means of suggesting distance do likewise suggest magnitude, so they suggest the

---

appear able to produce anything. The falling of a pebble may, for all we know, extinguish the sun; or the wish of a man control the planets in their orbits. It is only experience that teaches us the actual nature and bounds of cause and effect' (*Inquiry*, ch. XII. pt. 3). Here 'cause' means sign, and physical causation means natural signification.

In §§ 67–76, which are here omitted, Berkeley tries to verify the preceding doctrines, as to the visual signs of actual or tangible Magnitude, by applying them to solve a scientific puzzle of long standing—the fact of the greater visible magnitude of the moon and other heavenly bodies when in the horizon. See Berkeley's *Works*, vol. I.

[1] 'in the mind,' i. e. depend on being perceived.

[2] 'external,' i. e. given in touch, the data of which are (meantime) supposed to be possibly independent of perception.

one as immediately as the other. I say, they do not (vide sect. 53) first suggest distance, and then leave the mind from thence to infer or compute magnitude, but suggest magnitude as immediately and directly as they suggest distance [1].

78. This phenomenon of the horizontal moon is a clear instance of the insufficiency of lines and angles for explaining the way wherein the mind perceives and estimates the magnitude of outward objects. There is, nevertheless, a use of computation by them—in order to determine the apparent magnitude of things, so far as they have a connexion with and are proportional to those other ideas or perceptions which are the true and immediate occasions that suggest to the mind the apparent magnitude of things. But this in general may, I think, be observed concerning mathematical computation in optics—that it can never be very precise and exact, since the judgments we make of the magnitude of external things do often depend on several circumstances which are not proportional to or capable of being defined by lines and angles.

79. From what has been said, we may safely deduce this consequence, to wit, that a man born blind, and made to see, would, at first opening of his eyes, make a very different judgment of the magnitude of objects intromitted by them from what others do. He would not consider the ideas of sight with reference to, or as having any connexion with the ideas of touch. His view of them being entirely terminated within themselves, he can no otherwise judge them great or small than as they contain a greater or lesser number of visible points. Now, it being certain that any visible point can cover or exclude from view only one other visible point, it follows that whatever object intercepts the view

[1] Note the contrast here between 'inference' and 'suggestion': the former involves exercise of Intellect, while in the latter Habit takes the place of Intellect. See *Vindication*, sect. 42.

of another hath an equal number of visible points with it; and, consequently, they shall both be thought by him to have the same magnitude. Hence, it is evident one in those circumstances would judge his thumb, with which he might hide a tower, or hinder its being seen, equal to that tower: or his hand, the interposition whereof might conceal the firmament from his view, equal to the firmament: how great an inequality soever there may, in our apprehensions, seem to be betwixt those two things, because of the customary and close connexion that has grown up in our minds between the objects of sight and touch, whereby the very different and distinct ideas of those two senses are so blended and confounded together as to be mistaken for one and the same thing—out of which prejudice we cannot easily extricate ourselves.

. . . .

121. We have shewn the way wherein the mind, by mediation of visible ideas[1], doth perceive or apprehend the distance, magnitude, and situation of tangible objects.

I come now to inquire more particularly concerning the difference between the ideas of Sight and Touch which are called by the same names, and see whether there be any idea common to both senses. From what we have at large set forth and demonstrated in the foregoing parts of this treatise, it is plain there is no one self-same numerical Extension, perceived both by sight and touch; but that the particular figures and extensions perceived by sight, however they may be called by the same names, and reputed the same things with those perceived by touch, are nevertheless different, and have an existence very distinct and separate from them.

---

[1] 'visible ideas'—say rather *visible* and *visual* ideas; for he here includes not only colours which we *see*, but also the invisible 'sensations' in the visual organ—muscular and locomotive—which are *felt* and not seen.

So that the question is not now concerning the same *numerical* ideas, but whether there be any one and the same *sort* or *species* of ideas equally perceivable to both senses; or, in other words, whether extension, figure, and motion perceived by sight, are not *specifically distinct* from extension, figure, and motion perceived by touch?

. . . .

127. It having been shewn that there are no abstract ideas of figure, and that it is impossible for us, by any precision[1] of thought, to frame an abstract idea of extension, separate from all other visible and tangible qualities, which shall be common both to sight and touch, the question now remaining is, Whether the *particular* extensions, figures, and motions perceived by sight, be of the same *kind* with the *particular* extensions, figures, and motions perceived by touch? In answer to which I shall venture to lay down the following proposition :—*The extensions, figures, and motions perceived by sight are specifically distinct from the ideas of touch, called by the same names ; nor is there any such thing as one idea, or kind of idea, common to both senses*[2]. This proposition may, without much difficulty, be collected from what hath been said in several places of this Essay. But, because it

[1] 'precision,' i.e. separation produced by thinking.
[2] This seems to imply that there are no 'common sensibles,' as Aristotle called them, and as the primary qualities are by many held to be. That space may be a perception *necessarily* involved in all (or in some) perceptions of sense, while inconceivable apart from a particular perception, does not occur to Berkeley. He rightly insists on the impossibility of having a sensuous image of space in abstraction from data of sense; but he does not discuss the counter impossibility of sensuous data being perceived or conceived without space; nor whether perceptions which involve extension may be *evoked* by sensations in touch or in sight, without space being therefore *identified* either with sensations of contact and resistance or with sensations of colour. Is it the perception of extension thus called forth that *gives outness* to what we are conscious of in sense, and enables us to realise objects as 'in space'—not vaguely as unknown powers that are called 'external' because independent of our personal agency?

seems so remote from, and contrary to the received notions and settled opinion of mankind, I shall attempt to demonstrate it more particularly and at large by the following arguments:—

128. *First*, When, upon perception of an idea, I range it under this or that sort, it is because it is perceived after the same manner, or because it has a likeness or conformity with or affects me in the same way as the ideas of the sort I rank it under. In short, it must not be entirely new, but have something in it old and already perceived by me. It must, I say, have so much, at least, in common with the ideas I have before known and named, as to make me give it the same name with them. But, it has been, if I mistake not, clearly made out that a man *born* blind would not, *at first reception of his sight*, think the things he saw were of the same nature with the objects of touch, or had anything in common with them; but that they were a new set of ideas, perceived in a new manner, and entirely different from all he had ever perceived before. So that he would not call them by the same name, nor repute them to be of the same sort, with anything he had hitherto known.

129. *Secondly*, Light and colours are allowed by all to constitute a sort of species entirely different from the ideas of touch; nor will any man, I presume, say they can make themselves perceived by that sense. But there is no other immediate object of sight besides light and colours. It is therefore a direct consequence, that there is no idea common to both senses.

130. It is a prevailing opinion, even amongst those who have thought and writ most accurately concerning our ideas, and the ways whereby they enter into the understanding, that something *more* is perceived by sight than barely light and colours with their variations. Mr. Locke termeth sight 'the most comprehensive of all our senses, conveying to our minds the ideas of light and colours, which are peculiar only

to that sense; and also the far different ideas of space, figure, and motion.' (*Essay on Human Understanding*, b. II. ch. 9. s. 9.) *Space* or *distance*, we have shewn, is no otherwise the object of sight than of hearing. (Vid. sect. 46.) And, as for *figure* and *extension*, I leave it to any one that shall calmly attend to his own clear and distinct ideas to decide whether he has any idea intromitted immediately and properly by sight save only light and colours: or, whether it be possible for him to frame in his mind a distinct abstract idea of visible extension, or figure, exclusive of all colour; and, on the other hand, whether he can conceive colour without visible extension? For my own part, I must confess, I am not able to attain so great a nicety of abstraction. I know very well that, in a strict sense, I *see* nothing but light and colours, with their several shades and variations. He who beside these doth also perceive by sight ideas far different and distinct from them, hath that faculty in a degree more perfect and comprehensive than I can pretend to. It must be owned, indeed, that, by the mediation of light and colours, other far different ideas are *suggested* to my mind. But then, upon this score, I see no reason why the sight[1] should be thought more 'comprehensive' than the hearing, which, beside sounds which are peculiar to that sense, doth, by their mediation, suggest not only space, figure, and motion, but also all other ideas whatsoever that can be signified by words.

131. *Thirdly*, It is, I think, an axiom universally received, that 'quantities of the same kind may be added together and make one entire sum.' Mathematicians add lines together; but they do not add a line to a solid, or conceive it as making one sum with a surface. These three kinds of quantity being thought incapable of any such mutual

---

[1] 'the sight,' i.e. what we originally and immediately see, as distinguished from the 'suggestions' called forth by visible or visual signs.

addition, and consequently of being compared together in the several ways of proportion, are by them for that reason esteemed entirely disparate and heterogeneous. Now let any one try in his thoughts to add a *visible* line or surface to a *tangible* line or surface, so as to conceive them making one continued sum or whole. He that can do this may think them homogeneous; but he that cannot must, by the foregoing axiom, think them heterogeneous. A blue and a red line I can conceive added together into one sum and making one continued line; but to make, in my thoughts, one continued line of a visible and tangible line added together, is, I find, a task far more difficult, and even insurmountable; and I leave it to the reflection and experience of every particular person to determine for himself.

132. *Fourthly,* A farther confirmation of our tenet may be drawn from the solution of Mr. Molyneux's problem, published by Mr. Locke in his *Essay*: which I shall set down as it there lies, together with Mr. Locke's opinion of it:—
'Suppose a man born blind, and now adult, and taught by his touch to distinguish between a cube and a sphere of the same metal, and nighly of the same bigness, so as to tell when he felt one and the other, which is the cube and which the sphere. Suppose then the cube and sphere placed on a table, and the blind man made to see: Quære, Whether by his sight, before he touched them, he could now distinguish, and tell, which is the globe, which the cube. To which the acute and judicious proposer answers: Not. For, though he has obtained the experience of how a globe, how a cube affects his touch; yet he has not yet attained the experience, that what affects his touch so or so must affect his sight so or so: or that a protuberant angle in the cube, that pressed his hand unequally, shall appear to his eye as it doth in the cube. I agree with this thinking gentleman, whom I am proud to call my friend, in

his answer to this his problem; and am of opinion that the blind man, at first sight, would not be able with certainty to say, which was the globe, which the cube, whilst he only saw them.' (Locke's *Essay on Human Understanding*, b. II. ch. 9. s. 8[1].)

133. Now, if a square surface perceived by touch be of the *same sort* with a square surface perceived by sight, it is certain the blind man here mentioned might know a square surface as soon as he saw it. It is no more but introducing into his mind, by a new inlet, an idea he has been already well acquainted with. Since therefore he is supposed to have known by his touch that a cube is a body terminated by square surfaces; and that a sphere is not terminated by square surfaces—upon the supposition that a visible and tangible square differ only *in numero*, it follows that he might know, by the unerring mark of the square surfaces, which was the cube, and which not, while he only saw them. We must therefore allow, either that visible extension and figures are specifically distinct from tangible extension and figures, or else, that the solution of this problem, given by those two thoughtful and ingenious men, is wrong.

134. Much more might be laid together in proof of the proposition I have advanced. But, what has been said is, if I mistake not, sufficient to convince any one that shall yield a reasonable attention. And, as for those that will not be at the pains of a little thought, no multiplication of words will ever suffice to make them understand the truth, or rightly conceive my meaning.

135. I cannot let go the above-mentioned problem without some reflection on it. It hath been made evident that a man blind from his birth would not, at first sight, denominate anything he saw, by the names he had been used to

---

[1] This 'problem' first appeared in the second edition of Locke's *Essay*. See also Leibniz (*Nouveaux Essais*, liv. II. ch. 9), who disputes the alleged heterogeneity.

appropriate to ideas of touch. Cube, sphere, table are words he has known applied to things perceivable by touch, but to things perfectly intangible he never knew them applied. Those words, in their wonted application, always marked out to his mind bodies or solid things which were perceived by the resistance they gave. But there is no solidity, no resistance or protrusion, perceived by sight. In short, the ideas of sight are all new perceptions, to which there be no names annexed in his mind : he cannot therefore understand what is said to him concerning them. And to ask of the two bodies he saw placed on the table, which was the sphere, which the cube, were to him a question downright bantering and unintelligible ; nothing he sees being able to suggest to his thoughts the idea of body, distance, or, in general, of anything he had already known.

136. It is a mistake to think the same thing affects both sight and touch. If the same angle or square which is the object of touch be also the object of vision, what should hinder the blind man, at first sight, from knowing it ? For, though the manner wherein it affects the sight be different from that wherein it affected his touch, yet, there being, beside this manner or circumstance, which is new and unknown, the angle or figure, which is old and known, he cannot choose but discern it.

. . . . . .

138. I shall not enlarge any farther on this subject, but proceed to inquire what may be alleged, with greatest appearance of reason, against the proposition we have demonstrated to be true ; for, where there is so much prejudice to be encountered, a bare and naked demonstration of the truth will scarce suffice. We must also satisfy the scruples that men may start in favour of their preconceived notions, shew whence the mistake arises, how it came to spread, and carefully disclose and root out those false persuasions

that an early prejudice might have implanted in the mind.

139. It will be demanded how visible extension and figures come to be called by the same *name* with tangible extension and figures, if they are not of the same kind with them? It must be something more than humour or accident that could occasion a custom so constant and universal as this, which has obtained in all ages and nations of the world, and amongst all ranks of men, the learned as well as the illiterate.

140. To which I answer, we can no more argue a visible and tangible square to be of the same species, from their being called by the same name, than we can that a tangible square, and the monosyllable consisting of six letters whereby it is marked, are of the same species, because they are both called by the same name. It is customary to call written words, and the things they signify, by the same name: for, words not being regarded in their own nature, or otherwise than as they are marks of things, it had been superfluous, and beside the design of language, to have given them names distinct from those of the things marked by them. The same reason holds here also. Visible figures are the marks of tangible figures; and, from sect. 59, it is plain that in themselves they are little regarded, or upon any other score than for their connexion with tangible figures, which by nature they are ordained to signify. And, because this Language of Nature does not vary in different ages or nations, hence it is that in all times and places visible figures are called by the same names as the respective tangible figures suggested by them; and not because they are alike, or of the same sort with them.

141. But, say you, surely a tangible square is liker to a visible square than to a visible circle: it has four angles, and as many sides; so also has the visible square; but the visible circle has no such thing, being bounded by one

uniform curve, without right lines or angles, which makes it unfit to represent the tangible square, but very fit to represent the tangible circle. Whence it clearly follows, that visible figures are patterns of, or of the same species with, the respective tangible figures represented by them; that they are like unto them, and of their own nature fitted to represent them, as being of the same sort; and that they are in no respect arbitrary signs, as words.

142. I answer, it must be acknowledged the visible square is fitter than the visible circle to represent the tangible square; but then it is not because it is liker, or more of a species with it, but, because the visible square contains in it several distinct parts, whereby to mark the several distinct corresponding parts of a tangible square, whereas the visible circle doth not. The square perceived by touch hath four distinct equal sides, so also hath it four distinct equal angles. It is therefore necessary that the visible figure which shall be most proper to mark it contain four distinct equal parts, corresponding to the four sides of the tangible square; as likewise four other distinct and equal parts, whereby to denote the four equal angles of the tangible square. And accordingly we see the visible figures contain in them distinct visible parts, answering to the distinct tangible parts of the figures signified or suggested by them.

143. But it will not hence follow that any visible figure is like unto or of the same species with its corresponding tangible figure—unless it be also shewn that not only the *number*, but also the *kind* of the parts be the same in both. To illustrate this, I observe that visible figures represent tangible figures much after the same manner that written words do sounds. Now, in this respect, words are not arbitrary; it not being indifferent what written word stands for any sound. But, it is requisite that each word contain in it as many distinct characters as there are variations in the sound it stands for. Thus, the single letter *a* is proper

to mark one simple uniform sound; and the word *adultery* is accommodated to represent the sound annexed to it—in the formation whereof there being eight different collisions or modifications of the air by the organs of speech, each of which produces a difference of sound, it was fit the word representing it should consist of as many distinct characters, thereby to mark each particular difference or part of the whole sound. And yet nobody, I presume, will say the single letter *a*, or the word *adultery*, are alike unto or of the same species with the respective sounds by them represented. It is indeed arbitrary that, in general, letters of any language represent sounds at all; but, when that is once agreed, it is not arbitrary what combination of letters shall represent this or that particular sound. I leave this with the reader to pursue, and apply it in his own thoughts.

144. It must be confessed that we are not so apt to confound other signs with the things signified, or to think them of the same species, as we are visible and tangible ideas. But, a little consideration will shew us how this may well be, without our supposing them of a like nature. Visible signs are constant and universal; their connexion with tangible ideas has been learnt at our first entrance into the world; and ever since, almost every moment of our lives, it has been occurring to our thoughts, and fastening and striking deeper on our minds. When we observe that signs are variable, and of human institution: when we remember there was a time they were not connected in our minds with those things they now so readily suggest, but that their signification was learned by the slow steps of experience: this preserves us from confounding them. But, when we find the same signs suggest the same things all over the world; when we know they are not of human institution, and cannot remember that we ever learned their signification, but think that at first sight they would have suggested to us the same things they do now: all this persuades us they are

of the same species as the things respectively represented by them, and that it is by a natural resemblance they suggest them to our minds.

145. Add to this that whenever we make a nice survey of any object, successively directing the optic axis to each point thereof, there are certain lines and figures, described by the motion of the head or eye, which, being in truth perceived by *feeling*[1], do nevertheless so mix themselves, as it were, with the ideas of *sight* that we can scarce think but they appertain to that sense. Again, the ideas of sight enter into the mind several at once, more distinct and unmingled than is usual in the other senses beside the touch. Sounds, for example, perceived at the same instant, are apt to coalesce, if I may so say, into one sound : but we can perceive, at the same time, great variety of visible objects, very separate and distinct from each other. Now, tangible extension being made up of several distinct coexistent parts, we may hence gather another reason that may dispose us to imagine a likeness or analogy between the immediate objects of sight and touch. But nothing, certainly, does more contribute to blend and confound them together, than the strict and close connexion they have with each other. We cannot open our eyes but the ideas of distance[2], bodies, and tangible figures are suggested by them. So swift, and sudden, and unperceived is the transit from visible to tangible ideas that we can scarce forbear thinking them equally the immediate object of vision.

146. The prejudice which is grounded on these, and whatever other causes may be assigned thereof, sticks so fast on our understandings, that it is impossible, without obstinate striving and labour of the mind, to get entirely clear of it.

---

[1] These are *visual* as distinguished from *visible* signs of tactual phenomena.

[2] 'distance,' i. e. distance outward in the line of sight. Outwardness is invisible, and only ' suggested ' by what we see.

But then the reluctancy we find in rejecting any opinion can be no argument of its truth, to whoever considers what has been already shewn with regard to the prejudices we entertain concerning the distance, magnitude, and situation of objects; prejudices so familiar to our minds, so confirmed and inveterate, as they will hardly give way to the clearest demonstration.

147. Upon the whole, I think we may fairly conclude that the proper objects of vision[1] constitute the Universal Language of Nature[2]; whereby we are instructed how to regulate our actions, in order to attain those things that are necessary to the preservation and well-being of our bodies, as also to avoid whatever may be hurtful and destructive of them. It is by their information that we are principally guided in all the transactions and concerns of life. And the manner wherein they signify and mark out unto us the objects which are at a distance is the same with that of languages and signs of human appointment; which do not suggest the things signified by any likeness or identity of nature, but only by an habitual connexion that experience has made us to observe between them.

148. Suppose one who had always continued blind be told by his guide that after he has advanced so many steps he shall come to the brink of the precipice, or be stopped

---

[1] Is the 'proper object of vision' extended or unextended colour?

[2] In this and the next section Berkeley sums up the 'theory' to which the preceding analyses conduct;—after having, as he believed, shown the complete heterogeneity of the original data presented in the sense of Sight, and the original data presented in the sense of Touch. He had been gradually approaching this in the preceding sections, under his favourite metaphor of 'language' latent in nature, with the therein implied *arbitrariness* and *generality* in the sensible signs. When this theory is pushed into its issues, the mathematical as well as the physical sciences appear as if based on arbitrary relations among the data of the two senses, all their inferences being sustained by 'suggestions,' themselves not fully explained, which yield only *customary* not *necessary* or *universal* conclusions.

by a wall; must not this to him seem very admirable and surprising? He cannot conceive how it is possible for mortals to frame such predictions as these, which to him would seem as strange and unaccountable as prophecy does to others. Even they who are blessed with the visive faculty may (though familiarity make it less observed) find therein sufficient cause of admiration. The wonderful art and contrivance wherewith it is adjusted to those ends and purposes for which it was apparently designed; the vast extent, number, and variety of objects that are at once, with so much ease, and quickness, and pleasure, suggested by it— all these afford subject for much and pleasing speculation, and may, if anything, give us some glimmering analogous prænotion of things that are placed beyond the certain discovery and comprehension of our present state [1].

[1] The World of Vision is throughout a Book of God, which we are interpreting when we seem to be seeing, and which we find to be literally a Book of Prophecy.

Does Berkeley mean to maintain that the only proper object of sight is *unextended* colour—that even *superficial* extension is invisible—and that, apart from an experience of certain sensations and exertions in the motor organs, all *visibilia* are unextended points? Can coloured extension ever be *seen* without previous experience of organic movement and muscular resistance? Among British writers, Brown (*Lectures*, XXIX), J. S. Mill (*Exam. of Hamilton*, pp. 285-287), and Bain (*Senses and Intellect*, pp. 366-378) answer this question in the negative. They analyse our perception of extension, in length and breadth as well as in depth, into successive sensations of impeded and unimpeded organic movement, including muscular expansion and contraction. They deny that *form* can be seen in colour alone, or that what we mean by visible form can be conceived by one who has never been conscious of sensations of locomotion—at least in the eye. They interpret a 'round' form to signify something that presupposes a *felt* sweep of the eye to enable us to apprehend it. We must, it is argued, experience organic movement before we can find *extension* in our perceptions of colour. 'I cannot,' says Mill, 'admit that we could have what is meant by a perception of *superficial* space, unless we conceived it as something which the hand could be moved across.' Yet both Mill and Bain seem to allow that when the extended area is very small (less than $\frac{1}{10}$ of an inch in diameter), it can be seen without any motion even in the eye. On this subject see

Hamilton's Lectures on Metaphysics, vol. II. p. 165, where a reason is offered for concluding the *necessary* implication of superficial extension (as distinguished from outness or depth) in all perception of colours.

As to all this the question arises, whether perception of phenomena in motion does not presuppose perception of space or room, as a condition of our perceiving motion. If so, the proposed explanation of the latter by the former would involve *petitio principii*. Can the idea of motion from place to place be wholly resolved into experience of *successive* phenomena? One might also ask what conception of motion is possible to a person born blind?

Some hold that all sensuous impressions, in all the senses, are originally given as external to one another in place—in short, that we cannot have *any* organic sensation without an implied perception of extension—that sensation proper in our organism, and perception proper of the extended object exist only as they co-exist, though always in an inverse ratio—and that we are originally sentient and percipient of our own extended bodily organism, and of that only. 'All the senses,' says Hamilton, 'simply or in combination, afford conditions for the perception of the primary qualities' (Reid, *Works*, p. 864).

'Mind *alone*,' says Mansel, 'is not capable of sensation; for it is sentient only so far as it animates a bodily organism. That a *disembodied* spirit has consciousness we must believe;—at least it is impossible to conceive how spiritual existence can be otherwise manifested;—but it is impossible to conceive such consciousness as at all resembling our own, at any rate in the particular phenomena which are conveyed by means of the senses' (*Metaphysics*, p. 91). Berkeley elsewhere supposes that it is possible for us to be percipient of colours after death has dissolved the bodily organ of sight, of sounds after the bodily organ of hearing has been dissolved, and of the material world in all its qualities after the total dissolution of the body.

II

DIVINE VISUAL LANGUAGE

A DIALOGUE[1]

1. EARLY the next morning, as I looked out of my window, I saw *Alciphron* walking in the garden with all the signs of a man in deep thought. Upon which I went down to him.

[1] This is the Fourth of Seven Dialogues, published by Berkeley in 1732, under the title of *Alciphron, or the Minute Philosopher*. 'Minute philosophers' were sceptics, or, as we now call them, agnostics, whose narrow philosophy was limited to the empirical data of the senses. Alciphron and Lysicles represent this minute philosophy—the former as final philosophy, the latter merely as an apology for a life of sensuous pleasure : Euphranor and Crito argue for the reasonableness of religion. The following Dialogue examines the foundation of faith in the perpetual and omnipresent activity of God in external nature, taking its departure from the theory of seeing, and so looking at the visible world as a Book of God, because a system of sensible signs, more or less interpretable by man. As the Power that regulates the phenomena presented in sense is continually presenting to us in Sight *significant phenomena*, which are to all intents and purposes a Divine Language, it is argued that I have the same kind of evidence for the Universal Power being intelligent and intending Spirit as I have for the existence of a man when he is speaking to me. The explanation raises the inquiry,—Can one mind communicate with another mind, whether Divine or human, through the medium of a material world that consists only of sense-dependent phenomena?

The subject is introduced in §§ 1-7. The theory that much of what is called *seeing* is really *interpreting what is seen* is explained in §§ 8-15; where it is argued that, as the visible world has in itself no active power, the phenomena presented to Sight must derive their orderly and therefore significant relations to those of Touch from ordering Intelligence always omnipresent in nature. The remainder of the Dialogue

Alciphron, said I, this early and profound meditation puts me in no small fright.

How so?

Because I should be sorry to be convinced there was no God. The thought of *anarchy in Nature* is to me more shocking than in civil life: inasmuch as natural concerns are more important than civil, and the basis of all others.

I grant, replied *Alciphron*, that some inconvenience may possibly follow from disproving a God: but as to what you say of fright and shocking, all that is nothing but mere prejudice. Men frame an idea or chimera in their own minds, and then fall down and worship it. Notions govern mankind: but of all notions that of God's governing the world hath taken the deepest root and spread the farthest: it is therefore in philosophy an heroical achievement to dispossess this imaginary monarch of his government, and banish all those fears and spectres which the light of reason can alone dispel:

> Non radii solis, non lucida tela diei
> Discutiunt, sed naturae species ratioque[1].

My part, said I, shall be to stand by, as I have hitherto done, and take notes of all that passeth during this memorable event; while a minute philosopher, not six

---

(§§ 16-24) is devoted to a discussion of the human knowledge of this Universal Power that is continually speaking to us by visual signs, and in all the phenomena of the senses, which thus constitute a vast sense-symbolism, or language. Crito argues that our conception of this Power cannot be wholly negative; for total nescience makes faith impossible. We have reasonable assurance that the Power immanent in the visible world is Spirit. God is inferred from the intelligibility of the visible world, in the sort of way one's human neighbour is inferred from his words and actions.

.This Dialogue may be taken as a rationale of theism, founded on the orderliness, and therefore interpretability, of the data of the senses—especially those of sight.

[1] Lucretius.

feet high, attempts to dethrone the monarch of the universe.

Alas! replied *Alciphron*, arguments are not to be measured by feet and inches. One man may see more than a million; and a short argument, managed by a free-thinker, may be sufficient to overthrow the most gigantic chimera.

As we were engaged in this discourse, Crito and Euphranor joined us.

I find you have been beforehand with us to-day, said *Crito* to Alciphron, and taken the advantage of solitude and early hours, while Euphranor and I were asleep in our beds. We may, therefore, expect to see Atheism placed in the best light, and supported by the strongest arguments.

2. *Alc.* The being of a God is a subject upon which there has been a world of commonplace, which it is needless to repeat. Give me leave therefore to lay down certain rules and limitations, in order to shorten our present conference. For, as the end of debating is to persuade, all those things which are foreign to this end should be left out of our debate.

First then, let me tell you I am not to be persuaded by metaphysical arguments; such, for instance, as are drawn from the idea of an all-perfect being[1], or from the absurdity of an infinite progression of causes[2]. This sort of arguments I have always found dry and jejune: and, as they are not suited to my way of thinking they may perhaps puzzle, but never will convince me. Secondly, I am not to be persuaded by the authority either of past or present ages, of mankind in general, or of particular wise men, all which passeth for little or nothing with a man of sound argument and free thought. Thirdly, all proofs drawn from

---

[1] As proposed by Descartes for instance.
[2] A favourite argument of some theologians.

utility or convenience are foreign to the purpose. They may prove indeed the usefulness of the notion, but not the existence of the thing. Whatever legislators or statesmen may think, truth and convenience are very different things to the rigorous eye of a philosopher.

And now, that I may not seem partial, I will limit myself also not to object, in the first place, from anything that may seem irregular or unaccountable in the works of nature, against a cause of infinite power and wisdom; because I already know the answer you will make, to wit, that no one can judge of the symmetry and use of the parts of an infinite machine, which are all relative to each other, and to the whole, without being able to comprehend the entire machine, or the whole universe. And, in the second place, I shall engage myself not to object against the justice and providence of a Supreme Being from the evil that befalls good men, and the prosperity which is often the portion of wicked men in this life; because, I know that, instead of admitting this to be an objection against a Deity, you would make it an argument for a future state, in which there shall be such a retribution of rewards and punishments as may vindicate the Divine attributes, and set all things right in the end. Now, these answers, though they should be admitted for good ones, are in truth no proofs of the being of God, but only solutions of certain difficulties which might be objected, supposing it already proved by proper arguments. Thus much I thought fit to premise, in order to save time and trouble both to you and myself.

Cri. I think that as the proper end of our conference ought to be supposed the discovery and defence of truth, so truth may be justified, not only by persuading its adversaries, but, where that cannot be done, by shewing them to be unreasonable. Arguments, therefore, which carry light have their effect, even against an opponent who shuts his eyes, because they shew him to be obstinate and prejudiced.

Besides, this distinction between arguments that puzzle and that convince, is least of all observed by minute philosophers, and need not therefore be observed by others in their favour.—But perhaps, Euphranor may be willing to encounter you on your own terms, in which case I have nothing further to say.

3. *Euph.* Alciphron acts like a skilful general, who is bent upon gaining the advantage of the ground, and alluring the enemy out of their trenches. We who believe a God, are entrenched within tradition, custom, authority, and law. And, nevertheless, instead of attempting to force us, he proposes that we should voluntarily abandon these intrenchments and make the attack; when we may act on the defensive with much security and ease, leaving him the trouble to dispossess us of what we need not resign. Those reasons (continued he, addressing himself to Alciphron) which you have mustered up in this morning's meditation, if they do not weaken, must establish our belief of a God; for the utmost is to be expected from so great a master in his profession, when he set his strength to a point.

Alc. I hold the confused notion of a Deity, or some invisible power, to be of all prejudices the most unconquerable. When half-a-dozen ingenious men are got together over a glass of wine, by a cheerful fire, in a room well-lighted, we banish with ease all the spectres of fancy and education, and are very clear in our decisions. But, as I was taking a solitary walk before it was broad daylight in yonder grove, methought the point was not quite so clear; nor could I readily recollect the force of those arguments which used to appear so conclusive at other times. I had I know not what awe upon my mind, and seemed haunted by a sort of panic, which I cannot otherwise account for than by supposing it the effect of prejudice: for, you must know, that I, like the rest of the world, was once upon a time catechised and tutored into the belief of a God or Spirit. There is no surer mark of prejudice than the believing a thing without reason. What necessity then can there be that I should set myself the difficult task of proving a negative, when it is sufficient to observe that there is no proof of the affirmative, and that the admitting it without proof is unreasonable? Prove therefore your opinion; or, if you cannot, you may indeed remain in possession of it, but you will only be possessed of a prejudice.

Euph. O Alciphron, to content you we must prove, it seems, and we must prove upon your own terms. But, in the first place, let us see what sort of proof you expect.

Alc. Perhaps I may not expect it, but I will tell you what sort of proof I would have: and that is, in short—such proof as every man of sense requires of a matter of fact, or the existence of any other particular thing. For instance, should a man ask why I believe there is a king of Great Britain? I might answer—Because I had seen him. Or a king of Spain? Because I had seen those who saw him. But as for this King of kings, I neither saw him myself, or any one else that ever did see Him. Surely, if there be such a thing as God, it is very strange that He should leave Himself without a witness; that men should still dispute His being; and that there should be no one evident, sensible, plain proof of it, without recourse to philosophy or metaphysics. A matter of fact is not to be proved by notions, but by facts [1]. This is clear and full to the point.

[1] So Hume in *Inquiry concerning Understanding*, sect. 4, pt. 1. Those matters of fact for which we have not the direct evidence of sense cannot be ascertained in the same way as abstract conclusions which are demonstratively certain. 'The contrary of every matter of fact is still possible, because it can never imply a contradiction . . . That the sun will not rise to-morrow is no less intelligible a proposition, and implies no more contradiction, than the affirmation, that it will rise . . . If you ask a man why he believes *any matter of fact which is absent*, he would give you a reason, and this reason would be *some other fact*.'—But although a present fact can signify an absent fact,

You see what I would be at. Upon these principles I defy superstition.

Euph. You believe then as far as you can see?

Alc. That is my rule of faith.

Euph. How! will you not believe the existence of things which you hear, unless you also see them?

Alc. I will not say so neither. When I insisted on *seeing*, I would be understood to mean perceiving in general. Outward objects make very different impressions upon the animal spirits, all of which are comprised under the common name of *sense*. And whatever we can perceive by *any* sense we may be sure of.

4. *Euph.* What! do you believe then that there are such things as animal spirits?

Alc. Doubtless.

Euph. By what sense do you perceive them?

Alc. I do not perceive them immediately by any of my senses. I am nevertheless persuaded of their existence, because I can collect it from their effects and operations. They are the messengers which, running to and fro in the nerves, preserve a communication between the soul and outward objects.

Euph. You admit then the being of a soul?

Alc. Provided I do not admit an immaterial substance, I see no inconvenience in admitting there may be such a thing as a soul. And this may be no more than a thin fine texture of subtle parts or spirits residing in the brain.

Euph. I do not ask about its nature. I only ask whether

---

can an empirical fact, or any combination of them, prove Infinite and Eternal Power? Can an infinite conclusion be drawn from finite premises? 'The existence and nature of the Supreme Being,' says Reid (so far recognising this), 'is the *only real fact* that is *necessary*. Other real existences are the effects of will and power. They had a beginning and are mutable.' (Hamilton's Reid, p. 442.) In this respect God is unique, and so far out of analogy with embodied persons such as men.

you admit that there is a principle of thought and action, and whether *it* be perceivable by sense.

Alc. I grant that there is such a principle, and that it is not the object of sense itself, but inferred from appearances which are perceived by sense.

Euph. If I understand you rightly, from animal functions and motions you infer the existence of animal spirits, and from reasonable acts you infer the existence of a reasonable soul. Is it not so?

Alc. It is.

Euph. It should seem, therefore, that the being of things imperceptible to sense may be collected from effects and signs, or sensible tokens.

Alc. It may.

Euph. Tell me, Alciphron, is not the soul that which makes the principal distinction between a real person and a shadow, a living man and a carcass?

Alc. I grant it is.

Euph. I cannot, therefore, know that *you*, for instance, are a distinct thinking individual, or a real living man, by surer or other signs than those from which it can be inferred that you have a soul [1].

Alc. You cannot.

Euph. Pray tell me, are not all acts immediately and properly perceived by sense reducible to motion?

Alc. They are.

Euph. From motions, therefore, you infer a mover or cause; and from reasonable motions (or such as appear calculated for a reasonable end) a rational cause, soul or spirit?

Alc. Even so.

5. *Euph.* The soul of man actuates but a small body, an insignificant particle, in respect of the great masses of

[1] Accordingly, I cannot see another person. I can only see visible signs of him.

Nature, the elements, and heavenly bodies, and System of the World. And the wisdom that appears in those motions which are the effect of human reason is incomparably less than that which discovers itself in the structure and use of organised natural bodies, animal or vegetable. A man with his hand can make no machine so admirable as the hand itself; nor can any of those motions by which we trace out human reason approach the skill and contrivance of those wonderful motions of the heart, and brain, and other vital parts, which do not depend on the will of man.

Alc. All this is true.

Euph. Doth it not follow, then, that from natural motions, independent of man's will, may be inferred both power and wisdom incomparably greater than that of the human soul?

Alc. It should seem so.

Euph. Further, is there not in natural productions and effects a visible unity of counsel and design? Are not the rules fixed and immoveable? Do not the same laws of motion obtain throughout? The same in China and here, the same two thousand years ago and at this day?

Alc. All this I do not deny.

Euph. Is there not also a connexion or relation between animals and vegetables, between both and the elements, between the elements and heavenly bodies; so that, from their mutual respects, influences, subordinations, and uses, they may be collected to be parts of one whole, conspiring to one and the same end, and fulfilling the same design?

Alc. Supposing all this to be true.

Euph. Will it not then follow that this vastly great, or infinite, power and wisdom must be supposed in one and the same Agent, Spirit, or Mind; and that we have at least as clear, full, and immediate certainty of the being of this infinitely wise and powerful Spirit, as of any one human soul whatsoever besides our own?

Alc. Let me consider: I suspect we proceed too hastily. What! Do you pretend you can have the same assurance of the being of a God that you can have of mine, whom you actually *see* stand before you and talk to you?

Euph. The very same, if not greater.

Alc. How do you make this appear?

Euph. By the person Alciphron is meant an individual thinking thing, and not the hair, skin, or visible surface, or any part of the outward form, colour, or shape of Alciphron.

Alc. This I grant [1].

Euph. And, in granting this, you grant that, in a strict sense, I do not see Alciphron, i.e. that individual thinking thing, but only such visible signs and tokens as suggest and infer [2] the being of that invisible thinking principle or soul. Even so, in the self-same manner, it seems to me that, though I cannot with eyes of flesh behold the invisible God, yet I do in the strictest sense behold and perceive by all my senses such signs and tokens, such effects and operations, as suggest, indicate, and demonstrate an invisible God—as certainly, and with the same evidence, at least, as any other signs, perceived by sense, do suggest to me the existence of your soul, spirit, or thinking principle; which I am convinced of only by a few signs or effects, and the motions of one small organised body: whereas I do at all times and in all places perceive sensible signs which evince the being of God. The point, therefore, doubted or denied by you at the beginning, now seems manifestly to follow from the premises. Throughout this whole enquiry, have we not considered

---

[1] One is apt to object to this purely spiritual individuality, as an abstraction foreign to our experience of finite personality and agency, which we always find embodied;—rashly concluding from this that persons and all their conscious acts *ultimately* depend on matter, and then taking the bodily organism for the person.

[2] Here 'suggestion' and 'inference' are both included in the ground of our belief in the existence of other men.

every step with care, and made not the least advance without clear evidence? You and I examined and assented singly to each foregoing proposition: what shall we do then with the conclusion? For my part, if you do not help me out, I find myself under an absolute necessity of admitting it for true. You must therefore be content henceforward to bear the blame, if I live and die in the belief of a God[1].

6. *Alc.* It must be confessed, I do not readily find an answer. There seems to be some foundation for what you say. But, on the other hand, if the point was so clear as you pretend, I cannot conceive how so many sagacious men of our sect should be so much in the dark as not to know or believe one syllable of it.

Euph. O Alciphron, it is not our present business to account for the oversights, or vindicate the honour, of those great men the free-thinkers, when their very existence is in danger of being called in question.

Alc. How so?

Euph. Be pleased to recollect the concessions you have made, and then shew me, if the arguments for a Deity be not conclusive, by what better arguments you can prove the existence of that thinking thing which in strictness constitutes the free-thinker.

As soon as Euphranor had uttered these words, Alciphron stopped short, and stood in a posture of meditation, while the rest of us continued our walk and took two or three turns, after which he joined us again with a smiling countenance, like one who had made some discovery.

I have found, said he, what may clear up the point in

---

[1] The argument here ascends from finite facts given in sense to the Infinite Fact. It is based on the analogy of the proof from sensible facts of the existence of our fellow-men. But if *their* existence is only the existence of spirits that are embodied, are we to transfer this analogy to God? Or is the material universe an embodiment of Deity?

dispute, and give Euphranor entire satisfaction; I would say an argument which will prove the existence of a free-thinker, the like whereof cannot be applied to prove the existence of God. You must know then that your notion of our perceiving the existence of God, as certainly and immediately as we do that of a human person, I could by no means digest; though I must own it puzzled me, till I had considered the matter. At the first methought a particular structure, shape, or motion was a most certain proof of a thinking reasonable soul. But a little attention satisfied me that these things have no necessary connexion with reason, knowledge, and wisdom; and that, allowing them to be certain proofs of a living soul, they cannot be so of a thinking and reasonable one. Upon second thoughts, therefore, and a minute examination of this point, I have found that nothing so much convinces me of the existence of another person as *his speaking to me.* It is my hearing you talk that, in strict and philosophical truth, is to me the best argument for your being. And this is a peculiar argument, inapplicable to your purpose; for, you will not, I suppose, pretend that God speaks to man in the same clear and sensible manner as one man doth to another?

7. *Euph.* How! is then the impression of sound so much more evident than that of other senses? Or, if it be, is the voice of man louder than that of thunder?

Alc. Alas! you mistake the point. What I mean is not the sound of speech merely as such, but the arbitrary use of sensible signs, which have no similitude or necessary connexion with the things signified;—so as by the apposite management of them to suggest and exhibit to my mind an endless variety of things, differing in nature, time, and place; thereby informing me, entertaining me, and directing me how to act, not only with regard to things near and present, but also with regard to things distant and future. No matter whether these signs are pronounced or written; whether they enter by the eye or ear: they have the same use, and are equally proofs of an intelligent, thinking, designing cause.

Euph. But what if it should appear that God really speaks to man; would this content you?

Alc. I am for admitting no inward speech, no holy instincts, or suggestions of light or spirit. All that, you must know, passeth with men of sense for nothing[1]. If you do not make it plain to me that God speaks to men by outward sensible signs, of such sort and in such manner as I have defined, you do nothing.

Euph. But if it shall appear plainly that God speaks to men by the intervention and use of arbitrary, outward, sensible signs, having no resemblance or necessary connexion with the things they stand for and suggest: if it shall appear that, by innumerable combinations of these signs, an endless variety of things is discovered and made known to us; and that we are thereby instructed or informed in their different natures; that we are taught and admonished what to shun, and what to pursue; and are directed how to regulate our motions, and how to act with respect to things distant from us, as well in time as place, will this content you?

Alc. It is the very thing I would have you make out; for therein consists the force, and use, and nature of language.

8. *Euph.* Look, Alciphron, do you not see the castle upon yonder hill?

Alc. I do.

---

[1] If 'men of sense' could say that a man is only his living body, this might pass. But what if evidence of the presence and supremacy of God in the universe rests in our moral experience—evidence of a sort which if rejected would oblige us in consistency to disallow in external perception all that justifies us in treating the presented phenomena as signs and interpretable? What if the rise into acquired perception is itself inexplicable, except on grounds which require us to interpret experience under the presupposition that the universe is morally governed, and that *what ought to be* is thus the deepest and truest reality?

Euph. Is it not at a great distance from you?

Alc. It is.

Euph. Tell me, Alciphron, is not distance [1] a line turned endwise to the eye?

Alc. Doubtless.

Euph. And can a line, in that situation, project more than one single point on the bottom of the eye?

Alc. It cannot.

Euph. Therefore the appearance [2] of a long and of a short distance is of the same magnitude, or rather of no magnitude at all—being in all cases one single point.

Alc. It seems so.

Euph. Should it not follow from hence that distance is not immediately perceived by the eye?

Alc. It should [3].

Euph. Must it not then be perceived by the mediation of some other thing?

Alc. It must.

Euph. To discover what this is, let us examine what alteration there may be in the appearance of the same object placed at different distances from the eye. Now, I find by experience that when an object is removed still farther and

---

[1] i. e. distance outwards, or in the line of sight.

[2] 'appearance.' Does he mean here the *visible* appearance, and that we actually see the single point in the retina—which, as always of the same size, or rather of no size, cannot be a visible sign of distances that are of various degrees; or does he mean that, being of 'no magnitude,' the supposed appearance cannot be either a visible or invisible sign? In what follows he says nothing of instinct—a name for the unexplained—in his account of the way we learn to see things existing under space relations. To confess 'instinct' would be to allege that in the perception of placed things there lies an inexplicable fact. Berkeley tries so far to explain by means of 'suggestion' our perception of the significant phenomena we call the material world.

[3] Could it be *immediately* perceived in seeing, even if the 'appearance'—the point in the bottom of the eye—did vary according to the distance of the object seen?

farther off in a direct line from the eye, its visible appearance still grows lesser and fainter; and this change of appearance, being proportional and universal, seems to me to be that by which we apprehend the various degrees of distance.

Alc. I have nothing to object to this.

Euph. But littleness or faintness, in their own nature, seem to have no necessary connexion with greater length of distance?

Alc. I admit this to be true.

Euph. Will it not follow then that they could never suggest it but from experience?

Alc. It will.

Euph. That is to say—we perceive distance, not immediately, but by mediation of a sign, which hath no likeness to it, or necessary connexion with it, but only suggests it from repeated experience—as words do things [1].

Alc. Hold, Euphranor: now I think of it, the writers in optics tell us of an angle made by the two optic axes, where they meet in the visible point or object; which angle, the obtuser it is the nearer it shews the object to be, and by how much the acuter, by so much the farther off; and this from a necessary demonstrable connexion.

Euph. The mind then finds out the distance of things by geometry?

Alc. It doth.

Euph. Should it not follow, therefore, that nobody could see but those who had learned geometry, and knew something of lines and angles?

Alc. There is a sort of natural geometry which is got without learning.

Euph. Pray inform me, Alciphron, in order to frame a proof of any kind, or deduce one point from another, is it not necessary that I perceive the connexion of the terms in the premises, and the connexion of the premises with the

---

[1] Outness is only *signified* by its sensible signs—**not originally** *seen*.

conclusion; and, in general, to know one thing by means of another, must I not first know that other thing? When I perceive your meaning by your words, must I not first perceive the words themselves? and must I not know the premises before I infer the conclusion?

Alc. All this is true.

Euph. Whoever, therefore, collects a nearer distance from a wider angle, or a farther distance from an acuter angle, must first perceive the angles themselves. And he who doth not perceive those angles can infer nothing from them. Is it so or not?

Alc. It is as you say.

Euph. Ask now the first man you meet whether he perceives or knows anything of those optic angles? or whether he ever thinks about them, or makes any inferences from them, either by natural or artificial geometry? What answer do you think he would make?

Alc. To speak the truth, I believe his answer would be, that he knew nothing of these matters.

Euph. It cannot therefore be that men judge[1] of distance by angles: nor, consequently, can there be any force in the argument you drew from thence, to prove that distance is perceived by means of something which hath a necessary connexion with it.

Alc. I agree with you.

9. *Euph.* To me it seems that a man may know whether he perceives a thing or no; and, if he perceives it, whether it be immediately or mediately: and, if mediately, whether by means of something like or unlike, necessarily or arbitrarily connected with it.

Alc. It seems so.

Euph. And is it not certain that distance is perceived

---

[1] 'judge' here seems to include *demonstration through relations necessary in reason*, and so is different from Locke's 'judgment,' which is probable presumption based on analogy.

only by experience[1], if it be neither perceived immediately by itself, nor by means of any image, nor of any lines and angles which are like it, or have a necessary connexion with it?

Alc. It is.

Euph. Doth it not seem to follow, from what hath been said and allowed by you, that before all experience a man would not imagine the things he saw were at any distance from him?

Alc. How! let me see.

Euph. The littleness or faintness of appearance, or any other idea or sensation not necessarily connected with or resembling distance, can no more suggest different degrees of distance, or any distance at all, to the mind which hath not experienced a connexion of the things signifying and signified, than words can suggest notions before a man hath learned the language.

Alc. I allow this to be true.

Euph. Will it not thence follow that a man born blind, and made to see, would, upon first receiving his sight, take the things he saw not to be at any distance from him, but in his eye, or rather in his mind?

Alc. I must own it seems so. And yet, on the other hand, I can hardly persuade myself that, if I were in such a state, I should think those objects which I *now* see at so great distance to be at no distance at all.

Euph. It seems, then, that you now think[2] the objects of sight are at a distance from you?

---

[1] 'experience,' namely, of the connexion, established independently of human will, between what we see and movement among extra-organic bodies. But more than automatic sense-suggestion is surely latent in an acquired perception. Is not reason tacitly involved in *such* 'suggestions'?

[2] Think, i.e. judge—the judgment somehow emerging in the suggestion with which it is blended. Berkeley does not fully explain its appearance, or explicate it after it has appeared.

Alc. Doubtless I do. Can any one question but yonder castle is at a great distance?

Euph. Tell me, Alciphron, can you discern the doors, windows, and battlements of that same castle?

Alc. I cannot. At this distance it seems only a small round tower.

Euph. But I, who have been at it, know that it is no small round tower, but a large square building with battlements and turrets, which it seems you do not see.

Alc. What will you infer from thence?

Euph. I would infer that the very object which you strictly and properly perceive by sight is not that thing which is several miles distant.

Alc. Why so?

Euph. Because a little round object is one thing, and a great square object is another. Is it not?

Alc. I cannot deny it.

Euph. Tell me, is not the visible appearance alone the proper object of sight?

Alc. It is.

What think you now (said *Euphranor*, pointing towards the heavens) of the visible appearance of yonder planet? Is it not a round luminous flat, no bigger than a sixpence?

Alc. What then?

Euph. Tell me then, what you think of the planet itself. Do you not conceive it to be a vast opaque globe, with several unequal risings and valleys?

Alc. I do.

Euph. How can you therefore conclude that the proper object of your sight[1] exists at a distance?

---

[1] 'the proper object of sight,' i.e. the data that are due exclusively to sight,—before we have learned, in the way already explained, to read into them data of touch. This infant consciousness cannot be revived by the adult. And could the adult, one may ask, have read extension and space, with their mathematical relations, into the sensible data

Alc. I confess I know not.

Euph. For your further conviction, do but consider that crimson cloud. Think you that, if you were in the very place where it is, you would perceive anything like what you now see?

Alc. By no means. I should perceive only a dark mist.

Euph. Is it not plain, therefore, that neither the castle, the planet, nor the cloud, which you see here, are those real ones which you suppose exist at a distance?

10. *Alc.* What am I to think then? Do we see anything at all, or is it altogether fancy and illusion?

Euph. Upon the whole, it seems the proper objects of sight are light and colours, with their several shades and degrees; all which, being infinitely diversified and combined, do form a language wonderfully adapted to suggest and exhibit to us the distances, figures, situations, dimensions, and various qualities of tangible objects—not by similitude, nor yet by inference of necessary connexion, but by the arbitrary imposition of Providence [1], just as words suggest the things signified by them.

Alc. How! Do we not, strictly speaking, perceive by sight such things, as trees, houses, men, rivers, and the like?

Euph. We do, indeed, perceive or apprehend [2] those things by the faculty of sight. But will it follow from thence that

either of touch or of sight, unless extension and space had been presupposed?

[1] Modern doubt would not be satisfied by this unreasoned reference of material nature to Active Reason. Berkeley here takes no account of the supremacy of conscience, and the fundamental ethical postulates. It is in conscience, not in sensuous understanding, that our faith in God or divine optimism is rooted.

[2] 'perceive, or apprehend,' i.e. mediately—through 'suggestion,' or 'judgment according to sense,' as distinguished by Berkeley from direct apprehension, which also he calls 'perception'—both falling short of the scientific, and still more of the philosophic interpretation of the sensible world.

they are the proper and immediate objects of sight, any more than that all those things are the proper and immediate objects of hearing which are signified by the help of words or sounds?

Alc. You would have us think, then, that light, shades, and colours, variously combined, answer to the several articulations of sound in language; and that, by means thereof, all sorts of objects are suggested to the mind through the eye, in the same manner as they are suggested by words or sounds through the ear: that is, neither from necessary deduction to the judgment, nor from similitude to the fancy, but purely and solely from experience, custom, and habit.

Euph. I would not have you think anything more than the nature of things obligeth you to think, nor submit in the least to my judgment, but only to the force of truth: which is an imposition that I suppose the freest thinkers will not pretend to be exempt from.

Alc. You have led me, it seems, step by step, till I am got I know not where. But I shall try to get out again, if not by the way I came, yet by some other of my own finding.

Here *Alciphron*, having made a short pause, proceeded as follows—

11. Answer me, Euphranor, should it not follow from these principles that a man born blind, and made to see, would, at first sight, not only not perceive their distance, but also not so much as know the very things themselves which he saw, for instance, men or trees? which surely to suppose must be absurd.

Euph. I grant, in consequence of those principles, which both you and I have admitted, that such a one would never think of men, trees, or any other objects that he had been accustomed to perceive by touch, upon having his mind filled with new sensations of light and colours[1], whose various combinations he doth not yet understand, or know the meaning of; no more than a Chinese, upon first hearing the words *man* and *tree* would think of the things signified by them. In both cases, there must be time and experience, by repeated acts, to acquire a habit of knowing[2] the connexion between the signs and things signified; that is to say, of understanding the language, whether of the eyes or of the ears. And I conceive no absurdity in all this.

Alc. I see, therefore, in strict philosophical truth, that rock only in the same sense that I may be said to hear it, when the word *rock* is pronounced.

Euph. In the very same.

Alc. How comes it to pass then that every one shall say he sees, for instance, a rock or a house, when those things are before his eyes; but nobody will say he hears a rock or a house, but only the words or sounds themselves, by which those things are said to be signified or suggested but not heard? Besides, if vision be only a language speaking to the eyes, it may be asked, when did men learn this language? To acquire the knowledge of so many signs as go to the making up a language is a work of some difficulty. But,

---

[1] Here throughout he speaks of 'sensations of light and colours' as the visible language of vision, making no account of the visual but invisible signs *felt* in the organ of seeing.

[2] A 'habit of knowing.' Consider whether human science can be constituted only by habit or automatic suggestion. If not, what higher elements must it involve?—The office of custom must of course be recognised. It is at any rate a stage in the evolution of knowledge. 'Custom,' says Pascal, 'may be conceived as a secondary nature, and nature as a primary custom.' 'What,' he even asks, 'are all our natural principles but principles of custom, derived by hereditary descent from parents to children, as fear and flight in beasts of sport?' So too Wordsworth—

> 'And custom lie upon thee with a weight
> . . . . deep almost as life.'

will any man say he hath spent time, or been at pains, to learn this Language of Vision?

Euph. No wonder; we cannot assign a time beyond our remotest memory. If we have been all practising this language, ever since our first entrance into the world : if the Author of Nature constantly speaks to the eyes of all mankind, even in their earliest infancy, whenever the eyes are open in the light, whether alone or in company : it doth not seem to me at all strange that men should not be aware they had ever learned a language begun so early, and practised so constantly, as this of Vision. And, if we also consider that it is the same throughout the whole world, and not, like other languages, differing in different places, it will not seem unaccountable that men should mistake the connexion between the proper objects of sight and the things signified by them to be founded in necessary relation or likeness ; or, that they should even take them for the same things. Hence it seems easy to conceive why men who do not think should confound in this language of vision the signs with the things signified, otherwise than they are wont to do in the various particular languages formed by the several nations of men.

12. It may be also worth while to observe that signs, being little considered in themselves, or for their own sake, but only in their relative capacity, and for the sake of those things whereof they are signs, it comes to pass that the mind overlooks them, so as to carry its attention immediately on to the things signified. Thus, for example, in reading we run over the characters with the slightest regard, and pass on to the meaning. Hence it is frequent for men to say, they see words, and notions, and things in reading of a book ; whereas in strictness they see only the characters which suggest words, notions, and things. And, by parity of reason, may we not suppose that men, not resting in, but overlooking the immediate and proper objects of sight, as

in their own nature of small moment, carry their attention onward to the very things signified, and talk as if they saw the secondary objects? which, in truth and strictness, are not *seen*, but only *suggested* and *apprehended* by means of the proper objects of sight, which alone are seen.

Alc. To speak my mind freely, this dissertation grows tedious, and runs into points too dry and minute for a gentleman's attention.

I thought, said *Crito*, we had been told that minute philosophers loved to consider things closely and minutely.

Alc. That is true, but in so polite an age who would be a mere philosopher? There is a certain scholastic accuracy which ill suits the freedom and ease of a well-bred man. But, to cut short this chicane, I propound it fairly to your own conscience, whether you really think that God Himself speaks every day and in every place to the eyes of all men.

Euph. That is really and in truth my opinion; and it should be yours too, if you are consistent with yourself, and abide by your own definition of language. Since you cannot deny that the great Mover and Author of nature constantly explaineth Himself to the eyes of men by the sensible intervention of arbitrary signs, which have no similitude or connexion with the things signified; so as, by compounding and disposing them, to suggest and exhibit an endless variety of objects, differing in nature, time, and place; thereby informing and directing men how to act with respect to things distant and future, as well as near and present. In consequence, I say, of your own sentiments and concessions, you have as much reason to think the Universal Agent or God speaks to your eyes, as you can have for thinking any particular person speaks to your ears[1].

---

[1] This argument by implication universalises the fact of continuous personal existence, assumed to be given in our primary consciousness (*Principles*, § 2), and of which, in Berkeley's language, we have a

Alc. I cannot help thinking that some fallacy runs throughout this whole ratiocination, though perhaps I may not readily point it out. Hold! let me see. In language the signs are arbitrary, are they not?

Euph. They are.

Alc. And, consequently, they do not always suggest real matters of fact. Whereas this Natural Language, as you call it, or these visible signs, do always suggest things in the same uniform way, and have the same constant regular connexion with matters of fact: whence it should seem the connexion was necessary; and, therefore, according to the definition premised, it can be no language. How do you solve this objection?

Euph. You may solve it yourself by the help of a picture or looking-glass.

Alc. You are in the right. I see there is nothing in it. I know not what else to say to this opinion, more than that it is so odd and contrary to my way of thinking that I shall never assent to it.

13. *Euph.* Be pleased to recollect your own lectures upon prejudice, and apply them in the present case. Perhaps they may help you to follow where reason leads, and to suspect notions which are strongly rivetted, without having been ever examined.

Alc. I disdain the suspicion of prejudice. And I do not speak only for myself. I know a club of most ingenious

---

'notion.' He thus infers, by analogy, the constant omnipresence of God in nature. The argument is an application of an assumed analogy between the visible signs of the existence of a man, on the one hand, and the symbolism of the sensible world, on the other hand,—as premises of the conclusion that both are revelations of *spiritual* agency. It implies too that the causal demand can find rest only in an absolute cause—not in the caused causation, or sensible signs, of natural science. Is the sensible world to be viewed as the divine organism? Or is the analogy between the human organism and the material universe, as the supposed organism of God, incomplete?

men, the freest from prejudice of any men alive, who abhor the notion of a God, and I doubt not would be very able to untie this knot.

Upon which words of Alciphron, I, who had acted the part of an indifferent stander-by, observed to him—That it misbecame his character and repeated professions, to own an attachment to the judgment, or build upon the presumed abilities of other men, how ingenious soever; and that this proceeding might encourage his adversaries to have recourse to authority [1], in which perhaps they would find their account more than he.

Oh! said *Crito*, I have often observed the conduct of minute philosophers. When one of them has got a ring of disciples round him, his method is to exclaim against prejudice, and recommend thinking and reasoning, giving to understand that himself is a man of deep researches and close argument, one who examines impartially, and concludes warily. The same man, in other company, if he chance to be pressed with reason, shall laugh at logic, and assume the lazy supine airs of a fine gentleman, a wit, a *railleur*, to avoid the dryness of a regular and exact inquiry. This double face of the minute philosopher is of no small use to propagate and maintain his notions. Though to me it seems a plain case that if a fine gentleman will shake off authority, and appeal from religion to reason, unto reason he must go: and, if he cannot go without leading-strings, surely he had better be led by the authority of the public than by that of any knot of minute philosophers.

---

[1] 'authority,' i.e. fallible authority of trusted men—faith in the insight of experts, as distinguished from our own. But in Berkeley's view of language immanent in Nature, all reasonings about Nature are based on faith in God, and are thus reasonings about facts which are grounded on authority—the absolute or infallible authority of a personal God.

Alc. Gentlemen, this discourse is very irksome, and needless. For my part, I am a friend to inquiry. I am willing reason should have its full and free scope. I build on no man's authority. For my part, I have no interest in denying a God. Any man may believe or not believe a God, as he pleases, for me. But, after all, Euphranor must allow me to stare a little at his conclusions.

Euph. The conclusions are yours as much as mine, for you were led to them by your own concessions.

14. You, it seems, stare to find that God is not far from every one of us; and that in Him we live, and move, and have our being[1]. You, who, in the beginning of this morning's conference, thought it strange that God should leave Himself without a witness, do now think it strange the witness should be so full and clear.

Alc. I must own I do. I was aware, indeed, of a certain metaphysical hypothesis of our seeing all things in God by the union of the human soul with the intelligible substance of the Deity, which neither I nor any one else could make sense of[2]. But I never imagined it could be pretended that we saw God with our fleshly eyes as plain as we see any human person whatsoever, and that He daily speaks to our senses in a manifest and clear dialect.

Cri. As for that metaphysical hypothesis, I can make no more of it than you. But I think it plain this Optic Language hath a necessary connexion[3] with knowledge, wisdom and

---

[1] Because, on this view of things, God animates the whole sensible universe, like as a man animates the movements of his own body: God uses the physical system as the symbol and sacrament of the spiritual agency that is externalised in it: all *natural* changes and their laws are referred to the Divine Will. Nature would thus be throughout supernatural.

[2] This refers to Malebranche's hypothesis, which Berkeley here and elsewhere disclaims, for reasons which should be studied. It is perhaps less remote from his own philosophy, as developed in *Siris*, than at this earlier stage in his mental history he supposes it to be.

[3] He thus postulates a necessary connexion between the physical and

goodness. It is equivalent to a constant creation, betokening an immediate act of power and providence. It cannot be accounted for by mechanical principles, by atoms, attractions, or effluvia. The instantaneous production and reproduction of so many signs, combined, dissolved, transposed, diversified, and adapted to such an endless variety of purposes, ever shifting with the occasions and suited to them, being utterly inexplicable and unaccountable by the laws of motion, by chance, by fate, or the like blind principles, doth set forth and testify the immediate operation of a spirit or thinking being; and not merely of a spirit, which every motion or gravitation may possibly infer, but of one wise, good, and provident Spirit, which directs and rules and governs the world. Some philosophers, being convinced of the wisdom and power of the Creator, from the make and contrivance of organised bodies and orderly system of the world, did nevertheless imagine that he left this system with all its parts and contents well adjusted and put in motion, as an artist leaves a clock, to go thenceforward of itself for a certain period[1]. But this Visual Language proves, not a Creator merely, but a provident Governor, actually and intimately present, and attentive to all our interests and motions, who watches over our conduct, and takes care of our minutest actions and designs

---

the spiritual or moral government of the universe—without showing the 'necessity.' He implies that the former must be subordinate to the latter, which is supreme. Compare with Plato and the idea of the Good, or Butler and Kant on the Supremacy of Moral Reason.

[1] This is the philosophical theory of an established Harmony, by which Leibniz sought to explain the inter-dependent agency of conscious persons and unconscious things. Leibniz uses the analogy of the watch in his correspondence with Clarke. See *Collection of Papers between Leibnitz and Clarke, relating to the Principles of Natural Philosophy and Religion* (1717), pp. 2–6, 12–16, 28–34, &c. On the other hand, on Berkeley's conception of what the reality of the material world means, the interpretable Cosmos would relapse into a Chaos if the Divine providential action in it were for a moment withdrawn.

throughout the whole course of our lives, informing, admonishing, and directing incessantly, in a most evident and sensible manner. This is truly wonderful.

Euph. And is it not so, that men should be encompassed by such a wonder, without reflecting on it?

15. Something there is of Divine and admirable in this Language, addressed to our eyes, that may well awaken the mind, and deserve its utmost attention :—it is learned with so little pains: it expresseth the differences of things so clearly and aptly : it instructs with such facility and despatch, by one glance of the eye conveying a greater variety of advices, and a more distinct knowledge of things, than could be got by a discourse of several hours. And, while it informs, it amuses and entertains the mind with such singular pleasure and delight. It is of such excellent use in giving a stability and permanency to human discourse, in recording sounds and bestowing life on dead languages, enabling us to converse with men of remote ages and countries. And it answers so apposite to the uses and necessities of mankind, informing us more distinctly of those objects whose nearness and magnitude qualify them to be of greatest detriment or benefit to our bodies, and less exactly in proportion as their littleness or distance makes them of less concern to us [1].

Alc. And yet these strange things affect men but little.

Euph. But they are not strange, they are familiar ; and that makes them be overlooked. Things which rarely happen strike ; whereas frequency lessens the admiration of things, though in themselves ever so admirable. Hence, a common man, who is not used to think and make reflections, would probably be more convinced of the being of a God by one

---

[1] Berkeley makes much of the sensible evidence of the constant active presence of God being such that we may be said to *see* Him as we see a fellow-man. Does not faith in the constancy of natural order imply tacitly faith in Omnipotent Goodness?

single sentence heard once in his life from the sky than by all the experience he has had of this Visual Language, contrived with such exquisite skill, so constantly addressed to his eyes, and so plainly declaring the nearness, wisdom, and providence of Him with whom we have to do [1].

Alc. After all, I cannot satisfy myself how men should be so little surprised or amazed about this visive faculty, if it was really of a nature so surprising and amazing.

Euph. But let us suppose a nation of men blind from their infancy, among whom a stranger arrives, the only man who can see in all the country; let us suppose this stranger travelling with some of the natives, and that one while he foretells to them that, in case they walk straight forward, in half an hour they shall meet men or cattle, or come to a house; that, if they turn to the right and proceed, they shall in a few minutes be in danger of falling down a precipice; that, shaping their course to the left, they will in such a time arrive at a river, a wood, or a mountain. What think you? Must they not be infinitely surprised that one who had never been in their country before should know it so much better than themselves? And would not those predictions seem to them as unaccountable and incredible as Prophecy to a minute philosopher?

Alc. I cannot deny it.

Euph. But it seems to require intense thought to be able to unravel a prejudice that has been so long forming; to get over the vulgar errors or ideas common to both senses; and so to distinguish between the objects of Sight and Touch, which have grown (if I may so say), blended together [2] in

---

[1] 'In philosophy equally as in poetry,' says Coleridge, 'it is the highest and most useful prerogative of genius to produce the strongest impressions of novelty, while it rescues admitted truths from the neglect caused by the very circumstance of their universal admission.'

[2] 'blended together.' So in his Commonplace Book he says that

our fancy, as to be able to suppose ourselves exactly in the state that one of those men would be in, if he were made to see. And yet this I believe is possible, and might seem worth the pains of a little thinking, especially to those men whose proper employment and profession it is to think, and unravel prejudices, and confute mistakes.

Alc. I frankly own I cannot find my way out of this maze, and should gladly be set right by those who see better than myself.

Cri. The pursuing this subject in their own thoughts would possibly open a new scene to those speculative gentlemen of the minute philosophy. It puts me in mind of a passage in the Psalmist, where he represents God to be covered with light as with a garment, and would methinks be no ill comment on that ancient notion of some eastern sages — that God had light for His body, and truth for His soul[1].

This conversation lasted till a servant came to tell us the tea was ready: upon which we walked in, and found Lysicles at the tea-table.

16. As soon as we sat down, I am glad, said *Alciphron*, that I have here found my second, a fresh man to maintain our common cause, which, I doubt, Lysicles will think hath suffered by his absence.

Lys. Why so?

' extension is *blended with* tangible or visible ideas,' which might mean that it is a latent pre-condition of sense experience.

[1] According to this philosophy, the significant phenomena presented in the senses—conspicuously those given in sight—are types or symbols of spiritual and unseen realities : physical order is an instrument of ethical. The supporting argument for this might be, that the theistic explanation, and that alone, affords a trustworthy natural universe, fit to be reasoned about and interpreted. But Berkeley relies too exclusively on sense, and understanding judging according to suggestions of sense, and takes too little account of moral postulates.

Alc. I have been drawn into some concessions you will not like.

Lys. Let me know what they are.

Alc. Why, that there is such a thing as a God, and that His existence is very certain.

Lys. Bless me! How came you to entertain so wild a notion?

Alc. You know we profess to follow reason wherever it leads. And in short I have been reasoned into it.

Lys. Reasoned! You should say, amused with words, bewildered with sophistry.

Euph. Have you a mind to hear the same reasoning that led Alciphron and me step by step, that we may examine whether it be sophistry or no?

Lys. As to that I am very easy. I guess all that can be said on that head. It shall be my business to help my friend out, whatever arguments drew him in.

Euph. Will you admit the premises and deny the conclusions?

Lys. What if I admit the conclusion?

Euph. How! will you grant there is a God?

Lys. Perhaps I may.

Euph. Then we are agreed.

Lys. Perhaps not.

Euph. O Lysicles, you are a subtle adversary. I know not what you would be at.

Lys. You must know then that at bottom the being of a God is a point in itself of small consequence, and a man may make this concession without yielding much. The great point is what sense the word *God* is to be taken in [1].

---

[1] This is still a 'great point' in the philosophy of religion. Is God, so far as knowable by man, a conscious Person, incognisable by *us* otherwise;—or merely a name for the Reason presupposed in experience; or even for totally unknowable Power?

The very Epicureans allowed the being of gods; but then they were indolent gods, unconcerned with human affairs. Hobbes allowed a corporeal god: and Spinosa held the universe to be God. And yet nobody doubts they were staunch free-thinkers. I could wish indeed the word God were quite omitted; because in most minds it is coupled with a sort of superstitious awe, the very root of all religion. I shall not, nevertheless, be much disturbed, though the *name* be retained, and the being of a God allowed in any sense but in that of a Mind, which knows all things, and beholds human actions, like some judge or magistrate, with infinite observation and intelligence. The belief of a God in this sense fills a man's mind with scruples, lays him under constraints, and embitters his very being: but in another sense it may be attended with no great ill consequence. This I know was the opinion of our great Diagoras, who told me he would never have been at the pains to find out a demonstration that there was no God[1], if the received notion of God had been the same with that of some Fathers and Schoolmen.

Euph. Pray what was that?

17. *Lys.* You must know, Diagoras, a man of much reading and inquiry, had discovered that once upon a time the most profound and speculative divines, finding it impossible to reconcile the attributes of God—taken in the common sense, or in any known sense—with human reason, and the appearance of things, taught that the words *knowledge, wisdom, goodness,* and such like, when spoken of the Deity, must be understood in quite a different sense from what they signify in the vulgar acceptation, or from anything that we can form a notion of or conceive. Hence, whatever

---

[1] The most plausible objections to Theism are founded on the final insolubility of the universe of nature and man. Agnosticism is offered as the alternative to either Theism or Atheism,—'suspense of judgment' as the only possible position at last.

objections might be made against the attributes of God they easily solved—by denying those attributes belonged to God, in this, or that, or any known particular sense or notion; which was the same thing as to deny they belonged to Him at all. And, thus denying the attributes of God, they in effect denied His being, though perhaps they were not aware of it.

Suppose, for instance, a man should object that future contingencies were inconsistent with the Foreknowledge of God, because it is repugnant that certain knowledge should be of an uncertain thing: it was a ready and an easy answer to say that this may be true with respect to knowledge taken in the common sense, or in any sense that we can possibly form any notion of; but that there would not appear the same inconsistency between the contingent nature of things and Divine Foreknowledge, taken to signify somewhat that we know nothing of, which in God supplies the place of what we understand by knowledge; from which it differs not in quantity or degree of perfection, but altogether, and in kind, as light doth from sound;—and even more, since these agree in that they are both sensations; whereas knowledge in God hath no sort of resemblance or agreement with any notion that man can frame of knowledge. The like may be said of all the other attributes, which indeed may by this means be equally reconciled with everything or with nothing. But all men who think must needs see this is cutting knots and not untying them. For, how are things reconciled with the Divine attributes when these attributes themselves are in every intelligible sense denied; and, consequently, the very notion of God taken away, and nothing left but the name, without any meaning annexed to it? In short, the belief that there is an unknown subject of attributes absolutely unknown is a very innocent doctrine; which the acute Diagoras well saw, and was therefore wonderfully delighted with this system.

18. For, said he, if this could once make its way and obtain in the world, there would be an end to all natural or rational religion, which is the basis both of the Jewish and the Christian: for he who comes to God, or enters himself in the church of God, must first believe that there is a *God in some intelligible sense*; and not only that there is *Something in general, without any proper notion, though never so inadequate, of any of its qualities or attributes*: for this may be fate, or chaos, or plastic nature, or anything else as well as God.—Nor will it avail to say:—There is something in this unknown being *analogous* to knowledge and goodness; that is to say, which produceth those effects which we could not conceive to be produced by men, in any degree, without knowledge and goodness. For, this is in fact to give up the point in dispute between theists and atheists—the question having always been, not whether there was a Principle (which point was allowed by all philosophers, as well before as since Anaxagoras), but whether this principle was a νοῦς, a thinking intelligent being: that is to say, whether that order, and beauty, and use, visible in natural effects, could be produced by anything but a Mind of Intelligence, in the proper sense of the word? And whether there must not be true, real, and proper knowledge, in the First Cause? We will, therefore, acknowledge that all those natural effects which are vulgarly ascribed to knowledge and wisdom proceed from a being in which there is, properly speaking, no knowledge or wisdom at all, but only something else, which in reality is the cause of those things which men, for want of knowing better, ascribe to what they call knowledge and wisdom and understanding. You wonder perhaps to hear a man of pleasure, who diverts himself as I do, philosophize at this rate. But you should consider that much is to be got by conversing with ingenious men, which is a short way to knowledge, that saves a man the drudgery of reading and thinking.

And, now we have granted to you that there is a God in this indefinite sense, I would fain see what use you can make of this concession. You cannot argue from unknown attributes, or, which is the same thing, from attributes in an unknown sense. You cannot prove that God is to be loved for His goodness, or feared for His justice, or respected for His knowledge: all which consequences, we own, would follow from those attributes admitted in an intelligible sense. But we deny that those or any other consequences can be drawn from attributes admitted in no particular sense, or in a sense which none of us understand. Since, therefore, nothing can be inferred from such an account of God, about conscience, or worship, or religion, you may even make the best of it. And, not to be singular, we will use the name too, and so at once there is an end of atheism.

Euph. This account of a Deity is new to me. I do not like it, and therefore shall leave it to be maintained by those who do.

19. *Cri.* It is not new to me. I remember not long since to have heard a minute philosopher triumph upon this very point; which put me on inquiring what foundation there was for it in the Fathers or Schoolmen. And, for aught that I can find, it owes its original to those writings which have been published under the name of Dionysius the Areopagite[1]. The author of which, it must

---

[1] May we not say that reason in man at last necessarily merges in faith or moral trust in the omnipotent goodness of the Power at work in the physical and spiritual system in which, in our bodily and moral experience, we find ourselves included? Does not this, with its background of mystery, meet our intellectual inadequacy—God thus practically comprehended, while still scientifically incomprehensible? Does not Berkeley incline too much to the anthropomorphic Theism that is content to think of God as one Spirit among many? 'Knowledge,' 'wisdom,' and 'goodness,' so far as *our* experience can go, may be inadequate terms when applied to Deity, not because the Universal

be owned, hath written upon the Divine attributes in a very singular style. In his treatise *De Hierarchia Coelesti*, he saith that God is something above all essence and life, ὑπὲρ πᾶσαν οὐσίαν καὶ ζωήν; and again, in his treatise *De Divinis Nominibus*, that He is above all wisdom and understanding, ὑπὲρ πᾶσαν σοφίαν καὶ σύνεσιν, ineffable and innominable, ἄρρητος καὶ ἀνώνυμος; the wisdom of God he terms an unreasonable, unintelligent, and foolish wisdom, τὴν ἄλογον, καὶ ἄνουν, καὶ μωρὰν σοφίαν. But then the reason he gives for expressing himself in this strange manner is, that the Divine wisdom is the cause of all reason, wisdom, and understanding, and therein are contained the treasures of all wisdom and knowledge. He calls God ὑπέρσοφος and ὑπέρζως; as if wisdom and life were words not worthy to express the Divine perfections: and he adds that the attributes unintelligent and unperceiving must be ascribed to the Divinity, not κατ' ἔλλειψιν, by way of defect, but καθ' ὑπεροχήν, by way of eminency; which he explains by our giving the name of darkness to light inaccessible. And, notwithstanding the harshness of his expressions in some places, he affirms over and over in others—that God knows all things; not that He is beholden to the creatures for His knowledge, but by knowing Himself, from whom they all derive their being, and in whom they are contained as in their cause. It was late before these writings appear to have been known in the world; and, although they obtained credit during the age of the Schoolmen, yet, since critical learning hath been cultivated, they have lost that credit, and are at this day given up for spurious, as containing several evident marks of a much later date than the age of Dionysius.—Upon the whole, although this method of growing in expression and dwindling in notion, of clearing up doubts by nonsense, and avoiding difficulties by running

---

Power includes less, but because the Universal Power includes more than even our highest thought enables us to conceive.

into affected contradictions, may perhaps proceed from a well-meant zeal, yet it appears not to be according to knowledge; and, instead of reconciling atheists to the truth, hath, I doubt, a tendency to confirm them in their own persuasion. It should seem, therefore, very weak and rash in a Christian to adopt this harsh language of an apocryphal writer preferably to that of the Holy Scriptures. I remember, indeed, to have read of a certain philosopher, who lived some centuries ago, that used to say—if these supposed works of Dionysius had been known to the primitive Fathers, they would have furnished them admirable weapons against the heretics, and would have saved a world of pains But the event since their discovery hath by no means confirmed his opinion [1].

It must be owned, the celebrated Picus of Mirandula [2], among his nine hundred conclusions (which that prince, being very young, proposed to maintain by public disputation at Rome), hath this for one—to wit, that it is more improper to say of God, He is an intellect or intelligent Being, than to say of a reasonable soul that it is an angel:

---

[1] The books attributed to Dionysius the Areopagite, who was said to be a contemporary of the Apostles (Acts xvii. 34) and first Bishop of Athens. They belong probably to the fourth century after Christ, if not to a later period, and to the New Platonic school. They are entitled *De Hierarchia Coelesti, De Nominibus Divinis, De Hierarchia Ecclesiastica,* and *De Theologia Mystica.* Various editions appeared in the sixteenth and seventeenth centuries. In common with some Fathers of the Church, the pseudo-Dionysius expresses, in paradoxical language, the ultimate incomprehensibility of God, unbalanced by the counter truth that God may be truly known,—as at man's finite point of view, and relatively to the ends of human life. He ascends (or descends) to a point at which, by total abstraction of attributes, the Universal Power becomes wholly incognisable. The subject invites to the study of Kant's 'Dialectic,' B. II. ch. 3, in the *Kritik of Pure Reason.*

[2] John Picus, Count of Mirandula, lived in the fifteenth century. The disputation in which he proposed to defend his nine hundred theses never took place.

which doctrine it seems was not relished. And Picus, when he comes to defend it, supports himself altogether by the example and authority of Dionysius, and in effect explains it away into a mere verbal difference—affirming that neither Dionysius nor himself ever meant to deprive God of knowledge, or to deny that He knows all things; but that, as reason is of kind peculiar to man, so by intellection he understands a kind or manner of knowing peculiar to angels; and that the knowledge which is in God is more above the intellection of angels than angel is above man. He adds that, as his tenet consists with admitting the most perfect knowledge in God, so he would by no means be understood to exclude from the Deity intellection itself, taken in the common or general sense, but only that peculiar sort of intellection proper to angels, which he thinks ought not to be attributed to God any more than human reason. Picus, therefore, though he speaks as the apocryphal Dionysius, yet, when he explains himself, it is evident he speaks like other men. And, although the forementioned books of the Celestial Hierarchy and of the Divine Names, being attributed to a saint and martyr of the apostolical age, were respected by the Schoolmen, yet it is certain they rejected or softened his harsh expressions, and explained away or reduced his doctrine to the received notions taken from Holy Scripture and the light of nature.

20. Thomas Aquinas[1] expresseth his sense of this point in the following manner. All perfections, saith he, derived from God to the creatures are in a certain higher sense, or (as the Schoolmen term it) *eminently* in God. Whenever, therefore, a name borrowed from any perfection in the

[1] Thomas of Aquino (Aquinas), in the territory of Naples (1225-74), in whose works the philosophy called Scholastic reached its highest point, accommodating Aristotle to the teaching of the Catholic Church. His philosophical theology, or theological philosophy, is contained in his *Summa Thelogiae*.

creature is attributed to God, we must exclude from its signification everything that belongs to the imperfect manner wherein that attribute is found in the creature. Whence he concludes that knowledge in God is not a habit but a pure act. And again, the same Doctor observes that our intellect gets its notions of all sorts of perfections from the creatures, and that as it apprehends those perfections so it signifies them by names. Therefore, saith he, in attributing these names to God we are to consider two things: first, the perfections themselves, as goodness, life, and the like, which are properly in God; and secondly, the manner which is peculiar to the creature, and cannot, strictly and properly speaking, be said to agree to the Creator.

And although Suarez[1], with other Schoolmen, teacheth that the mind of man conceiveth knowledge and will to be in God as faculties or operations, by analogy only to created beings, yet he gives it plainly as his opinion that when knowledge is said not to be properly in God it must be understood in a sense including imperfection, such as discursive knowledge[2] or the like imperfect kind found in the creatures: and that none of those imperfections in the knowledge of men or angels belonging to the formal notion of knowledge, or to knowledge as such, it will not thence follow that knowledge, in its proper formal sense, may not be attributed to God. And of knowledge taken

---

[1] Suarez, the Spanish Thomist, who died in 1617. What follows is related in his *Disputationes Metaphysicae*, XXX. 'Quid Deus sit.'

[2] Knowledge reached only through the intervention of what is supposed to be already known, i. e. by means of premises, is called 'discursive,' and forms discursive as distinguished from intuitive knowledge. Discursive or syllogistic activity is a mark of the finitude of the mind that is obliged to have recourse to it. Were we able to know all things and all their relations in a single view, discursive thought would seem to be superfluous. It is in all-comprehensive intuition, we suppose, that Omniscient Intelligence knows.

in general for the clear evident understanding of all truth, he expressly affirms that it is in God, and that this was never denied by any philosopher who believed a God[1]. It was, indeed, a current opinion in the schools that even *being* itself should be attributed *analogically* to God and the creatures. That is, they held that God, the supreme, independent, self-originate cause and source of all beings, must not be supposed to *exist* in the same sense with created beings; not that he exists less truly, properly, or formally than they, but only because he exists in a more eminent and perfect manner[2].

21. But, to prevent any man's being led, by mistaking the scholastic use of the terms *analogy* and *analogical*, into an opinion that we cannot frame in any degree a true and proper notion of attributes applied by analogy, or, in the school phrase, predicated analogically, it may not be amiss to inquire into the true sense and meaning of those words. Every one knows that *analogy* is a Greek word used by mathematicians to signify a similitude of proportions. For instance, when we observe that two is to six as three is to nine, this similitude or equality of proportion is termed analogy. And, although proportion strictly signifies the habitude or relation of one quantity to another, yet, in a looser and translated sense, it hath been applied to signify every other habitude; and, consequently, the term analogy comes to signify all similitude of relations or habitudes whatsoever. Hence the Schoolmen tell us there

---

[1] But if Omniscience does not, like our limited or broken knowledge, presuppose a *succession* of conscious acts going on in God, contemporaneously with our own conscious acts and states—as we represent to ourselves the intellectual life of a fellow man—we cannot realise the 'clear evident understanding of all truth' by God: the act that is conceivable by us must be part of a succession.

[2] All this is very different from the materialistic dogma, that the Universal Power is *below*, instead of mysteriously *above*, the conscious life we experience, in which our spirits are revealed to ourselves.

is analogy between intellect and sight; forasmuch as intellect is to the mind what sight is to the body, and that he who governs the state is analogous to him who steers a ship. Hence a prince is analogically styled a pilot, being to the state as a pilot is to his vessel.

For the further clearing of this point, it is to be observed that a twofold analogy is distinguished by the Schoolmen—metaphorical and proper.—Of the first kind there are frequent instances in Holy Scripture, attributing human parts and passions to God. When He is represented as having a finger, an eye, or an ear; when He is said to repent, to be angry, or grieved; every one sees that analogy is metaphorical. Because those parts and passions, taken in the proper signification, must, in every degree, necessarily and from the formal nature of the thing, include imperfection. When, therefore, it is said—the finger of God appears in this or that event, men of common sense mean no more but that it is as truly ascribed to God as the works wrought by human fingers are to man: and so of the rest. But the case is different when wisdom and knowledge are attributed to God. Passions and senses, as such, imply defect; but in knowledge simply, or as such, there is no defect[1]. Knowledge, therefore, in the proper formal meaning of the word, may be attributed to God *proportionably*, that is preserving a proportion to the infinite nature of God[2]. We may say, therefore, that as God is infinitely above man, so is the knowledge of God infinitely above the knowledge of

---

[1] But what if there is something which forbids the resolution of the divinely constituted universe into a perfectly comprehended unity, by human intellectual power, and which obliges us, if we have regard to reason, to 'leave many things abrupt,' as Bacon says the philosophical theologian must at last do? The sceptical issue of attempted omniscience on man's part, as contrasted with the philosophy that begins and ends in moral faith, proves that the Infinite Reality refuses to be *fully* known in our 'little systems.'

[2] What does this apparently important qualification imply?

man, and this is what Cajetan calls *analogia proprie facta*. And after this same analogy we must understand all those attributes to belong to the Deity which in themselves simply, and as such, denote perfection. We may, therefore, consistently with what hath been premised, affirm that all sorts of perfection which we can conceive in a finite spirit are in God, but without any of that allay[1] which is found in the creatures. This doctrine, therefore, of analogical perfections in God, or our knowing God by analogy, seems very much misunderstood and misapplied by those who would infer from thence that we cannot frame any direct or proper notion, though never so inadequate, of knowledge or wisdom, as they are in the Deity; or understand any more of them than one born blind can of light and colours[2].

22. And now, gentlemen, it may be expected I should ask your pardon for having dwelt so long on a point of metaphysics, and introduced such unpolished and unfashionable writers as the Schoolmen into good company;

---

[1] 'allay,' i.e. alloy. 'Allay' in Bacon and other early writers.

[2] In what he says about an *analogical* knowledge of God, Berkeley had probably in view two contemporary theologians—both Irish bishops. Among other replies to Toland's *Christianity not Mysterious* (1696) was a *Letter* by Peter Browne, afterwards Bishop of Cork and Ross, which appeared in 1699. Browne maintains (so far in verbal agreement with Berkeley) that we have no *idea* of spirit; and further, that our knowledge of God and the spiritual world is gained by analogy from our knowledge of the operations of our own embodied spirit. Also in 1709, Archbishop King published a Sermon on the *Consistency of Predestination and Foreknowledge with the Freedom of Man's Will*, which he defended on the same foundation of analogy, in a way that seems to imply that our highest conception of God must be in metaphors, not in science. Browne's view of human theological knowledge is given in his *Procedure, Extent, and Limits of Human Understanding* (1728), and more fully in *Things Divine and Supernatural conceived by Analogy with Things Natural and Human* (1733).—Butler's 'analogy' between the constitution of nature and that larger constitution that is implied in Religion, is not to be confounded with Browne's analogical interpretation of the attributes of God.

but, as Lysicles gave the occasion, I leave him to answer for it.

Lys. I never dreamt of this dry dissertation. But, if I have been the occasion of discussing these scholastic points, by my unluckily mentioning the Schoolmen, it was my first fault of the kind, and I promise it shall be the last. The meddling with crabbed authors of any sort is none of my taste. I grant one meets now and then with a good notion in what we call dry writers, such a one for example as this I was speaking of, which I must own struck my fancy. But then, for these we have such as Prodicus or Diagoras, who look into obsolete books, and save the rest of us that trouble.

Cri. So you pin your faith upon them?

Lys. It is only for some odd opinions, and matters of fact, and critical points. Besides, we know the men to whom we give credit; they are judicious and honest, and have no end to serve but truth. And I am confident some author or other has maintained the forementioned notion in the same sense as Diagoras related it.

Cri. That may be. But it never was a received notion, and never will, so long as men believe a God: the same arguments that prove a First Cause proving an Intelligent Cause;—intelligent, I say, in the proper sense; wise and good in the true and formal acceptation of the words. Otherwise, it is evident that every syllogism brought to prove those attributes, or, which is the same thing, to prove the being of a God, will be found to consist of four terms, and consequently can conclude nothing[1]. But for your

---

[1] 'Four terms' in a syllogism—one of the commonest fallacies, due to the ambiguity of human language. The reference is to the position in Bishop Browne in his *Procedure of the Understanding* and *Divine Analogy*, where he argues that God's so-called 'knowledge' and 'goodness' are not knowledge or goodness as we understand those terms, but only words that represent mysteries which transcend human intelligence. Can this be reconciled with theistic faith?

part, *Alciphron*, you have been fully convinced that God is a thinking intelligent being, in the same sense with other spirits; though not in the same imperfect manner or degree.

23. *Alc.* And yet I am not without my scruples: for, with knowledge you infer wisdom, and with wisdom goodness. But how is it possible to conceive God so good and man so wicked? It may, perhaps, with some colour be alleged that a little soft shadowing of evil sets off the bright and luminous parts of the creation, and so contributes to the beauty of the whole piece; but for blots so large and so black it is impossible to account by that principle. That there should be so much vice, and so little virtue upon earth, and that the laws of God's kingdom should be so ill observed by His subjects, is what can never be reconciled with that surpassing wisdom and goodness of the supreme Monarch [1].

Euph. Tell me, *Alciphron*, would you argue that a state was ill administered, or judge of the manners of its citizens, by the disorders committed in the jail or dungeon?

Alc. I would not.

Euph. And, for aught we know, this spot, with the few sinners on it, bears no greater proportion to the universe of intelligences than a dungeon doth to a kingdom. It seems we are led, not only by revelation, but by common sense, observing and inferring from the analogy of visible things, to conclude there are innumerable orders of intelligent beings more happy and more perfect than man; whose life is but a span, and whose place, this earthly globe, is but a point, in respect of the whole system of God's

---

[1] This familiar difficulty does not rise, like that which occasioned the analogical hypothesis, from perplexities implied in a finite Intelligence. It is occasioned by the Evil which in fact men find in their own lives and around them.

creation. We are dazzled, indeed, with the glory and grandeur of things here below, because we know no better. But, I am apt to think, if we knew what it was to be an angel for one hour, we should return to this world, though it were to sit on the brightest throne in it, with vastly more loathing and reluctance than we would now descend into a loathsome dungeon or sepulchre [1].

24. *Cri.* To me it seems natural that such a weak, passionate, and short-sighted creature as man should be ever liable to scruples of one kind or other [2]. But, as this same creature is apt to be over-positive in judging, and over-hasty in concluding, it falls out that these difficulties and scruples about God's conduct are made objections to His being [3]. And so men come to argue from their own defects against the Divine perfections. And, as the views and humours of men are different and often opposite, you may sometimes see them deduce the same atheistical conclusions from contrary premises. I knew an instance of this in two minute philosophers of my acquaintance, who used to argue each from his own temper against a Providence. One of them, a man of a choleric and vindictive spirit, said he could not believe a Providence, because London was not swallowed up or consumed by fire from heaven;

---

[1] Astronomers tell us of thirty millions of stars or suns, with their respective planetary systems—it may be supposed the homes of self-conscious persons or moral agents, as well as merely sentient beings. With the conception thus formed of the population of the material universe, not to speak of unembodied spirits, what room is there for *a priori* dogmas regarding man?

[2] This suggested mitigation of the mystery of the sorrow and sin found on this planet is in the spirit of Butler's 'Analogy' rather than of Browne's, especially Butler's Sermon on the 'Ignorance of Man.'

[3] Thus much at least, as Butler might say, will be found not taken for granted but *proved*—that a reasonable man, who will consider the matter, may be as much assured as he is of his own being, that it is not so clear a case that there is nothing in our faith in theistic optimism and ethical supremacy in the universe, or in our own continued moral agency after physical death.

the streets being, as he said, full of people who shew no other belief or worship of God but perpetually praying that He would damn, rot, sink, and confound them. The other, being of an indolent easy temper, concluded there could be no such thing as Providence; for that a being of consummate wisdom must needs employ himself better than in minding the prayers and actions and little interests of mankind [1].

Alc. After all, if God have no passions, how can it be true that vengeance is His? Or how can He be said to be jealous of His glory?

Cri. We believe that God executes vengeance without revenge, and is jealous without weakness, just as the mind of man sees without eyes, and apprehends without hands.

25. *Alc.* To put a period to this discourse, we will grant there is a God in this dispassionate sense; but what then? What hath this to do with Religion or Divine worship? To what purpose are all these prayers, and praises, and thanksgivings, and singing of praises, which the foolish vulgar call serving God? What sense, or use, or end is there in all these things?

Cri. We worship God, we praise and pray to Him: not because we think that He is proud of our worship or fond of our praise or prayers, and affected with them as mankind are: or that all our service can contribute in the least degree to His happiness or good: but because it is good for *us* to be so disposed towards God: because it is just and right, and suitable to the nature of things, and

---

[1] A supreme law of Omnipresent Providential Adaptation is no more inapplicable to the 'little interests of mankind,' or even of the lowest orders of sentient beings, than the law of gravitation is inapplicable to the fall of a grain of sand. Is not the Universe of God adapted as much to the least as to the greatest thing and person contained in it?

becoming the relation we stand in to our supreme Lord and Governor.

Alc. If it be good for us to worship God, it should seem that the Christian Religion, which pretends to teach men the knowledge and worship of God, was of some use and benefit to mankind.

Cri. Doubtless.

Alc. If this can be made appear, I shall own myself very much mistaken.

Cri. It is now near dinner-time. Wherefore, if you please, we will put an end to this conversation for the present [1].

---

[1] Berkeley, in the preceding Dialogue, argues that faith in the existence and character of God may be vindicated in the same way as faith in the existence and character of our fellow-men. He realises the universe as consisting in a hierarchy of intercommunicating spirits—intercommunicating by means of the phenomena presented to each in sense; and all by like means in communion with the Divine Spirit Supreme. God is with him the Spirit, Supreme in the hierarchy, on whom all other conscious spirits and the universe depend.

But one may ask whether this conception enough recognises that ineffable mysteriousness of the Infinite Being, which nourishes the sentiment of reverence, so efficacious in our spiritual life, and which is involved in the faith, in its different degrees in individual men, on which human life ultimately rests?

At the opposite extreme God disappears in Unknowable Power—as with Herbert Spencer.

The difficulty of *an intermediate* between the extremes of *theistic anthropomorphism* and *total theological nescience* perplexes modern thought. A God fully comprehensible by us is no God: a God totally unknowable by man cannot engage faith. Berkeley seems unconscious of the difficulty. Out of it has arisen the theological agnosticism of modern physical science, and its counterpart gnosticism, in an Abstract God—personified in finite spirits. *Siris* carries us further into this subject.

The preceding Dialogue hardly recognises difficulties which are now apt to beset the inquirer in theology; for it encourages the assumption that there is no alternative between a fully comprehended God and dogmatic Atheism. Moreover, little is said that applies to later scientific agnosticism, initiated by Hume, which pronounces the final problem insoluble—in Hume's words, 'a riddle, an enigma, an inexplicable mystery'; with 'doubt, uncertainty, and suspense of judgment,' as 'the only result of our most accurate scrutiny into it'—and which thus holds us debarred from any ultimate satisfaction. We are now beginning to see that if the ultimate is total darkness, then even secular life, and the generalisations of science, may be unworthy of trust. The issue is thus total as well as theological agnosticism.

Many of the subjects that are touched in the preceding annotations and in those which follow are discussed in my *Philosophy of Theism*.

III

DIVINE VISUAL LANGUAGE

FURTHER VINDICATED AND EXPLAINED

. . . .

9. By a *sensible object* I understand that which is properly perceived by sense. Things properly perceived by sense are *immediately* perceived[1].—Besides things properly and immediately *perceived* by any sense, there may be also other things *suggested* to the mind by means of those proper and immediate objects:—which things so suggested are not objects of that sense, being in truth only objects of the imagination[2], and originally belonging to some other sense or faculty. Thus, sounds, are the proper object of hearing, being properly and immediately perceived by that, and by no other sense. But, by the mediation of sounds or words, all other things may be suggested to the mind; and yet things so suggested are not thought the object of hearing.

10. The peculiar objects of each sense, although they are

[1] Do we become immediately percipient—meaning by that cognisant of something that is more than a transient phenomenon contemporaneous only with the percipient act—in any one of our five senses, taken singly? Does externality so belong to all of them that in each we reach not only sensations, but also realise objects independent of the individual percipient? If so, what means this distinction, and how and why is it made?

[2] 'imagination,' i. e. expectant imagination. But is not reason *latent* in the automatic expectation, founded on trust in the constancy of natural order, which Berkeley calls 'suggestion'?

truly or strictly perceived by that sense alone, may yet be suggested to the imagination by some other sense. The objects therefore of all the senses may become objects of imagination—which faculty represents all sensible things. A colour, therefore, which is truly perceived by sight alone, may nevertheless, upon hearing the words blue or red, be apprehended by the imagination. It is in a primary and peculiar manner the object of sight; in a secondary manner it is the object of imagination: but cannot properly be supposed the object of hearing [1].

11. The *objects of sense*, being things immediately perceived, are otherwise called *ideas* [2].

The *cause* [3] of these ideas, or the power of producing them, is not the object of sense—not being itself perceived, but only inferred by reason from its effects, to wit, those objects or ideas which are perceived by sense. From our ideas of sense the inference of reason is good to Power, Cause, Agent. But we may not therefore infer that our ideas are *like* unto this Power, Cause, or Active Being. On the contrary, it seems evident that an idea can be only like another idea, and that in our ideas or immediate

---

[1] In this and the preceding section he distinguishes *sense-phenomena* that are *immediately perceived* in the several senses, and peculiar to each sense, from *suggestions*, in which more than one sense is involved, their respective data being interpreted as signs, by which our perception of extra-organic things is enlarged. Berkeley's 'immediate perception' is *direct consciousness* of phenomena in sense; his 'suggestion' is the automatic *interpretation* of the phenomena given in sense that is evoked after custom or experience.

[2] Elsewhere called 'sensations' and 'real ideas' (in contrast with 'chimeras' of fancy), and afterwards in *Siris* called 'phenomena.' Phenomenon is perhaps the most convenient term.

[3] 'Cause' here is not sign, i. e. constant antecedent or natural cause, but efficient or productive cause; and that with Berkeley must be *spirit*. It cannot be phenomenon of sense.

objects of sense, there is nothing of Power, Causality, or Agency included.

12. Hence it follows that the power or cause of ideas is not an object of sense, but of *reason*. Our knowledge of the cause is measured by the effect ; of the power, by our idea. To the absolute nature, therefore, of outward causes or powers, we have nothing to say : they are no objects of our sense or perception. Whenever, therefore, the appellation of *sensible object* is used in a determined intelligible sense, it is not applied to signify the absolutely existing outward cause or power, but the ideas themselves produced thereby [1].

13. Ideas which are observed to be connected together are vulgarly considered under the relation of cause and effect, whereas, in strict and philosophic truth, they are only related as the sign to the thing signified [2]. For, we know our ideas, and therefore know that one idea cannot be the cause of another. We know that our ideas of sense are not the cause of themselves. We know also that *we* do not cause them. Hence we know they *must* have some other efficient cause, distinct from *them* and *us*.

14. In treating of Vision, it was my purpose to consider the *effects* and *appearances*—the objects perceived by my senses—the ideas of sight as connected with those of touch ; to inquire how one idea comes to suggest another belonging

---

[1] This seems to say that the things of sense involve only phenomena *directly perceived* in sense, or *suggested* when the data of sense are interpreted as evidence of sense-phenomena to be expected. But the rational relations which the objects necessarily thus involve are not empirical phenomena; they are presupposed.

[2] He does not articulately show what is involved in our being obliged to refer sensuous phenomena to unperceived power; nor *why* we must connect them as sign and thing signified, i. e. under laws persistent. Mere *sense* cannot give more than a transient phenomenon. Of *suggestion* he only says that it is based on ' arbitrary institution.'

to a different sense; how things visible suggest things tangible; how present things suggest things more remote and future—whether by likeness, by necessary connexion, by geometrical inference, or by arbitrary institution.

15. It hath indeed been a prevailing opinion and undoubted principle among mathematicians and philosophers that there were certain ideas common to both senses: whence arose the distinction of primary and secondary qualities. But, I think it hath been demonstrated that there is no such thing as *a common object*—as an idea, or kind of idea, perceived both by sight and touch.

16. In order to treat with due exactness on the nature of Vision, it is necessary in the first place accurately to consider our own ideas; to distinguish where there is a difference; to call things by their right names; to define terms, and not confound ourselves and others by their ambiguous use; the want or neglect whereof hath so often produced mistakes. Hence it is that men talk as if one idea was the efficient cause of another; hence they mistake *inferences of reason* for *perceptions of sense*; hence they confound *the power residing in somewhat external*[1] with the *proper object of sense*—which is in truth no more than our own idea.

17. When we have well understood and considered the nature of Vision, we may, by reasoning from thence, be better able to collect some knowledge of the *external unseen cause* of our ideas;—whether it be one or many, intelligent or unintelligent, active or inert, body or spirit. But, in order to understand and comprehend this theory[2], and discover the true principles thereof, we should consider the likeliest way is not to attend to unknown substances, external causes,

---

[1] This 'power' is, with Berkeley, Divine Mind or Spirit—not immediately perceived by our senses, but found by 'inference,' if not by automatic suggestion.

[2] i.e. the theory of our power of interpreting phenomena.

agents, or powers; nor to reason or infer anything about or from things obscure, unperceived, and altogether unknown[1].

18. As in this inquiry we are concerned with what objects we perceive, or our own ideas, so, upon them our reasonings must proceed. To treat of things utterly unknown as if we knew them, and so lay our beginning in obscurity, would not surely seem the properest means for the discovering of truth. Hence it follows, that it would be wrong if one about to treat of the nature of Vision should, instead of attending to *visible ideas*, define the *object of sight* to be *that obscure cause, that invisible power or agent, which produced visible ideas in our minds*. Certainly such cause or power does not seem to be the object either of the sense or the science of Vision, inasmuch as what we know thereby we know only of the effects[2].

. . . .

[1] 'unknown'—so far as mere sense is concerned.

[2] The foregoing sections confine the question to the *objects* we are directly percipient of—namely, 'ideas of sense,' or 'phenomena' actually present—and to their *suggested* connexion with one another, in which connexion the reality of the material world consists. The *power* that presents phenomena to our senses, in an interpretable order, cannot itself be an 'object' of sense: its character is presupposed in our trust in the language of nature. We distinguish what *we can* produce, from visible and tangible phenomena which *we cannot* produce, and which we find ourselves in reason obliged to refer to a Spirit 'distinct from them and us' (§ 13). Causality—physical, formal, efficient, and final—as a fundamental principle of Universal Reason, is thus, as it were, proposed here for further philosophical analysis, by a student so inclined.

The *causal principle* has been used by some as a premiss in reasonings on behalf of the existence of Matter. The phenomena of sense, they argue, must be caused: we are not their cause (although they are perceived by us): they must therefore be *effects* of a Something, called Matter. Unable to accept this conclusion, Berkeley had asked, Must not the Power of which the phenomena presented to our senses and their interpretable order are effects—at least if the word 'power' is to have a meaning—be Mind or Spirit—like our own mind in kind, but

33. We not only impose on others but often on ourselves, by the unsteady or ambiguous use of terms. One would imagine that an *object* should be *perceived*[1]. I must own, when that word is employed in a different sense, that I am at a loss for its meaning, and consequently cannot comprehend any arguments or conclusions about it. And I am not sure that, on my own part, some inaccuracy of expression, as well as the peculiar nature of the subject, not always easy either to explain or conceive, may not have rendered my Treatise concerning Vision difficult to a cursory reader. But, to one of due attention, and who makes my words an occasion of his own thinking, I conceive the whole to be very intelligible: and, when it is rightly understood, I scarce doubt but it will be assented to. One thing at least I can affirm, that, if I am mistaken, I can plead neither haste nor

---

higher in degree—*not* a mere abstraction, as Matter divorced from living Mind is?—Others, Reid and Hamilton for instance, deny that Matter is thus *inferred*. Body and mind, in their view, exist face to face in perception—in the *sui generis* relation of *percipient* and *perceived*—each *equally* known to the perceiving mind, in an irreducible act; neither knowable independently of their phenomena.—Berkeley argues that we *may* infer that Active Spirit is the cause of sense-presented phenomena and of their significance, although we cannot infer that abstract Matter is so. And his implied reason for this seems to be, that *we have experience of what 'power' means*, in the free personal acts of which we recognise *ourselves* as the responsible, and therefore true causes, while we cannot connect *any* meaning with the term power when it is applied to 'matter': there *is* meaning in *spiritual* or morally responsible *power*; but *power in matter* is a meaningless abstraction.

A sort of *representative* perception of sensible things is implied in Berkeley's 'suggestion,' or acquired perception: 'real things' consist of phenomena that are significant of (and *thus represent*) other phenomena—under natural law, i. e. according to the rational order of ever acting Divine Providence.

[1] Berkeley's *suggested* 'objects of sense' imply both *actual* and *expected* phenomena of sense; the former signs of the latter, and the latter expected, but not actually given in sense. (Cf. § 39.) He regards what is suggested as mediately perceived, and so resolves inductive expectation into automatic suggestion and consequent trust.

inattention, having taken true pains and much thought about it.

. . . .

38. It is to be noted that, in formerly considering the Theory of Vision, I observed a certain known method, wherein, from false and popular suppositions, men do often arrive at truth [1]. Whereas in the synthetical method of delivering science or truth already found, we proceed in an inverted order, the conclusions in the analysis being assumed as principles in the synthesis. I shall therefore now begin with that conclusion—*That Vision is the Language of the Author of Nature*; from thence deducing theorems and solutions of phenomena, and explaining the nature of visible things and the visive faculty.

39. Ideas which are observed to be connected with other ideas come to be considered as signs [2], by means whereof things not actually perceived by *sense* are signified or suggested to the *imagination*; whose objects they are, and which alone perceives them. And, as sounds suggest other things, so characters suggest other sounds; and, in general, all signs suggest the things signified, there being no idea which may not offer to the mind another idea which hath been frequently joined with it. In certain cases a sign may suggest its correlate as an image, in others as an effect, in others as a cause [3]. But, where there is no such relation

---

[1] The juvenile *Essay on Vision* proceeds upwards from facts to the general principle which they exemplify.

[2] How do they 'come to be so considered'? Berkeley says through 'experience' or 'custom:' But the 'custom of nature' which the things of sense follow, commonly called 'law' of nature, presupposes an 'arbitrary (not capricious) institution' of the laws, by the *ethically perfect* will of God.

[3] Does this imply that efficient and final causes—free spiritual causes—are only 'suggested' automatically and blindly in sense, without being inferred under moral reason?

of similitude or causality, nor any necessary connexion whatsoever, two things, by their mere co-existence, or two ideas, merely by being perceived together, may suggest or signify one the other—their connexion being all the while arbitrary; for it is the connexion only, as such, that causeth this effect [1].

40. A great number of *arbitrary* signs, various and opposite, do constitute a Language. If such arbitrary connexion be instituted by men, it is an artificial Language; if by the Author of Nature, it is a Natural Language. Infinitely various are the modifications of light and sound, whence they are each capable of supplying an endless variety of signs, and, accordingly, have been each employed to form languages; the one by the arbitrary appointment of mankind, the other by that of God Himself. A connexion established by the Author of Nature, in the ordinary course of things, may surely be called natural, as that made by men will be named artificial. And yet this doth not hinder but the one may be as arbitrary as the other. And, in fact, there is no more likeness to exhibit, or necessity to infer, things tangible from the modifications of light, than there is in language to collect the meaning from the sound (*Essay on Vision*, sect. 144, 147). But, such as the connexion is of the various tones and articulations of voice

---

[1] *Association* seems to be here taken as an explanation of our trust in objective order in nature; and thus of our translation of the transitory phenomena of sense into fixed perceptions of solid and extended things. This might be compared with Kant's theory of perception, according to which sensations, received under necessary forms of *space*, are made intelligible by *categories of understanding*. The modern student has to determine between the two explanations. Berkeley assumes that each human being begins his conscious life with perception of phenomena presented to his senses independently of his will; he then finds by 'suggestion'—which here seems to mean little more than association of ideas—the externality of this experience, and then rises to inductive judgments of science.

with their several meanings, the same is it between the various modes of light and their respective correlates, or, in other words, between the ideas of sight and touch.

41. As to light, and its several modes or colours, all thinking men are agreed that they are ideas peculiar only to sight; neither common to the touch, nor of the same kind with any that are perceived by that sense. But herein lies the mistake, that, beside these, there are supposed other ideas common to both senses, being equally perceived by sight and touch—such as Extension, Size, Figure, and Motion. But that there are in reality no such common ideas, and that the objects of sight, marked by these words, are entirely different and heterogeneous from whatever is the object of feeling, marked by the same names, hath been proved in the *Theory* (*A New Theory of Vision*, sect. 127).

42. To *perceive* is one thing; *to judge* is another. So likewise, to be *suggested* is one thing, and to be *inferred* another. Things are suggested and perceived by Sense. We make judgments and inferences by the Understanding. (*a*) What we immediately and properly perceive by sight is its primary object—*light and colours*. (*b*) What is suggested, or perceived by mediation thereof, are *tangible ideas*—which may be considered as secondary and improper objects of sight. (*c*) We infer causes from effects, effects from causes, and properties one from another, *where the connexion is necessary* [1].

---

[1] Note in this a fuller recognition of universal and necessary human judgments, having their evidence in themselves, the source of intuitive truths above sense,—designated by some the Common Sense. According to Berkeley, in his earlier writings, our ability to read into what we see *more than is directly seen* is due to 'suggestion' of phenomena previously perceived, especially in touch. In all this Intellect is latent. Judgment and inference, on the other hand, manifest Intellect proper. Higher development of mind, in which Sense is subordinate to Intellect, is now more prominent in his view.

What does Berkeley here and elsewhere mean by '*necessity*' of connexion; and how, on his theory of knowledge, does he account for

How comes it to pass that we apprehend by the ideas of sight certain other ideas, which neither resemble them, nor cause them, nor are caused by them, nor have any necessary connexion with them? The solution of this Problem, in its full extent, doth comprehend the whole Theory of Vision. This stating of the matter placeth it on a new foot, and in a different light from all preceding theories.

43. To which the proper answer is—*That this is done in virtue of an arbitrary connexion, instituted by the Author of Nature*[1].

44. The proper, immediate object of vision is light, in all its modes and variations, various colours in kind, in degree, in quantity; some lively, others faint; more of some and less of others; various in their bounds or limits; various in their order and situation. A blind man, when first made to see, might perceive these objects, in which there is an endless variety; but he would neither perceive nor imagine any resemblance or connexion between these visible objects and those perceived by feeling[2]. Lights, shades, and colours would suggest nothing to him about bodies, hard or soft, rough or smooth: nor would their quantities, limits or order suggest to him geometrical figures, or extension, or situation—which they must do upon the received supposition, that these objects are common to sight and touch.

---

the 'necessity'? He finds 'judgments' of reason rising out of 'suggestions,' but he does not define precisely what they are, or unfold them articulately. In short, he does not anticipate either Kant or Reid.

[1] The philosophical inquirer still asks *On what ultimate ground of reason* we in any case proceed from the known to the unknown—from the *perceived sign* to the *suggested thing signified*. More than a mere datum of sense is needed to explain this mental transition; and to justify the assumption of steady order in nature, which is involved in expectation and inductive inference.

[2] 'feeling,' i.e. touch, which here, as elsewhere with Berkeley, includes the muscular sense, and the sense of locomotive activity.

45. All the various sorts, combinations, quantities, degrees, and dispositions of light and colours, would, upon the first perception thereof, be considered in themselves only as a new set of sensations and ideas. As they are wholly new and unknown, a man born blind would not, at first sight, give them the names of things formerly known and perceived by his touch. But, after some experience, he would perceive their connexion with tangible things, and would, therefore, consider them as signs, and give them (as is usual in other cases) the same names with the things signified.

71. Before I conclude, it may not be amiss to add the following extract from the *Philosophical Transactions* (No. 400), relating to a person blind from his infancy, and long after made to see: 'When he first saw, he was so far from making any judgment about distances that he thought all objects whatever touched his eyes (as he expressed it) as what he felt did his skin, and thought no objects so agreeable as those which were smooth and regular, though he could form no judgment of their shape, or guess what it was in any object that was pleasing to him. He knew not the shape of anything, nor any one thing from another, however different in shape or magnitude: but upon being told what things were, whose form he before knew from Feeling, he would carefully observe them that he might know them again; but having too many objects to learn at once, he forgot many of them; and (as he said) at first he learned to know, and again forgot, a thousand things in a day. Several weeks after he was couched being deceived by pictures, he asked which was the lying sense—Feeling or Seeing? He was never able to imagine any lines beyond the bounds he saw. The room he was in, he said, he knew to be part of the house, yet he could not conceive that the whole house could look bigger. He said every new object

was a new delight, and the pleasure was so great that he wanted ways to express it[1].'—Thus, by fact and experiment, those points of the theory which seem the most remote from common apprehension were not a little confirmed, many years after I had been led into the discovery of them by reasoning.

[1] Berkeley here quotes the noted experiment of Cheselden, recorded in the *Philosophical Transactions* for 1728. It is offered as evidence that *our power of interpreting sensible signs* is neither (*a*) an instinct nor (*b*) a necessary inference, but (*c*) an expectation suggested by our customary experience.—Cheselden's is among the first of several recorded examples of persons born blind and made to see, whose mental experience, immediately consequent upon their acquirement of sight, has been (more or less accurately) described. Berkeley's comparative indifference to experiments of the sort, and to the relative physiology of the senses, is not difficult to understand. His appeal to our inward consciousness, to show that we cannot originally see outward distances, magnitudes, or situations, nor touch what is visible, nor see what is tangible; along with the evidence he offers that our inclination to unite visible and tangible phenomena, as 'qualities' of the same 'substance,' may all be explained by the constant mental association of the latter with the former—perhaps seemed to make testimony of the born-blind unnecessary. Our inadequate records of experiments like Cheselden's illustrate the remark of Diderot, that an adequate cross-examination of persons born blind would be employment enough for the combined powers of Newton, Descartes, Locke, and Leibniz.

Besides the first experience of the born-blind when made to see, the experiences of children, and of the lower animals, during the evolution of distinct visual perception, have also been recorded, with a view to show the nature and genesis of adult visual perception,—instead of Berkeley's introspective inferences. The former is an example of the method of external observation in psychology—more obvious, but apt to overlook the spiritual facts. The latter is the method of introspective analysis—more subtle and difficult, but more fundamental. Our physiological psychology is of later growth.

THIRD PART

A CHAIN OF PHILOSOPHICAL REFLECTIONS

OR

THE UNIVERSE SPIRITUALLY UNITED IN GOD

SELECTIONS FROM

BERKELEY'S 'SIRIS'

In God we live and move and have our being.

PREFATORY NOTE

Siris (σειρὰ, a chain) appeared when Berkeley was about sixty. It contains the philosophy of his later life, in which he rises from Locke to Plato. He ingeniously starts from the supposed medicinal virtues of tar-water, invites us to follow the ascending links which connect sensible things with one another, through supreme and pervading Divine Will, and then revels in his favourite thought of the natural world in constant, because necessary, dependence on Active Reason.

In the English metaphysical literature of the eighteenth century no work more abounds in seeds of thought than *Siris*. Its immediate purpose was to confirm the conjecture that Tar yields a 'water of health' for the relief of diseases, from which the animal world might draw fresh supplies of vital activity. In a series of aphorisms, connected by subtle association, the thoughts of ancient and medieval philosophers are interwoven, the whole forming a study at once in medicine and in metaphysics. The work breathes the spirit of Plato, in the least Platonic generation in England since the rise of modern philosophy, all with the unexpectedness of genius, inspired by a thing so commonplace as tar.

More than half of *Siris* is occupied with physical conjectures meant to improve the art of healing. The Selections which follow are almost all taken from the metaphysical aphorisms. They may be studied apart from tar-water; simply as meditations upon the world viewed in its Divine spiritual unity.

In this curious work medicine thus passes into metaphysics. Doubt regarding the medicinal virtues of tar-water need not disturb enjoyment of the philosophical speculations about the rational concatenation of the Universe of which tar is merely the occasion. The medical aphorisms may misinterpret the meaning that is latent in the phenomena of tar; this must not hinder us from learning through *Siris* to see, in an unsubstantial and powerless material world, a constant manifestation of God.

When we compare *Siris* with the *Principles*, published nearly forty years earlier, we find important developments of Berkeley's philosophy. The Universals of Reason here overshadow the changing phenomena presented in Sense and the suggestions of sensuous Imagination. Sensible things are looked at as adumbrations of a reality beyond Nature, which philosophy helps us to recognise. The objects presented in sense are in *Siris* called *phenomena*, instead of *ideas* or *sensations*; while Ideas (not in Berkeley's early meaning of the term but in Plato's) are recognised as the supreme objects of meditative thought.

An increase of intellectual tolerance and of eclecticism appears in *Siris*, and less disposition to insist with merely controversial acuteness upon the dependence of the sensible world on sentient mind, as a final solution of difficulties. That *esse* is *percipi* is felt to be the beginning rather than the end of philosophy. Recluse meditation—long continued, with more study of human philosophy in the past—has given Berkeley a larger conception of the final problem of the Universe, and a feeling that it is neither so easily nor so perfectly intelligible under this old formula as it seemed in his ardent and less considerate youth. Awe of its mysteriousness is shown, and also readiness to allow different ages and countries, each in its own way, to recognise Divine Reason and Will as supreme,—with still irreducible data too in the explanation finally offered. He now welcomes an acknowledgment of God in any intellectual form of faith that consists with supremacy of Reason in the universe. His last work in philosophy more than any breathes and helps to educate the philosophic spirit; which begins in infantile wonder, but is found at the end to issue in wonder deepened by reflection. *Siris* illustrates his spiritual growth in later life. We find him intellectually broader, more modest, and more liberal; more ready to accept with reverence the 'broken' philosophy, with its sense of mystery, to which deep and patient insight at last conducts us; more aware that in this mortal state, under its present limitations, we must be satisfied to make the best of any openings which occur;—yet not without hope, there being 'no subject so obscure but we may discern some glimpse of truth by long poring on it,' if we cultivate love for truth—'the cry of all,' while it is really 'the game of only a few.'

Thus thought in the life of Berkeley, taken in chronological order, begins with Matter and ends with God. Intellect is latent in the senses: the phenomena of the external world find their ultimate explanation in the omnipresent meaning which makes science possible: Sense-perception connects conscious Spirit and unconscious phenomena, with their unfathomable mysteries of Space and Time: Reason essays the Divine meaning of what in Sense is revealed under conditions of co-existence and succession. Here are the three great objects of meditative thought—the conscious Ego and the Material World, mutually related in and through God. The correlation of Self and Sense—Spirit and Matter—is prominent in the *Principles*; the ultimate unity of the Universe in Divine Spirit is prominent in *Siris*, which enforces the harmony of science of Nature with the constant orderly agency of Omnipresent Reason and Will. Natural causation is a revelation of the Divine Agent who is immanent and yet manifested in the natural world and in man.

A CHAIN OF PHILOSOPHICAL REFLECTIONS

154. The order and course of things, and the experiments we daily make, shew there is a Mind that governs and actuates this mundane system, as the proper real agent and cause. . . . We have no proof, either from experiment or reason, of any other agent or efficient cause than Mind or Spirit. When, therefore, we speak of corporeal agents or corporeal causes, this is to be understood in a different, subordinate, and improper sense [1].

155. The *principles* whereof a thing is compounded, the *instrument* used in its production, and the *end* for which it was intended, are all in vulgar use termed 'causes,'—though none of them be, strictly speaking, agent or efficient. There is not any proof that an extended corporeal or mechanical cause doth really and properly *act*—even motion itself being in truth a passion. . . . They are, nevertheless, sometimes termed 'agents' and 'causes,' although they are by no means

---

[1] This and the following sections express Berkeley's later thoughts about Active Reason as the Universal Power, and so the insufficiency of the atomic or any other merely physical hypothesis, as our ultimate explanation of the universe, although it may satisfy science. His implied premiss is, that every change must at last have *sufficient* cause, and that the only sufficient ultimate cause must be God; but that in physical nature, *anything* might *a priori* have been made by God the previsive trustworthy sign, i. e. natural cause, of any change.

active in a strict and proper signification. When therefore force, power, virtue, or action is mentioned as subsisting in an extended and corporeal or mechanical being, this is not to be taken in a true, genuine, and real, but only in a gross and popular sense, which sticks in appearances, and doth not analyse things to their first principles [1]. In compliance with established language and the use of the world, we must employ the popular current phrase. But then in regard to truth we ought to distinguish its meaning.

. . . .

160. The mind of man acts by an instrument necessarily [2]. The τὸ ἡγεμονικὸν, or Mind presiding in the world, acts by an instrument freely [3]. Without instrumental and second causes, there could be no regular course of nature. And without a regular course, nature could never be understood; mankind must always be at a loss, not knowing what to expect, or how to govern themselves, or direct their actions for the obtaining of any end. Therefore in the government of the world physical agents—improperly so called—or mechanical or second causes, or natural causes or instruments, are necessary to assist, not the governor, but the governed [4].

. . . .

---

[1] This is urged and illustrated in Thomas Brown's *Inquiry into the Relation of Cause and Effect*.

[2] This is in the spirit of the opening aphorisms of the *Novum Organum*, which teach that, in order to be able to produce beneficial changes in nature, man must observe and understand the established connexions, or laws of change, in nature. A divinely-established sense-symbolism is the basis of trustworthy science of nature.

[3] The 'laws of nature,' to which man must conform his actions, are here assumed to be themselves the issue of the will of God—so that nature is essentially supernatural, although merely physical science disregards its supernatural side, while philosophy is bound to recognise both sides.

[4] Cf. *Principles*, §§ 60-66, in which Berkeley urges the utility to man of *elaborate order* in nature, which needs to be interpreted in science, and its consistency with constant dependence of matter and its changes upon Spirit.

231. The laws of attraction and repulsion are to be regarded as laws of motion; and these only as rules or methods observed in the productions of natural effects,—the efficient and final causes whereof are not of mechanical consideration. Certainly, if the *explaining* a phænomenon be to assign its proper efficient and final cause, it should seem that Mechanical Philosophers never explained any thing; their province being only to discover the laws of nature, that is, the general rules and methods of motion, and to account for particular phænomena by reducing them under, or shewing their conformity to, such general rules.

232. Some corpuscularian philosophers of the last age have indeed attempted to explain the formation of this world and its phænomena by a few simple laws of mechanism. But, if we consider the various productions of nature, in the mineral, vegetable, and animal parts of the creation, I believe we shall see cause to affirm, that not any one of them has hitherto been, or can be, accounted for on principles merely mechanical; and that nothing could be more vain and imaginary than to suppose with Descartes, that merely from a circular motion's being impressed by the supreme Agent on the particles of extended substance, the whole world, with all its several parts, appurtenances, and phænomena, might be produced, by a necessary consequence, from the laws of motion [1].

233. Others suppose that God did more at the beginning, having then made the seeds of all vegetables and animals, containing their solid organical parts in miniature, the

---

[1] This is part of the scientific cosmogony of Descartes. He explained the stellar system, and the motions of stars and planets, as the issue of vortices, or vortical motions, in an original chaos coextensive with space. But this must be taken in connexion with what he taught about the apparent interaction of mind and body being really due to the constant efficient agency of God. The notion of constant Divine agency was carried further by Malebranche and other Cartesians, in their theory of 'occasional' causes.

gradual filling and evolution of which, by the influx of proper juices, doth constitute the generation and growth of a living body. So that the artificial structure of plants and animals daily generated requires no *present* exercise of art to produce it, having been already framed at the origin of the world, which with all its parts hath ever since subsisted;—going like a clock or machine by itself, according to the laws of nature, without the immediate hand of the artist[1]. But how can this hypothesis explain the blended features of different species in mules and other mongrels? or the parts added or changed, and sometimes whole limbs lost, by marking in the womb? or how can it account for the resurrection of a tree from its stump, or the vegetative power in its cuttings? in which cases we must necessarily conceive something more than the mere evolution of a seed[2].

234. Mechanical laws of nature or motion direct us how to act, and teach us what to expect. Where Intellect presides there will be method and order, and therefore rules, which if not stated and constant, would cease to be rules. There is therefore a constancy in things, which is styled the Course of Nature[3]. All the phænomena in nature are pro-

---

[1] This is the theory of Leibniz, according to which the force or energy originally infused into the universe remains the same, only subject to transformations, agreeably to laws of nature, in a harmony pre-established by God between *thoughts* and *motions*. Mind and body in man thus agree like two clocks moving in concert. And thus the material world is always in harmony with intelligence, and thus interpretable. With Cartesians and with Leibniz, *matter* is neither that of which we are actually percipient, nor is it the efficient cause of our being percipient: we are percipient by *present* (Cartesians), or *previous* (Leibnizians) agency and design of God.

[2] We cannot, he virtually argues, find sufficient cause of the effects in mere data of sense and their changes, so that there must be more than an evolution of phenomena to explain the issue trustworthily. The issue presupposes the constant orderly agency of evolving Mind, evolution itself being manifestation of power in the evolving Mind.

[3] Faith, i.e. trust in the supremacy of Moral Reason at the root

duced by motion. There appears an uniform working in things great and small, by attracting and repelling forces. But the particular laws of attraction and repulsion are various. Nor are we concerned at all about the forces, neither can we know or measure them otherwise than by their effects, that is to say, the motions; which motions only, and not the forces, are indeed in the bodies. Bodies are moved to or from each other, and this is performed according to different laws. The natural or mechanic philosopher endeavours to discover those laws by experiment and reasoning. But what is said of *forces residing in bodies*, whether attracting or repelling, is to be regarded only as a mathematical hypothesis, and not as any thing really existing in nature [1].

235. We are not therefore seriously to suppose, with certain mechanic philosophers, that the minute particles of bodies have *real* forces or powers, by which they act on each other, to produce the various phenomena in nature. The minute corpuscles are impelled and directed, that is to say, moved to and from each other, according to various rules or laws of motion. The laws of gravity, magnetism, and electricity are divers. And it is not known what other different rules or laws of motion might be established by the Author of Nature [2].

.   .   .   .

237. These and numberless other effects seem inexplic-

---

of all, is in short the basis of our inductive reliance on constant physical order.

[1] That is to say, even if all changes in natural phenomena could be resolved according to laws of motion, these laws would be themselves only effects, not true causes. But Intellect, thus omnipresent in motions and their laws, cannot be an effect of the motion which reveals it.

[2] The 'arbitrariness' of the existing constitution of nature means dependence, not on caprice, but on Divine Will. The ultimate dependence of the physical world on the moral world is suggested.

able on mechanical principles; or otherwise than by recourse to a mind or Spiritual Agent. Nor will it suffice from present phænomena and effects, through a chain of natural causes and subordinate blind agents, to trace a Divine Intellect as the remote original cause, that first created the world, and then set it a going. We cannot make even one single step in accounting for the phænomena, without admitting the immediate presence and immediate action of an incorporeal Agent, who connects, moves, and disposes all things, according to such rules, and for such purposes, as seem good to Him [1].

.   .   .   .

247. Though it be supposed the chief business of a natural philosopher to trace out causes from the effects, yet this is to be understood not of agents, but of component parts, in one sense, or of laws or rules, in another. In strict truth, *all agents are incorporeal, and as such are not properly of physical consideration.* The astronomer, therefore, the mechanic, or the chemist, not as such, but by accident only, treat of real causes, agents, or efficients. Neither doth it seem, as is supposed by the greatest of mechanical philosophers, that the true way of proceeding in their science is, from known notions in nature to investigate the moving forces. Forasmuch as *force* is neither corporeal, nor belongs to any corporeal thing; nor yet to be discovered by experiments or mathematical reasonings, which reach no farther

---

[1] In short, there are no active or responsible causes in the material world as interpreted in physical science. Yet there is the supreme agency of the Universal Mind, and the occasional agency of morally responsible persons. The Divine agency Berkeley, like Descartes, seems to say must be constant, not, as with Leibniz, remote in past time. But perhaps the alternative, as between Descartes and Leibniz, is one which man cannot settle; nor the involved question of time and the timeless, in relation to Divine Mind.

than discernible effects, and motions in things passive and moved.

248. *Vis* or force is to the soul what extension is to the body, saith St. Augustin, in his tract concerning the Quantity of the Soul; and without force there is nothing done or made, and consequently there can be no agent. Authority is not to decide in this case. Let any one consult his own notions and reason, as well as experience, concerning the origin of motion, and the respective natures, properties, and differences of soul and body, and he will, if I mistake not, evidently perceive, that there is nothing active in the latter. Nor are they natural agents or corporeal forces which make the particles of bodies to cohere. Nor is it the business of experimental philosophers to find them out.

249. The mechanical philosopher, as hath been already observed, inquires properly concerning the rules and modes of operation alone, and not concerning the cause; forasmuch as nothing mechanical is or really can be a *cause*. And although a mechanical or mathematical philosopher may speak of absolute space, absolute motion, and of force, as existing in bodies, causing such motion and proportional thereto; yet *what* these 'forces' are, which are supposed to be lodged in bodies, to be impressed on bodies, to be multiplied, divided, and communicated from one body to another, and which seem to animate bodies like abstract spirits, or souls, hath been found very difficult, not to say impossible, for thinking men to conceive and explain.

250. Nor, if we consider the proclivity of mankind to realise their notions[1], will it seem strange that mechanic philosophers and geometricians should, like other men, be misled by prejudice, and take mathematical hypotheses for

---

[1] 'realise their notions,'—by assuming for instance that the abstractions of natural philosophy, such as 'force' or 'power' in matter, stand for something that may be perceived and imagined, instead of being empty abstractions.

real beings existing in bodies, so far as even to make it the very aim and end of their science to compute or measure those phantoms; whereas it is very certain that nothing in truth can be measured or computed, besides the very effects or motions themselves. Sir Isaac Newton asks, Have not the minute particles of bodies certain forces or powers by which *they* act on one another, as well as on the particles of light, for producing most of the phænomena in nature? But, in reality, those minute particles are only agitated, according to certain laws of nature, *by some other agent*, wherein the force exists, and not in them, which have only the motion; which motion in the body moved, the Peripatetics rightly judge to be a mere passion, but in the mover to be ἐνέργεια or act[1].

251. It passeth with many, I know not how, that mechanical principles give a clear solution of the phænomena. The Democritic hypothesis, saith Dr. Cudworth, doth much more handsomely and intelligibly solve the phænomena, than that of Aristotle and Plato[2]. But, things rightly considered, perhaps it will be found not to solve any phænomenon at all: for all *phænomena*[3] are, to speak truly, *appear-*

---

[1] The relation of *motion* (as a sense-presented idea or phenomenon) to *active power* (a notion to which no mere sense-phenomenon corresponds) is the subject of Berkeley's tract *De Motu* (*Works*, vol. III. pp. 75-100).

[2] The passage in Cudworth (1619-1688) is as follows:—'The whole Aristotelical system of philosophy is infinitely to be preferred before the whole Democritical; though the former hath been so much disparaged, and the other cried up of late amongst us. Because, though it cannot be denied but that the Democritic hypothesis doth much more handsomely and intelligibly solve the *corporeal* phænomena, yet *in all other things which are of far the greater moment, it is rather a madness than a Philosophy.*'—*Intellectual System*, b. I. ch. 1. § 45. The atomic hypothesis may be the boundary of merely physical science, but not of philosophy. Plato (B.C. 427-347) and Aristotle (B.C. 384-322), in contrast to the atomism of Democritus (B.C. 460-370), occupy many of the sections which follow. Bacon and others had extolled Democritus and the pre-Socratics, in comparison with Socrates and his school.

[3] 'phenomena,' I may say again, correspond to the 'sensations,' or

ances in the soul or mind; and it hath never been explained, nor can it be explained, how external bodies, figures, and motions, should produce an appearance in the mind. These principles, therefore, do not solve—if by solving is meant assigning the real, either efficient or final, cause of appearances—but only reduce them to general rules.

252. [1]'There is a certain *analogy*, *constancy*, and *uniformity* in the phænomena or appearances of nature, which are a foundation for general rules: and these are a Grammar for the understanding of Nature, or that series of effects in the Visible World whereby we are enabled to foresee what will come to pass in the natural course of things. Plotinus [2] observes, in his third Ennead, that the art of presaging is in some sort the reading of natural letters denoting order, and that so far forth as analogy obtains in the universe, there may be vaticination. And in reality, he that foretells the motions of the planets, or the effects of medicines, or the results of chemical or mechanical experiments, may be said to do it by natural vaticination [3].

253. We know a thing when we understand it; and we understand it when we can interpret or tell what it signifies. Strictly, the Sense knows nothing [4]. We perceive indeed

---

'ideas of sense,' of Berkeley's earlier works; as to which he had argued that their real existence depends upon their being perceived. In order to become real, mind must be percipient of them; but they do not depend on my individual mind.

[1] The following sections place Nature in some new lights, when regarded as an interpretable and prophetic Language.

[2] The celebrated Neoplatonist.

[3] This remarkable passage in its own way anticipates the modern scientific conception of *prevision*. It treats perception in sense as obscure science, disclosed when we emerge from mere sense, and enter, through divine reason in which we share, into the true meaning of things.

[4] So Cudworth, who carefully distinguishes *intellectual notions* from *sensuous imaginations*: 'Sense,' he argues, 'cannot be the knowledge which comprehends a thing as it is. If the Sense had no other power

sounds by hearing, and characters by sight. But we are not therefore said to understand them. After the same manner, the phænomena of nature are alike visible to all: but all have not alike learned the connexion of natural things, or understand what they signify, or know how to vaticinate by them.

254. As the natural connexion of *signs* with the *things signified* is regular and constant, it forms a sort of Rational Discourse, and is therefore the immediate effect of an intelligent Cause. This is agreeable to the philosophy of Plato, and other ancients. Plotinus indeed saith, that which acts naturally is not intellection, but a certain power of moving matter, which doth not know but only do.—And it must be owned that, as faculties are multiplied by philosophers according to their operations, the *will* may be distinguished from the *intellect*. But it will not therefore follow that the Will which operates in the course of nature is not conducted and applied by intellect [1], although it be granted that neither will understands, nor intellect wills. Therefore, the phænomena of nature, which strike on the senses and are understood by the mind, do form not only a magnificent spectacle, but also a most coherent, entertaining, and instructive Discourse; and to effect this, they are conducted, adjusted, and ranged by the greatest wisdom. This language or Discourse is studied with different attention, and interpreted with different degrees of skill. But so far as men have studied and remarked its rules, and can interpret right, so far they may be said to be knowing in nature. A beast is

---

but this of passion or sensation (as Protagoras supposed), then there could be no such thing as truth or knowledge. But that hypothesis contradicts itself. For that which pronounces that sensible ideas of things are phantastical and relative, must itself be something superior to Sense, and able to judge what really and absolutely is and is not. See Cudworth's *Immutable Morality*.

[1] It is not imperfectly reasonable wills, as in man, but Will in Divine Active Reason.

like a man who hears a strange tongue but understands nothing¹.

255. Nature, saith the learned Doctor Cudworth, is not master of art or wisdom : nature is *ratio mersa et confusa* — reason immersed and plunged into matter, and as it were fuddled in it and confounded with it. But the formation of plants and animals, the motions of natural bodies, their various properties, appearances, and vicissitudes, in a word, the whole series of things in this visible world, which we call the Course of Nature, is so wisely managed and carried on that the most improved human reason cannot *thoroughly* comprehend even the least particle thereof;—so far is it from seeming to be produced by fuddled or confounded reason².

256. Natural productions, it is true, are not all equally perfect. But neither doth it suit with the order of things, the structure of the universe, or the ends of Providence, that they should be so. General rules are necessary to make the world intelligible : and from the constant observations of such rules, natural evils will sometimes unavoidably ensue : things will be produced in a slow length of time, and arrive at different degrees of perfection.

257. It must be owned, we are not conscious of the systole and diastole of the heart, or the motion of the diaphragm. It may not nevertheless be thence inferred, that *unknowing nature* can act regularly, as well as ourselves. The true inference is—that the self-thinking in-

---

[1] This section applies to external nature the theory, implied in Bacon and expressed in Berkeley, that what we see, or perceive in any of our senses, is to all intents a Divine Language. Bacon's favourite conception of the *interpretability* of Nature is in harmony with this. Physical science is attainment by human mind of some of the divine thoughts that are expressed by the sensible world.

[2] Since we cannot fully know any one thing without knowing all its relations to all other things, *knowledge in its highest meaning* must be Omniscience.

dividual, or human person, is not the real author of those natural motions. And, in fact, no man blames himself if they are wrong, or values himself if they are right[1]. The same may be said of the fingers of a musician, which some object to be moved by habit which understands not; it being evident that what is done by rule must proceed from something that understands the rule; therefore, if not from the musician himself, from *some other active Intelligence*, the same perhaps which governs bees and spiders, and moves the limbs of those who walk in their sleep[2].

258. *Instruments, occasions*, and *signs* (sect. 160) occur in, or rather make up, the whole visible Course of Nature. These, being no agents themselves, are under the direction of One Agent, concerting all for one end, the supreme good. All these motions, whether in animal bodies, or in other parts of the system of nature, which are not effects of *particular wills*, seem to spring from the same general cause

---

[1] The *moral* judgment seems to be here taken (by implication) as the test for distinguishing *agents proper* from the physical laws or methods of action that are maintained by God in nature. Conscience makes it impossible to explain moral or immoral acts by physical law; and presupposes moral ideals, not derived from, but which may be illustrated in experience. Conscience points to our *only* known example of a true cause, in pointing to the free creative agency of persons—moral and immoral agents. Phenomena presented in sense can only be divinely appointed *signs* of unpresented phenomena—not agents; and, as far as one can see, any phenomenon might have been made the sign (*physical* cause or effect) of any other.

[2] So Cudworth (*Intellectual System*, b. I. chap. 3. §§ 12-14). A vein of speculation somewhat similar appears in Aristotle's *Physics*. The facts here referred to, with others analogous, have given rise to hypotheses of 'sub-conscious mental agency,' 'unconscious cerebral agency,' and 'automatic activity.' That our habits and instincts *involve thoughts of which the person who is the subject of them is unconscious*, is not, however, to be taken as evidence that thought may issue from what is blind or unintelligent. It rather shows that *our* genuine instincts express immanent Divine Reason. An artist need not possess *consciously* the ideal that determines the work by which he is practically inspired, and which determines his artistic activity.

with the vegetation of plants—an æthereal spirit actuated by a Mind[1].

259. The first poets and theologers of Greece and the East considered the generation of things as ascribed rather to a Divine Cause, but the *physici* to natural causes, subordinate to and directed still by a Divine; except some corporealists and mechanics, who vainly pretended to make a world without a God. The hidden force that unites, adjusts, and causeth all things to hang together, and move in harmony—which Orpheus and Empedocles styled Love—this principle of union is no blind principle, but acts with intellect. This Divine Love and Intellect are not themselves obvious to our view, or otherwise discerned than in their effects. Intellect enlightens, Love connects, and the Sovereign Good attracts all things.

260. All things are made for the Supreme Good, all things tend to that end: and we may be said to *account* for a thing, when we shew that it is so best. In the Phædon, Socrates declares it to be his opinion that he who supposed all things to have been disposed and ordered by a Mind should not pretend to assign any other cause of them. He blames physiologers for attempting to account for phænomena, particularly for gravity and cohesion, by vortexes and æther; overlooking the τὸ ἀγαθὸν and τὸ δέον, the strongest bond and cement which holds together in all parts of the universe, and not discerning the Cause itself from those things which only attend it[2].

---

[1] In short, wicked acts, for which finite *persons* are *responsible*, are the *only* effects in the universe that are *not* to be referred to the Universal Power : *finite persons* are real, because responsible, causes.

[2] In Berkeley's philosophy, as one cannot be too often reminded, the physical inquirer has to do only with *powerless phenomena*, and with the constant laws or rules which they are made by God to follow in their natural metamorphoses. Phenomena (i.e. the data of the *senses*), as also their laws, are *effects*—not active causes—through which Divine Reason and Will are to some extent revealed to human minds : physical

262. As for the blots and defects which appear in the course of this world—which some have thought to proceed from a fatality or necessity in nature, and others from an evil principle—that same philosopher observes, that it may be the Governing Reason produceth and ordaineth all those things; and, not intending that all parts should be equally good, maketh some worse than others by design; as all parts in an animal are not eyes; and in a city, comedy, or picture, all ranks, characters, and colours are not equal or alike; even so excesses, defects, and contrary qualities conspire to the beauty and harmony of the world.

263. It cannot be denied that, with respect to the universe of things, we in this mortal state are like men educated in Plato's cave, looking on shadows with our backs turned to the light. But though our light be dim, and our situation bad, yet if the best use be made of both, perhaps something may be seen [1].—Proclus, in his Commentary on the Theology of Plato, observes there are two sorts of philosophers. The one placed Body first in the order of beings, and made the faculty of thinking depend thereupon, supposing that the principles of all things are corporeal: that Body most really or principally exists, and all other things in a secondary sense, and by virtue of that. Others, making all corporeal things to be dependent upon Soul or Mind, think this to exist in the first place and primary sense, and the being of

---

'causation' is the divinely caused—constant and arbitrary, but not capricious—connexion of sensible signs with other phenomena of sense, which they signify under what is commonly called 'law' in nature.

[1] The tone in this and other parts of *Siris* may be compared with that in the first five sections of the Introduction to the *Principles of Human Knowledge*, in which Berkeley attributes the difficulties of philosophy, not to the facts of the case, but to 'our having first raised a dust, and then complaining that we cannot see'—misled thus by our empty verbal abstractions.

Bodies to be altogether derived from and to presuppose that of the Mind[1].

264. Sense and Experience[2] acquaint us with the course and analogy of appearance or *natural effects*. Thought, Reason, Intellect introduce us into the knowledge of their *causes*. Sensible appearances, though of a flowing, unstable, and uncertain nature, yet having first occupied the mind, they do by an early prevention render the aftertask of thought more difficult; and, as they amuse the eyes and ears, and are more suited to vulgar uses and the mechanic arts of life, they easily obtain a preference, in the opinion of most men, to those superior principles, which are the later growth of the human mind, arrived to maturity and perfection, but, not affecting the corporeal sense, are thought to be so far deficient in point of solidity and reality—*sensible* and *real*, to common apprehensions, being the same thing. Although it be certain that the *principles* of science are neither objects of Sense nor Imagination; and that Intellect and Reason are alone the sure guides to truth[3].

---

[1] This expresses the contrast between Materialism and Spiritual Realism. Proclus, the Neoplatonist, lived in the fifth century after Christ.

[2] 'Experience' seems to be here limited to the fluctuating phenomena presented to the senses, connected by automatic mental association, as distinguished from the intellectual notions under which we rise into reasoned knowledge.

[3] This section is one of the best expressions of Berkeley's later philosophy, influenced by Plato and Plotinus, with its recognition of Intellect (νοῦς) as supreme, distinguished from mere Sense, as well as from the Suggestions to which custom gives rise. It may be contrasted with the attack on abstractions, in the Introduction to the *Principles*, and with the account of the factors of human knowledge with which he starts in the *Principles*, §§ 1, 2. *Siris*, animated by a higher Idealism, finds reality in 'principles'—'universal relations'— only tacitly contained in ordinary sense-perception and sense-suggestion. In his early works, Berkeley speaks as if scepticism consisted in doubting the reality of sensible things. Here he speaks lightly of the phenomena of sense. Can these views be reconciled, and if so, how?

265. The successful curiosity of the present age, in arts, and experiments, and new systems, is apt to elate men, and make them overlook the Ancients. But, notwithstanding that the encouragement and purse of princes, and the united endeavours of great societies in these later ages, have extended experimental and mechanical knowledge very far, yet it must be owned that the Ancients too were not ignorant of many things, as well in Physics or Metaphysics, which perhaps are more generally, though not first, known in these modern times.

266. The *Pythagoreans* and *Platonists* had a notion of the true System of the World. They allowed of mechanical principles, but actuated by soul or mind: they distinguished the primary qualities in bodies from the secondary, making the former to be physical causes, and they understood physical causes in a right sense: they saw that a mind infinite in power, unextended, invisible, immortal, governed, connected, and contained all things: they saw there was no such thing as real absolute space: that mind, soul, or spirit truly and really exists: that bodies exist only in a secondary and dependent sense: that the soul is the place of forms: that the sensible qualities are to be regarded as acts only in the cause, and as passions to us: they accurately considered the differences of intellect, rational soul, and sensitive soul, with their distinct acts of intellection, reasoning, and sensation; points wherein the Cartesians and their followers, who consider sensation as a mode of thinking, seem to have failed. They knew the whole mass of corporeal beings was itself actually moved and directed by a mind; and that physical causes were only instruments, or rather marks and signs[1].

.   .   .   .

[1] This section helps to show what Berkeley had come to consider 'the true system of the world.' It may also be used as a text for

270. Plotinus acknowledgeth no place but soul or mind, expressly affirming that the soul is not in the world, but the world in the soul. And farther, the place of the soul, saith he, is not body, but soul is in mind, and body in the soul.

273. It was an opinion of remote antiquity that the World was an *animal*. If we may trust the Hermaic writings, the Egyptians thought all things did partake of life. This opinion was also so general and current among the Greeks that Plutarch asserts all others held the world to be an animal, and governed by Providence, except Leucippus, Democritus, and Epicurus. And although an animal containing all bodies within itself could not be touched or sensibly affected from without, yet it is plain they attributed to it an inward sense and feeling, as well as appetites and aversions; and that from all the various tones, actions, and passions of the universe, they suppose one symphony, one animal act and life to result.

274. Jamblichus declares the world to be *one* animal, in which the parts, however distant each from other, are nevertheless related and connected by one common nature. And he teacheth, what is also a received notion of the Pythagoreans and Platonics, that there is no chasm in nature, but a Chain or Scale of beings rising by gentle uninterrupted gradations from the lowest to the highest, each nature being informed and perfected by the participation of a higher[1]. As air becomes igneous, so the purest fire becomes

comparing speculations about the universe among the Platonists and Neoplatonists with those of the moderns, in the Cartesian and Lockian era in which Berkeley was educated.

[1] The thought of a Chain (σειρὰ) in nature, connecting all the phenomena of the universe with one another and with God, the omnipresent providential Mind, in a Cosmos in which phenomena are regularly linked with phenomena, is the governing thought in *Siris*. This and the next section may be compared with Milton, *Par. Lost*, V. 469-490.

animal, and the animal soul becomes intellectual: which is to be understood not of the change of one nature into another, but of the connexion of different natures; each lower nature being, according to those philosophers, as it were a receptacle or subject for the next above it to reside and act in.

275. It is also the doctrine of Platonic philosophers, that *intellect* is the very life of living things, the first principle and exemplar of all, from whence by different degrees are derived the inferior classes of life : first the rational, then the sensitive, after that the vegetal ; but so as in the rational animal there is still somewhat intellectual, again, in the sensitive there is somewhat rational, and in the vegetal somewhat sensitive, and lastly, in mixed bodies, as metals and minerals, somewhat of vegetation. By which means the whole is thought to be more perfectly connected. Which doctrine implies that all the faculties, instincts, and motions of inferior beings, in their several respective subordinations, are derived from, and depend upon Mind and Intellect.

276. Both Stoics and Platonics held the world to be alive ; though sometimes it be mentioned as a sentient animal, sometimes as a plant or vegetable. But in this, notwithstanding what hath been surmised by some learned men, there seems to be no Atheism[1]. For, so long as the world is supposed to be quickened by elementary fire or spirit, which is itself animated by soul, and directed by under-

---

[1] Faith in the absolute supremacy of Active Reason in the universe is here recognised, under its various forms in the Divine language of the senses ; in particular in the graduated evolution of vegetable into animal life, of animal into rational life, and generally in the order of nature. 'Evolution' itself is a scientific, not a philosophical or ultimate conception. It is a physical law ; and although moral ideas and universal truths have gradually emerged in human consciousness in harmony with this law, the result is unaccountable by this or any other merely physical law.

standing, it follows that all parts thereof originally depend upon, and may be reduced unto the same indivisible stem or principle, to wit, a Supreme Mind—which is the concurrent doctrine of Pythagoreans, Platonics, and Stoics.

277. There is, according to those philosophers, a *life* infused throughout all things: the πῦρ νοερὸν, πῦρ τεχνικὸν, an intellectual and artificial fire—an inward principle, animal spirit, or natural life, producing and forming within as art doth without; regulating, moderating, and reconciling the various motions, qualities, and parts of this Mundane System. By virtue of this life the great masses are held together in their orderly courses, as well as the minutest particles governed in their natural motions, according to the several laws of attraction, gravity, electricity, magnetism, and the rest. It is this gives instincts[1], teaches the spider her web, and the bee her honey. This it is that directs the roots of plants to draw forth juices from the earth, and the leaves and corticle vessels to separate and attract such particles of air, and elementary fire, as suit their respective natures.

278. Nature seems to be not otherwise distinguished from the *anima mundi* than as life is from soul, and, upon the principles of the oldest philosophers, may not improperly or incongruously be styled the life of the world. Some Platonics, indeed, regard life as the act of nature, in like manner as intellection is of the mind or intellect. As the First Intellect acts by understanding, so nature according to them acts or generates by living. But life is the act of the soul, and seems to be very nature itself, which is not the principle, but the result of another and higher principle, being a life resulting from soul, as cogitation from intellect[2].

---

[1] Compare § 257, and note.
[2] 'soul,' i.e. animating power, as distinguished from its physical manifestations. The phenomena constitute the material world—that world being, by the supposition, virtually *animated organism*. Soul (ψυχή) was distinguished from body (σάρξ), on the one hand, and from reason (νοῦς), on the other—mediating between them. The ancient notion

279. If nature be the life of the world, animated by one soul, compacted into one frame, and directed or governed in all parts by one mind: this system cannot be accused of Atheism; though perhaps it may of mistake or impropriety. And yet, as one presiding mind gives unity to the infinite aggregate of things, by a mutual communion of actions and passions, and an adjustment of parts, causing all to concur in one view to one and the same end—the ultimate and supreme good of the whole, it should seem reasonable to say, with Ocellus Lucanus the Pythagorean, that as life holds together the bodies of animals, the cause whereof is the soul; and as a city is held together by concord, the cause whereof is law, even so the world is held together by harmony, the cause whereof is God. And in this sense the world or universe may be considered either as one *animal* or one *city*[1].

284. * * Thus much the schools of Plato and Pythagoras seem agreed in, to wit, that the Soul of the World, whether having a distinct mind of its own, or directed by a superior mind, doth embrace all its parts, connect them by an invisible and indissoluble Chain, and preserve them ever well adjusted and in good order.

285. Naturalists, whose proper province it is to consider phænomena, experiments, mechanical organs and motions, principally regard the visible frame of things or corporeal world—supposing soul to be contained in body. And this hypothesis may be tolerated in physics, as it is not necessary in the arts of dialling or navigation to mention the true

---

of the animation of the universe may be found, in one form or another, among physical philosophers of the sixteenth and seventeenth centuries. It is often difficult to distinguish from Hylozoism, or the hypothesis that the universe is Eternal Matter of which conscious life is an attribute.

[1] The *De Legibus* of Ocellus Lucanus is here referred to—now, along with other fragments, rejected as spurious.

system or earth's motion. But those who, not content with sensible appearances, would penetrate into the real and true causes (the object of Theology, Metaphysics, or the *Philosophia Prima*[1]), will rectify this error, and speak of the world as contained by the soul, and not the soul by the world.

 . . . .

287. If we suppose that *one and the same Mind* is the Universal Principle of order and harmony throughout the world, containing and connecting all its parts, and giving unity to the system, there seems to be nothing atheistical or impious in this supposition.

288. Number is no object of sense: it is an act of the mind. The same thing in a different conception is one or many. Comprehending God and the creatures in one general notion, we may say that all things together make one Universe, or τὸ πᾶν. But if we should say that all things make one God, this would, indeed, be an erroneous notion of God, but would not amount to Atheism, so long as mind or intellect was admitted to be the τὸ ἡγεμονικὸν, the governing part[2]. It is, nevertheless, more respectful, and consequently the truer notion of God, to suppose Him neither made up of parts, nor to be himself a part of any whole whatsoever.

289. All those who conceived the universe to be an

---

[1] With Aristotle these are one. See *Metaph.* lib. VI. c. 1, and lib. XI. c. 7. This section again contrasts 'sensible appearances,' i.e. the data of *sense* and *suggestion*, in their sequences and coexistences, with true causes. (Cf. *Vindication*, §§ 9-13, and 42.)

[2] This is a Theism difficult to reconcile with moral agency in men, and therefore with a finally spiritual or ethical conception of the universe—unless we distinguish persons or moral agents from 'things.' But his disposition, especially in *Siris*, is to acknowledge that, in defect of a perfect knowledge of God, men may nevertheless struggle to become like God—so far as God is revealed in the sense-signs of nature, in conscience, and in history—and be victorious in the struggle.

animal must, in consequence of that notion, suppose all things to be one. But to conceive God to be the sentient soul of an animal is altogether unworthy and absurd. There is no sense nor sensory, nor any thing like a sense or sensory, in God. Sense implies an impression from some other being, and denotes a dependence in the soul which hath it. Sense is a passion: and passions imply imperfection. God knoweth all things, as pure mind or intellect; but nothing by sense, nor in nor through a sensory. Therefore to suppose a sensory of any kind—whether space or any other—in God, would be very wrong, and lead us into false conceptions of His nature[1].

290. *Body* is opposite to *spirit* or *mind*. We have a notion of spirit from thought and action. We have a notion of body from resistance. So far forth as there is real power, there is spirit. So far forth as there is resistance, there is inability or want of power: that is, there is negation of spirit. We are embodied, that is, we are clogged by weight, and hindered by resistance. But in respect of a perfect spirit, there is nothing hard or impenetrable: there is no resistance to the Deity: nor hath he any body: nor is the supreme Being united to the world as the soul of an animal is to its body; which necessarily implieth defect, both as an instrument, and as a constant weight and impediment[2].

[1] Berkeley here rejects the supposition that things exist *as phenomena of sense* in the Divine Mind. He says that they exist in God *intellectually*, whatever that implies. And the sublime mystery of infinite uncreated space again repels him.—Note what is said in this section of dependence on *Power external to ourselves* being implied in the passivity of sense. Thus sense, by contrast with our own self-activity, awakens in us the conviction of our personal individuality, rounded off by Power other than our own.

[2] He assigns solidity (not extension) as the essential mark of body. So too in his early philosophical works. How are tactual phenomena tests of sensible reality more than visible phenomena? Are they our fundamental experience in sense, into which that of the other senses has to be translated?

291. Nor is this doctrine less philosophical than pious. We see all nature alive or in motion. We see water turned into air, and air rarefied and made elastic by the attraction of another medium, more pure indeed, more subtle, and more volatile, than air. But still, as this is a moveable, extended, and consequently a corporeal being, it cannot be itself the principle of motion, but leads us naturally and necessarily to an incorporeal Spirit or Agent. We are conscious that a Spirit can begin, alter, or determine motion; but nothing of this appears in body. Nay, the contrary is evident, both to experiment and reflexion [1].

292. Natural phænomena are only natural appearances. They are, therefore, such as we see and perceive them. Their real and objective [2] natures are, therefore, the same; passive without anything active, fluent and changing without anything permanent in them. However, as these make the first impressions, and the mind takes her first flight and spring, as it were, by resting her foot on these objects, they are not only first considered by all men, but most considered by most men. They and the phantoms that result from those appearances, the children of imagination grafted upon sense—such for example as pure space—are thought by many the very first in existence and stability, and to embrace and comprehend all other beings.

293. Now, although such phantoms as corporeal forces, absolute motions, and real spaces do pass in physics for

---

[1] Here he finds what the word power means in a consciousness of self-activity, but without sufficient reference to this activity as morally responsible, and *therefore* self-originated. And he grounds his allegation of the total powerlessness of matter on our not having any evidence of true causality in sensible *things*, which we have in the case of morally responsible *persons*.

[2] 'objective'—here equivalent to presented in sense. Contrast its other applications, (*a*) to what is extended, and so supposed to be a manifestation of something other than mind, and (*b*) to relations that are universal and necessary, because involved in the constitution of reason.

causes and principles, yet are they in truth but hypotheses; nor can they be the objects of real science. They pass nevertheless in physics, conversant about things of sense, and confined to experiments and mechanics. But when we enter the province of the *philosophia prima*, we discover another order of beings—*mind and its acts—permanent being*—not dependent on corporeal things, nor resulting, nor connected, nor contained; but containing, connecting, enlivening the whole frame; and imparting those motions, forms, qualities, and that order and symmetry, to all those transient phænomena which we term the Course of Nature.

294. It is with our faculties as with our affections: what first seizes holds fast. It is a vulgar theme, that man is a compound of contrarieties, which breed a restless struggle in his nature, between flesh and spirit, the beast and the angel, earth and heaven, ever weighed down and ever bearing up. During which conflict the character fluctuates: when either side prevails, it is then fixed for vice or virtue. And life from different principles takes a different issue.— It is the same in regard to our faculties. Sense at first besets and overbears the mind. The sensible appearances are all in all: our reasonings are employed about them: our desires terminate in them: we look no farther for realities or causes; till intellect begins to dawn, and cast a ray on this shadowy scene. We then perceive the true principle of unity, identity, and existence. Those things that before seemed to constitute the whole of Being, upon taking an intellectual view of things, prove to be but fleeting phantoms [1].

295. From the outward form of gross masses which occupy the vulgar, a curious inquirer proceeds to examine the inward structure and minute parts, and, from observing

---

[1] This section suggests that gradual development of intellect and spirit in man which it is the office of psychology to describe, along with the conditions on which it depends. Cf. §§ 255 and 264.

the motions in nature, to discover the laws of those motions. By the way, he frames his hypothesis and suits his language to this natural philosophy. And these fit the occasion and answer the end of a maker of experiments or mechanic, who means only to apply the powers of nature, and reduce the phænomena to rules. But if, proceeding still in his analysis and inquiry, he ascends from the sensible into the intellectual world, and beholds things in a new light and a new order, he will then change his system, and perceive that what he took for substances and causes are but fleeting shadows: that the mind contains all, and acts all, and is to all created beings the source of unity and identity, harmony and order, existence and stability [1].

296. It is neither acid, nor salt, nor sulphur, nor air, nor æther, nor visible corporeal fire—much less the phantom *fate* or *necessity*—that is the real agent, but, by a certain analysis, a regular connexion and climax, we ascend through all those mediums to a glimpse of the First Mover, invisible, incorporeal, unextended, intellectual source of life and being. There is, it must be owned, a mixture of obscurity and prejudice in human speech and reasonings. This is unavoidable, since the veils of prejudice and error are slowly and singly taken off one by one. But, if there are many links in the Chain which connects the two extremes of what

---

[1] In this and the foregoing section intellect, as an element in the formation of knowledge, is recognised, in contrast to the physical phenomena of sense and their automatic suggestions. We hardly find this in Berkeley's earlier writings. In his *Commonplace Book* especially, 'mind' is little more than *sense*; and necessities of reason are not distinctly acknowledged in the construction of our knowledge. 'Pure intellect I understand not.' 'We must with the mob place certainty in the senses.' 'If it were not for the senses mind could have no knowledge, no thought, at all.' 'Mind is a congeries of perceptions. Take away perceptions and you take away the mind. Put the perceptions and you put the mind.' 'Sensual pleasure is the *summum bonum*. This the great principle of morality.' The sensuous utilitarianism of the juvenile *Commonplace Book* rises in *Siris* into spiritual ethic.

is *grossly sensible* and *purely intelligible*, and it seems a tedious work, by the slow helps of memory, imagination, and reason [1]—oppressed and overwhelmed, as we are, by the senses, through erroneous principles, and long ambages of words and notions—to struggle upwards into the light of truth, yet, as this gradually dawns, farther discoveries still correct the style and clear up the notions.

297. The Mind, her acts and faculties, furnish a new and distinct class of objects, from the contemplation whereof arise certain other notions, principles, and verities, so remote from, and even so repugnant to, the first prejudices which surprise the sense of mankind that they may well be excluded from vulgar speech and books, as abstract from sensible matters [2], and more fit for the speculation of truth, the labour and aim of a few, than for the practice of the world, or the subjects of experimental or mechanical inquiry.

. . . .

300. Plato and Aristotle considered God as abstracted or distinct from the natural world [3]. But the Egyptians considered God and Nature as making one whole, or all things together as making one Universe. In doing which they did not exclude the Intelligent Mind, but considered it as containing all things. Therefore, whatever was wrong in their way of thinking, it doth not, nevertheless, imply or lead to Atheism [4].

---

[1] 'reason'—here used for reasoning, as by Locke and others.

[2] The 'abstract' is here contrasted with the 'sensible'—in a tone foreign to his earlier thought.

[3] This is confirmed by passages in Plato. As regards Aristotle the case is not so clear. He distinguishes Deity from Nature, and recognises final causes—but not God in any analogy to a person: the world with him is eternal—an endless succession of changes, developed according to the essences of their species, and in relation to their ends.

[4] As in his early works, Berkeley expressly raised the question of what should be meant when we use the word *Matter*, so in *Siris* (as previously in the Dialogue on *Visual Language*), he raises the deeper

301. The human mind is so much clogged and borne downward by the strong and early impressions of sense, that it is wonderful how the ancients should have made even such a progress, and seen so far into intellectual matters, without some glimmering of a divine tradition. Whoever considers a parcel of rude savages left to themselves, how they are sunk and swallowed up in sense and prejudice, and how unqualified by their natural force to emerge from this state, will be apt to think that the first spark of philosophy was derived from heaven.

302. Theology and philosophy gently unbind the ligaments that chain the soul down to the earth, and assist her flight towards the sovereign Good. There is an instinct or tendency of the mind upwards, which sheweth a natural endeavour to recover and raise ourselves from our present sensual and low condition, into a state of light, order, and purity[1].

303. The Perceptions of Sense are gross: but even in the senses there is a difference. Though harmony and proportion are not objects of sense, yet the eye and the ear are organs which offer to the mind such materials by means whereof she may apprehend both the one and the other. By experiments of sense we become acquainted with the lower faculties of the soul; and from them, whether by a gradual evolution or ascent, we arrive at the highest.— Sense supplies images to memory. These become subjects

question of what should be meant when we use the word *God*, and what Atheism essentially consists in. He says less here than in the Dialogue about verifying faith in God by sense and its suggestions, and more about finding God in the constitution of reason, if not in the final supremacy of moral reason.

[1] Evil, as Plato represents, is due to apostasy from the original Good. To the Good philosophy and religion struggle to return; the former through intellect, and the latter in the ethical or spiritual life through which we become like, and thus learn to know, 'the Good', or God, in Theistic optimism.

for Fancy to work upon.—Reason considers and judges of the imaginations. And these acts of reason become new objects to the Understanding.—In this scale, each lower faculty is a step that leads to one above it. And the uppermost naturally leads to the Deity; which is rather the object of intellectual knowledge than even of the discursive faculty, not to mention the sensitive [1].—There runs a Chain throughout the whole system of beings. In this Chain one link drags another. The meanest things are connected with the highest. The calamity therefore is neither strange nor much to be complained of, if a low sensual reader shall, from mere love of the animal life, find himself drawn on, surprised and betrayed, into some curiosity concerning the intellectual.

304. There is, according to Plato, properly no *knowledge*, but only *opinion* concerning things sensible and perishing; not because they are naturally abstruse and involved in darkness, but because their nature and existence are uncertain, ever fleeting and changing. Or rather, because they do not in strict truth exist at all, being always generating or *in fieri*, that is, in a perpetual flux, without any thing stable or permanent in them to constitute an object of real science. The Pythagoreans and Platonics distinguish between τὸ γιγνόμενον and τὸ ὄν, that which ever generated and that which exists. Sensible things and corporeal forms are perpetually producing and perishing, appearing and disappearing,

---

[1] This important passage contains hints of the interdependent gradation of faculties that is involved in the development of Intellect in man. In proportion as Intellect awakens in the individual, the universe becomes more intelligible. The ascent is through (*a*) sense-perception to (*b*) sensuous imagination, determined by automatic laws of suggestion. These are the lower 'faculties,' which provide material for (*c*) scientific inferences; all culminating in (*d*) 'intellectual knowledge' of God sustained in faith. Philosophy gradually ascends towards God, and culminates in theology.

never resting in one state, but always in motion and change; and therefore, in effect, not one being but a succession of beings: while τὸ ὂν is understood to be somewhat of an abstract or spiritual nature, and the proper object of intellectual knowledge. Therefore, as there can be no knowledge of things flowing and unstable, the opinion of Protagoras and Theætetus, that *sense was science*, is absurd[1].

305. As understanding perceiveth not, that is, doth not hear, or see, or feel, so sense knoweth not: and although the mind may use both sense and fancy, as means whereby to arrive at knowledge, yet sense or soul, *so far forth as sensitive*, knoweth nothing. For, as it is rightly observed in the *Theætetus* of Plato, *science* consists not in the passive perceptions, but in the reasoning upon them—τῷ περὶ ἐκείνων συλλογισμῷ[2].

* * * * * * * *

[1] The reference is to the *homo mensura* of Protagoras—argued against in the *Theætetus* by Plato—with whom God, not each individual man, least of all man as a merely sensuous animal, is the criterion of truth. But man in the fulness of his spiritual integrity is, *for man*, the only possible final criterion. This is the *homo mensura* in its highest significance, or the *Divina mensura* humanised.

If there can be no 'knowledge' of what is 'flowing and unstable,' how do transitory sensations ever become knowledge? Also, how can customary sequences of phenomena be *known* to be *invariable*? These questions hardly rise in Berkeley.

Here, as in his earlier writings, what he teaches is in harmony with the *divine arbitrariness* of natural law. Throughout he resists the hypothesis that laws of nature can be so necessary that they are independent of the Reason and Will that is Supreme. To those who argue that, in interpreting nature, we *must* see that natural laws are eternally necessary, and that the opposite conception is irreconcilable with our having experience—he might answer that, in this meaning of 'knowledge,' we have *no* knowledge of things sensible.

[2] Does this imply that isolated phenomena of sense are unintelligible, so that we cannot be even percipient of them—unless 'perception' means only blind sensuous feeling?

307. Aristotle maketh a threefold distinction of objects, according to the three speculative sciences. Physics he supposeth to be conversant about such things as have a principle of motion in themselves; Mathematics about things permanent but not abstracted; and Theology about Being abstracted and immoveable. Which distinction may be seen in the ninth book of his *Metaphysics*, where by abstracted, χωριστὸν, he understands separable from corporeal beings and sensible qualities.

308. That philosopher held that the mind of man was a *tabula rasa*, and that there were no innate ideas. Plato, on the contrary, held original ideas in the mind; that is, notions which never were or can be in the sense, such as being, beauty, goodness, likeness, parity. Some, perhaps, may think the truth to be this :—that there are properly no *ideas*, or passive objects, in the mind but what were derived from sense : but that there are also besides these her own acts or operations; such as *notions*[1].

309. It is a maxim of the Platonic philosophy, that the soul of man was originally furnished with native inbred notions, and stands in need of sensible occasions, not absolutely for producing them, but only for awakening, rousing, or exciting into act what was already pre-existent, dormant, and latent in the soul; as things are said to be laid up in the memory, though not actually perceived until they happen

---

[1] In this important sentence we again touch the contrast yet, correlation, of Sense and Intellect. Berkeley's 'ideas or passive objects' represent the former; his 'notions' the latter. What he says here is in curious contrast to what he says in the *Commonplace Book* of his early youth, where he expressly accepts the sensationalist answer— 'Nihil est in intellectu quod non prius fuit in *sensu*'; adding that if the Schoolmen had stuck to this, 'it had never taught them the doctrine of abstract ideas.' Here, in *Siris*, the work of his old age, he virtually accepts the famous addition of Leibniz—'Nihil est in intellectu quod non prius fuit in sensu, *nisi intellectus ipse*'; in which the activity of intellect is recognised as necessary to the constitution of knowledge.

to be called forth and brought into view by other objects. This notion seemeth somewhat different from that of innate ideas, as understood by those moderns who have attempted to explode them[1]. To *understand* and to *be* are, according to Parmenides, the same thing. And Plato in his seventh Letter makes no difference between νοῦς and ἐπιστήμη, mind and knowledge. Whence it follows that mind, knowledge, and notions, either in habit or in act, always go together.

310. And albeit Aristotle considered the soul in its original state as a blank paper, yet he held it to be the proper place of *forms*—τὴν ψυχὴν εἶναι τόπον εἰδῶν; which doctrine, first maintained by others, he admits, under this restriction, that it is not to be understood of the whole soul, but only of the νοητική; as is to be seen in his third book *De Anima*[2].

311. As to an *absolute actual existence*[3] of Sensible or Corporeal Things (sect. 264, 292, 294), it doth not seem to have been admitted either by Plato or Aristotle. In the

---

[1] He probably refers to Locke, who fails in his *Essay* to recognise the distinction between *conscious* and *sub-conscious* intellectual activity, in his argument against innate ideas and knowledge.

[2] In the passage referred to, Aristotle identifies the αἰσθητικὸν with the αἰσθητὸν, and the ἐπιστημονικὸν with the ἐπιστητὸν, through their forms (εἴδη)—the potential intellect being with him, as with Plato, the place of forms—τόπος εἰδῶν. The illustration of blank paper is used by Locke. 'Let us suppose the mind to be, as we say, white paper, void of all character, without any ideas—how comes it to be furnished?' (*Essay*, b. II. ch. i. § 2.)

[3] In §§ 311-319, Berkeley, in contemplating the transitoriness of all that appears in the senses, returns (but in a more meditative and less argumentative spirit) to the favourite speculation of his youth—the meaning of *real*, when the term is applied to *sensible things*, and the distinction between *visible* and *tangible* space. He summons Plato and Aristotle as witnesses, that the existence of matter and space is dependent upon a living percipient; so that what is unperceived must be mere negation. ('Sensible things' are not to be confounded with the ἄπειρον of Plato, or the ὕλη of Aristotle.)

Theætetus we are told that if any one saith a thing is, or is made, he must withal say, for what, or of what, or in respect of what, it is, or is made; for, that any thing should exist *in itself* or *absolutely* is absurd. Agreeably to which doctrine it is also farther affirmed by Plato, that it is impossible a thing should be sweet and sweet to nobody[1]. It must, nevertheless, be owned with regard to Aristotle, that even in his *Metaphysics* there are some expressions which seem to favour the absolute existence of corporeal things. For instance, in the eleventh book, speaking of corporeal sensible things, what wonder, saith he, if they never appear to us the same, no more than to sick men, since we are always changing and never remain the same ourselves? And again, he saith, sensible things, *although they receive no change in themselves*, do nevertheless in sick persons produce different sensations and not the same. These passages would seem to imply a distinct and absolute existence of the objects of sense[2].

312. But it must be observed, that Aristotle distinguisheth a twofold existence—*potential* and *actual*. It will not therefore follow that, according to Aristotle, because a thing is, it must *actually* exist[3]. This is evident from the eighth book of his *Metaphysics*, where he animadverts on the Megaric philosophers, as not admitting a possible existence distinct from the actual: from whence, saith he, it must follow, that there is nothing cold, or hot, or sweet, or any sensible thing

---

[1] So Berkeley on the qualities of matter.

[2] See b. X. (XI. ch. 6, where Aristotle argues against Protagoras and the sceptics, in behalf of *permanence* in sensible things. He does not thereby contradict the doctrine of the *De Anima*, as to the creative activity of mind, and the share contributed by perception. Only he implies that *things* are more than sensations in a sentient being.

[3] Although the *actual* being of the things of sense depends on a living perception of their qualities, may they not have a *potential* existence that is independent of all percipients?

at all, where there is no perception. He adds that, in consequence of that Megaric doctrine, we can have no sense but while we actually exert it: we are blind when we do not see, and therefore both blind and deaf several times a day [1].

313. The ἐντελέχειαι πρῶται of the Peripatetics, that is, the sciences, arts, and habits, were by them distinguished from the acts or ἐντελέχειαι δεύτεραι, and supposed to exist in the mind, though not exerted or put into act [2]. This seems to illustrate the manner in which Socrates, Plato, and their followers, conceive *innate notions* to be in the soul of man (sect. 309). It was the Platonic doctrine, that human souls or minds descended from above, and were sowed in generation; that they were stunned, stupefied, and intoxicated by this descent and immersion into animal nature; and that the soul, in this ὀνείρωξις or slumber, forgets her original notions, which are smothered and oppressed by many false tenets and prejudices of sense. Insomuch that Proclus compares the soul in her descent, invested with growing prejudices, to Glaucus diving to the bottom of the sea, and there contracting divers coats of seaweed, coral, and

---

[1] The distinction of potential and actual is amongst the most fruitful in Aristotle, and one might reconsider Berkeley's theory of the *reality* of the material world in the light of it. In this passage, potential (ἐν δυνάμει) is contrasted with actualised existence (ἐν ἐνεργείᾳ, or ἐν ἐντελεχείᾳ); and the Megaric theory, limiting 'being' to the latter, is identified with the sceptical individualism of Protagoras. Berkeley, on the other hand, might mean that, as far as individual percipients or agents are concerned, the things of sense might always exist in ἐν δυνάμει; inasmuch as, when unperceived by *them*, they exist potentially in the Divine Reason and Will.—What is to be understood by a 'potential' existence in God? Is a thing in the Divine Idea like the thing as known by us in sense? Is the universe unbeginning and endless under God, or was it created in time? Berkeley hardly recognises these questions, but he rejects the supposition that the material world has a *sentient* existence in God, i. e. that it exists in the form of *divine sensations*.

[2] The *acquisition* of a habit implies previous capacity in those who can acquire the habit.

shells, which stick close to him, and conceal his true shape[1].

314. Hence, according to this philosophy, the mind of man is so restless to shake off that slumber, to disengage and emancipate herself from those prejudices and false opinions that so straitly beset and cling to her, to rub off those covers that disguise her original form, and to regain her primeval state and first notions: hence that perpetual struggle to recover the lost region of light, that ardent thirst and endeavour after truth and intellectual ideas, which she would neither seek to attain, nor rejoice in, nor know when attained, except she had some prenotion or anticipation of them, and they had lain innate and dormant, like habits and sciences in the mind, or things laid up, which are called out and roused by recollection or reminiscence. So that learning seemeth in effect reminiscence[2].

315. The Peripatetics themselves distinguish between reminiscence and mere memory. Themistius observes that the best memories commonly go with the worst parts; but that reminiscence is most perfect in the most ingenious minds. And, notwithstanding the *tabula rasa* of Aristotle, yet some of his followers have undertaken to make him speak Plato's sense[3].

. . . .

---

[1] *Commentaria* of the Neoplatonist Proclus (A.D. 412-485).

[2] There is blind or automatic suggestion, founded on coexistence in the person's past experience. It is distinguished from active 'reminiscence' i.e. the rise in consciousness of what was previously latent in a person—born with him, and as some would say, retained at birth from a preceding life.

[3] Themistius, the first-named of those Peripatetics, lived in the fourth century. To Simplicius, a Neoplatonist of the sixth century, we owe valuable expositions of Aristotle, especially of the *De Anima*. He attempted to reconcile Aristotle with Plato. 'Plutarch the Peripatetic' seems to be Plutarch son of Nestorius, the Neoplatonist, who is said to have written a commentary, now lost, on the *De Anima*. With Aristotle, reminiscence (ἀνάμνησις) implies less than Plato meant by

317. Neither Plato nor Aristotle by Matter, ὕλη, understood *corporeal substance*, whatever the moderns may understand by that word. To them certainly it signified no positive actual being. Aristotle describes it as made up of negatives, having neither quantity, nor quality, nor essence [1]. And not only the Platonists and Pythagoreans, but also the Peripatetics themselves declare it to be known, neither by sense, nor by any direct and just reasoning, but only by some spurious or adulterine method, as hath been observed before. That Matter is actually nothing, but potentially all things, is the doctrine of Aristotle, Theophrastus, and all the ancient Peripatetics.

318. According to those philosophers, Matter is only a *pura potentia*, a mere possibility. Plato observes that we dream, as it were, when we think of place, and believe it necessary that whatever exists should exist in some place. Which place or space, he also observes, is μετ' ἀναισθησίας ἁπτόν, that is, to be felt as darkness is seen, or silence heard, being a mere privation [2].

---

pre-existing yet latent ideals, gradually evoked into consciousness with growing clearness through reflective activity.

[1] The ἄπειρον, or ἕτερον of Plato—according to Hegel, a *world-necessitated* 'otherness.' The material world *realised* in living perception, must not be confounded with the formless Matter of Aristotle. This last is that dark, undefinable, *pre-condition* of the actuality of things, for which Berkeley substitutes God and constant creation, in the form of divinely-sustained regularity of nature.

[2] Space, in total abstraction from sense, is neither 'notion,' nor 'idea,' nor 'phenomenon' (according to Berkeley's use of these terms). We cannot when we try imagine space emptied of all sensuous data. But on the other hand, data of sense cannot be conceived as *outward* apart from space, which is necessarily blended with the phenomena that we perceive, giving them outwardness, and suggesting that boundlessness or spacial infinity which is one of the ultimate mysteries.

Berkeley sees in *the successive phenomena of sense* and in *intellectual notions* two elements of concrete reality. In his early philosophy he concerned himself chiefly with the former; in *Siris* rather with the

319. If any one should think to infer the reality or actual being of Matter from the modern tenet—that gravity is always proportionable to the quantity of matter, let him but narrowly scan the modern demonstration of that tenet, and he will find it to be a vain circle, concluding in truth no more than this—that gravity is proportionable to weight, that is, to itself. Since Matter is conceived only as defect and mere possibility; and since God is absolute perfection and act; it follows there is the greatest distance and opposition imaginable between God and Matter. Insomuch that a material God would be altogether inconsistent.

320. The *force* that produces, the *intellect* that orders, the *goodness* that perfects all things in the Supreme Being. Evil, defect, negation, is not the object of God's creative power.

326. Now, whether the νοῦς be abstracted from the sensible world, and considered by itself, as distinct from, and presiding over, the created system; or whether the whole Universe, including mind together with the mundane body, is conceived to be God, and the creatures to be partial manifestations of the Divine essence—there is no Atheism in either case, whatever misconceptions there may be; so long as Mind or Intellect is understood to preside over, govern, and conduct, the whole frame of things [1].

---

latter. Space, abstracted from sense, being neither a phenomenon nor a notion, must, he concluded, be an illusion. He did not contemplate space relations as necessary to the constitution of our experience of the world of sense.

Sect. 320-329, in accumulating authorities favourable to the dependence of all phenomena ultimately on Mind, approach the question of what the term God means.

[1] He seems satisfied to think of God either as *transcending* the dependent universe of things and persons, or as *omnipresent* in nature and spirit—provided only that there is a practical acknowledgment of Goodness at the heart of the universe. The 'must' of speculative reason, and the 'ought' of moral reason, cannot be reduced to the 'is' or 'is not' of sense.

328. Might we not conceive that God may be said to be ALL in divers senses;—as he is the cause and origin of all beings; as the νοῦς is the νοητά, a doctrine both of Platonics and Peripatetics; as the νοῦς is the place of all forms; and as it is the same which comprehends and orders and sustains the whole mundane system? Aristotle declares that the Divine force or influence permeates the entire universe, and that what the pilot is in a ship, the driver in a chariot, the precentor in a choir, the law in a city, the general in an army, the same God is in the world. This he amply sets forth in his book *De Mundo*; a treatise which, having been anciently ascribed to him, ought not to be set aside from the difference of style; which (as Patricius rightly observes), being in a letter to a king, might well be supposed to differ from the other dry and crabbed parts of his writings[1].

329. And although there are some expressions to be met with in the philosophers, even of the Platonic and Aristotelic sects, which speak of God as mixing with, or pervading all nature and all the elements; yet this must be explained by *force* and not by *extension*, which was never attributed to the mind, either by Aristotle or Plato.

330. These disquisitions will probably seem dry and useless to such readers as are accustomed to consider only sensible objects. The employment of the mind on things purely intellectual is to most men irksome; whereas the sensitive powers, by constant use, acquire strength. Hence, the objects of sense more forcibly affect us, and are too often counted the chief good. For these things men fight,

---

[1] The *De Mundo* is not now accepted as Aristotle's. That God is Moral Order vivified or personified—not capricious interference with order—is the profound lesson at once of science and of religion. As so conceived, theistic faith is an indispensable tacit postulate of science.

cheat, and scramble. Therefore, in order to tame mankind, and introduce a sense of virtue, the best human means is to exercise their understanding, to give them a glimpse of another world, superior to the sensible, and, while they take pains to cherish and maintain the animal life, to teach them not to neglect the intellectual[1].

331. Prevailing studies are of no small consequence to a state, the religion, manners, and civil government of a country ever taking some bias from its philosophy, which affects not only the minds of its professors and students, but also the opinions of all the better sort, and the practice of the whole people, remotely and consequentially indeed, though not inconsiderably. Have not the polemic and scholastic philosophy been observed to produce controversies in law and religion? And have not Fatalism and Sadducism gained ground, during the general passion for the corpuscularian and mechanical philosophy, which hath prevailed for about a century? This, indeed, might usefully enough have employed some share of the leisure and curiosity of inquisitive persons. But when it entered the seminaries of learning as a necessary accomplishment, and most important part of education, by engrossing men's thoughts, and fixing their minds so much on corporeal objects, and the laws of motion, it hath, however undesignedly, indirectly, and by accident, yet not a little indisposed them for spiritual, moral, and intellectual matters. Certainly had the philosophy of Socrates and Pythagoras prevailed in this age, among those who think themselves too wise to receive the dictates of the Gospel, we should not have seen interest take so general and fast hold on the minds of men, nor public spirit reputed to be γενναίαν ἀήθειαν, a generous folly, among those who are reckoned to

---

[1] The eloquent protest on behalf of Plato and against Materialism, in this and following sections, is the prelude in *Siris* to abstruse speculation as to the Personality and Trinity of God, and the dependence of the Personality on the Trinity, which is omitted here.

be the most knowing as well as the most getting part of mankind [1].

332. It might very well be thought serious trifling to tell my readers that the greatest men had ever a high esteem for Plato; whose writings are the touchstone of a hasty and shallow mind; whose philosophy has been the admiration of ages; which supplied patriots, magistrates, and lawgivers to the most flourishing states, as well as fathers to the Church, and doctors to the schools. Albeit in these days the depths of that old learning are rarely fathomed; and yet it were happy for these lands if our young nobility and gentry, instead of modern maxims, would imbibe the notions of the great men of antiquity. But, in these freethinking times, many an empty head is shook at Aristotle and Plato, as well as at the Holy Scriptures. And the writings of those celebrated ancients are by most men treated on a foot with the dry and barbarous lucubrations of the schoolmen. It may be modestly presumed there are not many among us, even of those who are called the better sort, who have more sense, virtue, and love of their country than Cicero, who in a Letter to Atticus could not forbear exclaiming, *O Socrates et Socratici viri! nunquam vobis gratiam referam.* Would to God many of our countrymen had the same obligations to those Socratic writers! Certainly, where the people are well educated, the art of piloting a state is best learned from the writings of Plato. But among bad men, void of discipline and education, Plato, Pythagoras, and Aristotle themselves, were they living, could do but little good.

334. Socrates in the First Alcibiades teacheth that the contemplation of God is the proper means to know or under-

---

[1] In short, the superiority of, *often latent*, universal Reason to the accidents of human experience, and to the transitory opinions of individuals and societies, would be recognised as they cannot be in a materialistic age, when experience is dogmatically confined within the limits of the physical.

stand our own soul. As the eye, saith he, looking steadfastly at the visive part or pupil of another eye, beholds itself, even so the soul beholds and understands herself, while she contemplates the Deity, which is wisdom and virtue, or like thereunto. In the Phædon, Socrates speaks of God as being τὸ ἀγαθὸν and τὸ δέον; Plotinus represents God as Order; Aristotle as Law[1].

335. It may seem, perhaps, to those who have been taught to discourse about substratums, more reasonable and pious to attribute to the Deity a more substantial being than the notional entities of wisdom, order, law, virtue, or goodness, which being only complex ideas, framed and put together by the understanding, are its own creatures, and have nothing substantial, real, or independent in them. But it must be considered that, in the Platonic system, order, virtue, law, goodness, and wisdom are not creatures of the soul of man, but innate and originally existent therein, not as an accident in a substance, but as light to enlighten, and as a guide to govern. In Plato's style, the term *Idea* doth not merely signify an inert inactive object of the understanding, but is used as synonymous with αἴτιον and ἀρχή, cause and principle. According to that philosopher, goodness, beauty, virtue, and such like are not figments of the mind, nor mere mixed modes, nor yet abstract ideas in the modern sense, but the most real beings, intellectual and unchangeable: and therefore more real than the fleeting, transient objects of sense, which, wanting stability, cannot be subjects of science, much less of intellectual knowledge[2].

---

[1] These doctrines present God as abstract reason and goodness, towards which we are ethically bound to struggle, rather than as reason and goodness vivified or personified.

[2] Mark the contrast between 'abstract ideas' as criticised in Berkeley's early writings, and what he now appreciates in the Ideas of Plato. Without Ideas, according to Plato, the material universe could not exist really; by participation in them sensible things are constituted; in

337. The most refined human intellect, exerted to its utmost reach, can only seize some imperfect glimpses of the Divine Ideas—abstracted from all things corporeal, sensible, and imaginable. Therefore Pythagoras and Plato treated them in a mysterious manner, concealing rather than exposing them to vulgar eyes; so far were they from thinking that those abstract things, although the most real, were the fittest to influence common minds, or become principles of knowledge, not to say duty and virtue, to the generality of mankind.

340. Human souls in this low situation, bordering on mere animal life, bear the weight and see through the dusk of a gross atmosphere, gathered from wrong judgments daily passed, false opinions daily learned, and early habits of an older date than either judgment or opinion. Through such a medium the sharpest eye cannot see clearly. And if by some extraordinary effort the mind should surmount this dusky region, and snatch a glimpse of pure light, she is soon drawn backwards, and depressed by the heaviness of the animal nature to which she is chained. And if again she chanceth, amidst the agitation of wild fancies and strong affections, to spring upwards, a second relapse speedily succeeds into this region of darkness and dreams.

· · · · · · · ·

350. The displeasure of some readers may perhaps be incurred, by surprising them into certain reflexions and

discovery of them, by reminiscence or otherwise, philosophy seeks satisfaction. Inductive research is only our tentative endeavour to see things under laws, according to their divine meaning. Its provisional but useful generalisations, limited by the data of our experience, are far short of the Divine Thought which Idealist systems have hitherto vainly tried to grasp and fully comprehend. Yet our scientific inferences involve trustful 'leaps' not wholly 'in the dark,' for even science of nature is rooted in theistic faith in the moral constitution of the universe.

inquiries for which they have no curiosity. But perhaps some others may be pleased to find a dry subject varied by digressions, traced through remote inferences, and carried into ancient times, whose hoary maxims, scattered in this Essay, are not proposed as principles, but barely as hints to awaken and exercise the inquisitive reader, on points not beneath the attention of the ablest men. Those great men, Pythagoras, Plato, and Aristotle, the most consummate in politics, who founded states, or instructed princes, or wrote most accurately on public government, were at the same time most acute at all abstracted and sublime speculations; the clearest light being ever necessary to guide the most important actions. And, whatever the world thinks, he who hath not much meditated upon God, the human mind, and the *summum bonum*, may possibly make a thriving earthworm, but will most indubitably make a sorry patriot and a sorry statesman.

. . . .

367. As for the perfect intuition of divine things, *that* Plato supposeth to be the lot of pure souls, beholding by a pure light, initiated, happy, free and unstained from those bodies, wherein we are now imprisoned like oysters. But, in this mortal state, we must be satisfied to make the best of those glimpses within our reach. It is Plato's remark, in his *Theætetus*, that while we sit still we are never the wiser, but going into the river, and moving up and down, is the way to discover its depths and shallows. If we exercise and bestir ourselves, we may even here discover something.

368. The eye by long use comes to see even in the darkest cavern: and there is no subject so obscure but we may discern some glimpse of truth by long poring on it. Truth is the cry of all, but the game of a few. Certainly, where it is the chief passion, it doth not give way to vulgar cares and views; nor is it contented with a little ardour in the early time of life: active perhaps, to pursue, but not so fit to

weigh and revise. He that would make a real progress in knowledge must dedicate his age as well as youth, the later growth as well as first fruits, at the altar of Truth [1].

[1] *Siris* concludes with sentences which confess that human knowledge of the infinite universe of reality must in the end be incomplete, with a residuum of mystery that demands faith or moral trust in the Universal Power. We know enough to know that *our* knowledge cannot become Omniscience; that our philosophy cannot solve all the questions to which physical and moral experience gives birth; that in its progressive advance, there must be an ever receding, yet always present, horizon of faith. But—although by 'exercise,' if we 'bestir ourselves,' we may 'discover something,' Omniscience is not indispensable to our living wisely and religiously. Universally victorious science is not the human way of finally separating gold from dross in this transitory life, which may be a life of final faith, although it must be one of incomplete conceptions and constant controversy—of slowly enlarging experience—of ever unfinished, and therefore faith-constituted, knowledge.

INDEX

Abstraction and Abstract Ideas, xx, 3-4, 11-23, 35-36, 96.
Activity, unconscious mental, 298 *n.*
Agent. *See* Causality.
Analogy, 259; laws of nature founded on, 295; God conceived by, 259, 261 *n.*; Butler's use of, 261 *n.*, 264 *n.*
Angles, cannot judge near distance by, 179, 204-205, 235.
Anima mundi, 305.
Aquinas, Thomas, 257.
Arbitrariness, of physical law or natural causation, xxx, xl, 74 *n.*, 178-186.
Archetypes of ideas, 39, 64, 92.
Aristotle, his *materia prima*, 41; his four causes, 52 *n.*; on essence, 99 *n.*; on the association of ideas, 185 *n.*; Cudworth on, 294; on unconscious human activity, 298 *n.*; Theology and Metaphysics identical according to, 307 *n.*; makes threefold distinction in objects, 316; mind at first like blank paper, 317; on matter, 318, 321; God immanent in the universe, 323.
Association, subjective, 185 *n.*
Atheism, 58, 100, 322.
Attraction, 289.
Augustine, St., 293.

Bacon, xvi, 7 *n.*, 51 *n.*, 80 *n.*, 294 *n.*
Bain, Alexander, 218 *n.*
Being, comprehends ideas or phenomena and also self-conscious persons, 94.

Berkeley, why a good introduction to the problems of modern thought, ix; outline of his life, x-xii; his precursors, xiii; his new question, xxiv; his starting-point, xxvi; outline of his system, xxvii-xxxvi; modern thought since, xxxvi-xlv; reply to Hume by anticipation, xxxviii; his new principles unfolded, 3; the lesson of the Introduction, 3; aim of his inquiries, 8 *n.*; question of his philosophy, 34 *n.*; charged with begging the question, 34 *n.*; does not show in what form sense ideas exist in the Divine mind, 37 *n.*; Can spirit be unconscious? 37 *n.*, 49 *n.*; on causality, 51 *n.*; his distinction between perception and imagination, 56 *n.*, 59 *n.*; the permanence and identity of sensible things *the* difficulty of his system, 67 *n.*, 68 *n.*, 69 *n.*, 90 *n.*, 93 *n.*; consistency of order in nature with his system, 46 *n.*, 78 *n.*; divine naturalism, 99 *n.*; the relation of free finite spirits to God, 104 *n.*; on death, 105 *n.*; germs of Kantism in, 108 *n.*; our communication with other persons is through phenomena presented in sense, 109 *n.*; his theory of vision, 170-173; on necessary connexion in mathematics, 176 *n.*, 177 *n.*; on suggestion, 180 *n.*; assumes the existence of an associative tendency, 185; on unextended colour,

218 *n.*; his philosophy deepened in *Siris*, 284-286.
Biran, Maine de, 52 *n.*
Blind (i. e. men born blind), have at first no idea of distance or outness by sight, 187, 239, 278—do not at first associate phenomena of sight and touch, 205; cases of sight when first awakened in the born blind, 278.
Body, perceived in our sense of resistance, 308; connexion of soul and, 105.
Brown, Thomas, 51 *n.*, 218 *n.*
Browne, Bp. Peter, x, 261 *n.*, 262 *n.*
Butler, Bp., 106 *n.*, 116 *n.*, 202 *n.*, 261 *n.*, 264 *n.*

Causation, xxxi-xxxiv, xxxix-xli, xli *n.*; dogma of materialists regarding, 69 *n.*; moral agents the only active causes, 51 *n.*; ideas or phenomena of sense are not real causes, 51, 72; no idea, but a notion of, 52; not an object of sense, 269; an object of reason, 301; physical causes, merely signs, xxx, 51, 72, 79, 288; occasional causes, 82.
Cheselden's case, 278.
Clarke, Samuel, xxxiv, 246 *n.*
Colour, idea of, abstracted from extension, 12; abstract general idea of, 13; the proper object of sight, 188, 208, 238; admitted not to exist without percipient mind, 38.
Common Sense, 8; Reid's, synonymous with Common Reason, 71 *n.*
Conception, as a criterion of objective possibility, 48.
Concepts, 17 *n.*, 19 *n.*
Condillac, 181 *n.*
Consciousness, xxvii.
Cosmos, 104 *n.*, 113 *n.*, 114 *n.*
Creation, constant, 64, 65, 78 *n.*, 246.
Cudworth, Ralph, 294, 295 *n.*, 297, 298 *n.*
Custom, xli, 51 *n.*, 201, 201 *n.*, 240 *n.*

Death and unbodied spirits, Berkeley and Butler on, 105 *n.*

Definition, 24-25, 99.
Democritus, 294, 303.
Descartes, his tentative doubt, xiii; his Dualism, xiv; Substance and Causality according to, *ib.*; scientific cosmogony of, 289; holds Divine agency to be constant, 292 *n.*; Cartesians and Platonists compared, 302.
Diderot, 279 *n.*
Dionysius the Areopagite, 256.
Distance, outness in the line of sight, 175 *n.*—Outness, admitted not to be a direct object of vision, 175; also admitted that remote outness is only suggested by visible signs, 176; the signs of near distance said to be necessary, 177; this rejected, for reasons given, 178-180; signs by which near distance is suggested, 180-186, 234; one born blind has at first sight no idea of outness, 187, 239. Is lateral, or superficial, an original object of sight with Berkeley? 278 *n.*
Divisibility, of matter, 65, 218.
Dreams, 45, 61.

Ego. *See* Spirit.
Empedocles, 299.
Epicurus, 303.
Error, causes of, 8.
Esse, of sensible things is *percipi*, 34; of spirits is *percipere*, 98 *n.*
Evil, physical, 113, 300; moral, 222, 263.
Existence, consists of spirits and their ideas or phenomena, 94; abstract idea of, incomprehensible, 80; of sensible things, 39, 66, 87, *et passim*; of our own spirit, 33, 94, 97; of other finite spirits, 94, 108; of God, 109, 228, 245.
Expectation. *See* Suggestion.
Experience, teaches us the scientific interpretability of sense ideas or phenomena, xxvii-xxxi, 54; inferences of geometry and their relation to knowledge of causes, 301.

...tension, is realised only in a mind perceiving, 40; so exists only by way of idea or phenomena, but not as a mode of mind, 67, 196 *n.*; extension not the same in sight and in touch, 207; no absolutely necessary connexion between visible and tangible phenomena, 201.
...xternality, real meaning of, 92.

...aculties, human, their finitude and its relation to scepticism, 8; are not mere ideas or phenomena, 108; cannot be abstracted from mind, *ib.*; gradation of, 314.
...aith, or trust, moral, xlvii, 8, 329 *n.*
...ichte, 95 *n.*
...orce. *See* Power.

...assendi, xxiv.
...eometry, 206, 234.
...eulinx, xv, 71 *n.*, 289 *n.*
...od, existence of, contained by implication in phenomena of sense, 110, 245; laws of nature express the Reason and Will of, xxxii–xxxiv, 54, 111,—and constitute His language, xxix–xxxii, 63, 80, 239–249, 295–297; His Ideas the archetypes of ours, 86 *n.*; the relation of free finite spirits to, 104 *n.*; objection from physical pain to the goodness of, 113; from moral evil, 222, 262–263; What is to be understood by the word 'God,' and in what respect God is knowable by man, 250.

Hamilton, Sir W., 93, 219, 273 *n.*
Hegel, x, 321 *n.*
Helmholtz, 186 *n.*
Hermaic writings, 303.
Hobbes, xxiv, 251.
Hume, xxxvi; on self as an idea or phenomenon, xxxviii; on human agency and will, xxxix; on order in nature, xl; resolves intellect into sense, xli; on abstract ideas, 11 *n.*; impressions or sensations, 56 *n.*; on substance, 44 *n.*; on causality, 52 *n.*; on Berkeley's argument against matter, xxxvii,

104 *n.*; on representative perception, 93 *n.*; his sceptical nescience, 267 *n.*; the universe a 'singular effect,' 116 *n.*; customary connexion is physical causation according to, 181 *n.*, 201 *n.*

Idea or phenomenon or appearance, xvii, xx *n.*, 10 *n.*, 11, 32 *n.*, 91 *n.*, 269 *n.*; restricted to the perceivable, and the imaginable, in Berkeley's early works, 55; can be like nothing but another idea, 38, 95; not equivalent to 'notion,' 15, 20; distinguished from 'mode,' 67; ideas of sense and their potential existence in God, 36, 67, 82, 96; do not imply abstract substance, xxvii, 44; are not true causes, 51, 98, 269; but only natural signs, 54, 79; those presented in sense are real things, in contradistinction to mere fancies or dreams, 55, 61, 92; in *Siris* those of sense and imagination are called phenomena, and 'idea' is used in its Platonic meaning, xx *n.*, 294 *n.*, &c. Ideas, abstract. *See* Abstraction. Ideas, how they become general, 17. Ideas, and language, 24–31.
Identity, of sensible things, 64–66, 82, 90 *n.*
Imagination, 32, 54, 268; affords no proof that sensible things can exist really when unperceived, 48; Locke, Leibniz, and Hume on, 56 *n.*
Immaterialism, xxviii, xlvii.
Immortality of man, 105, 106 *n.*
Induction, and its ground, xviii *n.*, xx *n.*, 180, 295.
Inference, rational, contrasted with automatic suggestion, and adapted to finite intelligence, 205, 274 *n.*, 276 *n.*
Infinity, 8 *n.*

Jamblichus, 303.
Judgment, 176 *n.*, 199 *n.*

Kant, xliv; on causation, 52 *n.*; on

identity of things, 82 *n.*; on physical and mathematical science, 98 *n.*; on knowledge of ego or self, 103 *n.*; on the origin of knowledge, 108 *n.*; on the constitutive principles of knowledge, 180 *n.*

King, Abp., 261 *n.*

Knowledge, objects of, 32, 91; does not include abstract ideas, 20; ideal, 96; real, 23 *n.*; incompleteness of human, 328; automatic suggestion, 240 *n.*; intuitive and discursive, 258 *n.*; symbolical, Leibniz, 25 *n.*; and opinion, Plato, 314.

Language, 275; nature and abuse of, 10, 28; does not require general ideas to be abstract, 17; universality in, 20; ends of, 26; Language of Nature, particularly of visual signs, xxxi, 62, 63; its arbitrariness, or dependence on Will, 217, 239; its reasonableness, 182 *n.*, 225; differs from artificial languages of man, 241.

Law, in nature, 54, 55.

Leibniz, x, xlii, 25 *n.*, 56 *n.*, 116 *n.*, 211 *n.*, 246 *n.*, 290 *n.*, 292 *n.*, 316 *n.*

Leucippus, 303.

Locke, influence of, on Berkeley, x, xiii, xvi-xxiv; begins with introspective study of mind, xvi; finds our experience made up of ideas of the senses and of reflexion, xvii; tacitly assumes *a priori* principles, *ib.*, 38; distinguishes primary from secondary qualities of matter, xviii; 'idea' and its meaning according to, xx, 192 *n.*; on 'abstract ideas,' xx, 15, 18; idea of 'substance,' xxi, 45 *n.*; 'perception,' according to, xx *n.*; on causation, 51 *n.*; on the perplexities of philosophy, 8 *n.*; holds that abstraction distinguishes man from brute, 15; on physical science and its indemonstrability, 40 *n.*; on judgment in his special meaning of the term, 176 *n.*; on sight and touch, 208, 210; on innate ideas, 317 *n.*; does not distinguish potential from actual knowledge, 317 *n.*

Lotze, 186 *n.*

Mackintosh, Sir J., 10 *n.*
Malebranche, x, xv, xxiv, 71 *n.*, 111 *n.*, 245 *n.*, 289 *n.*
Manichæism, 116 *n.*
Mansel, Dean, 17 *n.*
Materia prima, Aristotle's, 41.
Materialism, xxiv, 45 *n.*, 68 *n.*, 69 *n.*
Mathematics, 98, 316 *n.*
Matter, abstract, xxiv-xxxvi, 39; supposed support of accidents, 43; as such, cannot be known, 45; as such, useless, 46, 70, 81; as such, either contradictory or unintelligible, 44 *n.*, 49 *n.*; its total powerlessness, 50 *n.*, 53 *n.*, 309 *n.*, &c.; as such, independent material substance or power not needed in natural philosophy, 69; origin of belief in, 72-73; not the unknowable cause of ideas, 81; nor the unknowable support of qualities, 87; nor an unknown Somewhat, neither substance nor accident, 88; erroneous conception of matter the root of materialism and scepticism or total nescience, 94.
Megaric philosophy, 318.
Metaphysics, xiii, 11.
Mill, J. S., 11 *n.*, 51 *n.*, 113 *n.*, 218 *n.*
Mind. *See* Spirit.
Miracles, physical, 78 *n.*
Mirandula, Picus of, 256.
Molyneux, x, 210.
Motion, 12, 39, 50, 218 *n.*
Müller, 186 *n.*

Nature, laws of, xxx, xl, 54, 55, 112-115; language of. *See* Language. Berkeley's conception of natural law, 47 *n.*, 65 *n.*, 70 *n.*, 74 *n.*, 78 *n.*, 90 *n.*
Necessity, physical, xxx; mathematical, 177; ancients on, 303-304.
Newton, Sir Isaac, x, 294.
Nominalism, Berkeley's, 11-31.

Notion, as distinguished by Berkeley from sensuous idea or phenomenon, xxxii, xxxv, xxxviii, 11 *n.*, 15, 53, 94, 108, 316 *n.*, 217 *n.*, 321 *n.*
Number, 41, 307.

Occasional causes. *See* Cause.
Ocellus Lucanus, 306.
Outness. *See* Distance.

Parmenides, 317.
Pascal, 114 *n.*, 240 *n.*
Perception, xx *n.*; mediate, acquired or suggested, as distinguished from immediate, 178, 192, 272; distinguished from imagination, 53; in the ascending 'chain of faculties,' 313; representative, 38, 91 *n.*, 93 *n.*, 273 *n.*
Peripatetics, 319, 320, 321, 323.
Phenomenon, instead of idea, in *Siris*, xx *n.*, 294 *n.*
Philosophy, What? 7-10.
Philosophy of Theism, 267 *n.*
Plato, Ideas of, xx *n.*, 11 *n.*, 326-329; *Theaetetus*, quoted, 315, 318, 328; *Phaedo*, 326; *Timaeus*, 321; on the personality of God, 312; on evil, 313 *n.*; on knowledge and opinion, 314; on matter, 318, 321; on the soul, 319; on innate notions, 316; on sensible qualities, 321, 322; on God, 323; protest on behalf of, 324.
Platonists, 302-306, 314, 321, 323.
Plotinus, 295, 296, 303, 326.
Plutarch, 303.
Portius, Simon, 320 *n.*
Power, xxxii, 50, 51 *n.* *See* Causation.
Powers of mind. *See* Faculties.
Proclus, 300, 301 *n.*, 319.
Psychology, the facts with which it is concerned, 32; Berkeley's early, 32 *n.*; rational, 103 *n.*
Pythagoreans, 302, 305, 306, 314, 321, 327.

Qualities of Matter, primary and secondary, xviii, 38, 84. *See* Ideas and Phenomena.

Reality, admits of degrees, 58.
Reason, 269, 272 *n.*, 301.
Reasoning, *a priori* and *posteriori*, 47 *n.*
Reid, xliii, 52 *n.*, 71 *n.*, 72 *n.*, 93 *n.*, 180 *n.*, 219 *n.*, 226 *n.*, 273 *n.*
Relations, 'notions' of, 94, 108; presupposed in knowledge, 47 *n.*, 108, 268.
Responsibility, moral, and true or active causation, xxxii, 298.

Scepticism, xxxvi-xlii, 8, 61 *n.*, 94, 100, 238 *n.*
Schoolmen, 23, 65, 67 *n.*
Science, xxix, 73, 101 *n.*
Self. *See* Spirit.
Sensations, can exist only in a sentient mind, 33; cannot be true causes, 50; are significant through the constant Divine Orderly Activity, 90 *n.*; contain nothing but what is perceived, 92.
Sense, why the presentations of are called ideas, 59; abstract matter not an object of, 43; nor the spiritual ego, 101; *per se*, knows nothing, 295; antithesis of sense and reason, 271, 301.
Sight, immediate and mediate objects of, 188, 204, 208; objects of sight and of touch, 202, 206, 207.
Signs, material world a system of sense-given, and as such can be interpreted, xxix, 51 *n.*, 90 *n.*; material causes are only signs, 79, 275; of the agency of spirits, 109.
Simplicius, 320 *n.*
Socrates, 319, 324-326.
Solidity, 39, 191.
Soul. *See* Spirit.
Space, no such thing as real absolute, 302; in its three dimensions not an immediate object of sight, 192, 218 *n.*
Spinoza, xvi, 251.
Spirit, xxii, xxxii, xxxviii, 33, 34, 101; the only substance, 37, 51 *n.*, 95, 101; the only real cause, 51 *n.*; thinks always, 37 *n.*, 97; we have a notion, not an idea or image of, 53, 104, 107; the Supreme, how

known by an individual mind, 53, 73, 224; other finite spirits, how known one by another, 33, 53 *n*., 107, 227.
Stewart, Dugald, 26 *n*., 52 *n*., 181 *n*.
Stoics, 304.
Suarez, 258.
Substance, xix, xxi, xxiii, 37, 53, 103. *See* Spirit and Matter.
Suggestion, automatic, xxix, 62, 63, 180, 202, 268; contrasted with rational inference, 276.

Tangibile minimum, 201.
Themistius, 320.
Theophrastus, 321.
Thing, xxviii, 55, 60, 94. *See* Existence, Being, Matter, Spirit, Reality.

Time, 96, 97.
Toland, 261 *n*.
Touch, 63 *n*., 188 *n*., 191; sight and, 63, 202, 207.
Truth, 28; the cry of all but the game of few, 328.

Ueberweg, 34 *n*., 37.
Unity, the aim of philosophy, and how far attainable in a human or incomplete knowledge of existence, 7 *n*., 8 *n*.; of consciousness, 103 *n*.

Visibile minimum, 201.
Vision. *See* Sight.

Will, or moral agency, xl, xli, 52; Divine, 57.

THE END

Printed in England at the Oxford University Press